Tender Mercies

Inside the World
of a Child Abuse Investigator

Keith N. Richards

The Noble Press, Inc.
Chicago

and

The Child Welfare League of America, Inc.
Washington, DC

Printed in the United States of America
Published by The Noble Press and the Child Welfare League of
America

Library of Congress Cataloging-in-Publication Data

Richards, Keith N., 1951-
  Tender mercies : inside the world of a child abuse
investigator / Keith N. Richards.
    p. cm.
  ISBN 1-879360-07-1 (pbk.) : $12.95
  1. Richards, Keith N., 1951- . 2. Social workers—New
York (State)—Biography. 3. Child abuse—New York (State)—
Investigation—Case studies. I. Title.
  HV40.32.R53A3 1991
  363.2'595554'092—dc20   91-50624
                                                                CIP

Noble Press books are available in bulk at discount prices.
Single copies are available prepaid direct from the publishers:
The Noble Press, Inc.
213 W. Institute Place, Suite 508
Chicago, Illinois 60610
(800) 486-7737

Child Welfare League of America, Inc.
c/o CSSC
P.O. Box 7816
300 Raritan Center Parkway
Edison, New Jersey 08818
(908) 225-1900
FAX (908) 417-0482

Cover photograph by Jim Hubbard
Cover design by Mike Jaynes

To my Mother and Father, who taught me well;
to my Daughter and Son, who still teach;
and to my loving Wife, who continues
to learn along with me

The Child Welfare League of America, founded in 1920, is the oldest and largest voluntary membership organization in North America devoted entirely to protecting and promoting the well-being of children. CWLA's 670 member agencies, both government and voluntary organizations, annually serve over two million abused, neglected, abandoned, and otherwise troubled children, youths, and their families. CWLA Publications is the world's largest publisher of child welfare materials, including policy and practice books, a scholarly journal, newsletters, a quarterly magazine, and training curricula with videos. For more information or for a CWLA Publications catalog contact:

Child Welfare League of America, Inc.
440 First Street, NW, Suite 310
Washington, DC 20001-2085
(202) 638-2952

Author's Note

The names and identifying characteristics of people, hospitals, and schools have been changed in order to protect and preserve the confidentiality of the people I have encountered as clients, their families, and other professionals with whom I have worked.

FOREWORD

Much has been written about the crisis in America surrounding children and the child welfare system. One of every five children lives in poverty. Two and a half million children are reported to be abused and neglected each year. More than 100,000 children are homeless, and half of all high school students in our major cities drop out before graduation.

Our nation's child welfare system serves more than 400,000 children and teenagers—kids who need foster care and adoptive homes, who have been abused and neglected, who need to stay for periods in residential treatment facilities, who require prenatal or parenting help, or who need the services of drug treatment centers. Child welfare professionals also work with children who are homeless or abandoned or dying of AIDS.

For many readers, Keith Richards's first-hand account of life as a child abuse investigator will be an eye-opener. To read this compelling story of one case worker's experience is to learn about life as a Child Protective Services worker. That life entails tough decisions, disappointments, and pressures.

The truth is, the dramatic encounters and ordeals you will read about in this real-life account are experienced over and over by thousands of dedicated child welfare professionals in cities across America.

Those who choose a career in caring—a career working

with at-risk children and teens and their families—are individuals who want to help others change their lives. These individuals know that they can target strengths families have, and start there to encourage change. They know that they can earn the trust and confidence of frightened children and lonely teenagers. And they know of the satisfaction gained from serving those who are vulnerable and needy.

Life as a child protective worker is challenging and difficult, by any measure. Caseloads that child protective workers carry are dangerously high in too many areas of the country, sometimes soaring upwards of seventy cases per worker. It is the children who suffer as a result.

We need to do all we can to support and facilitate the work of dedicated professionals like Keith Richards, for they are the ones who have the knowledge, skill, and determination to nurture change and rekindle hope for those who depend on our country's child welfare system.

David S. Liederman
Executive Director
Child Welfare League of America
October, 1991

CHAPTER ONE

"**I**'m glad I don't have your job!"
I hear it all the time.

Trash collectors, morticians, nurses, and air traffic controllers have told me they couldn't do it, because of the stressful toll it takes. It drains me emotionally, I'm held accountable when something goes wrong, and although it takes a long time to train me to do it properly, odds are I won't last very long.

Even when I do it right, I can cause misery, suffering, anguish, and trauma; I try to defuse emotional time-bombs with every bit of the delicacy that a bomb squad affords the mechanical kind. I'm not a detective, a pediatrician, an attorney, or an educator, though I work closely with each and at times must function as they do.

I'm on call every hour of the day and every day of the year. I visit the mansions of the wealthy and the hovels of the poor, yet my own paycheck is small compensation for what I have to do.

I am charged by the state to investigate allegations of child maltreatment. I must first determine whether a child is "at risk" of being abused or neglected before I can act further. Yet, it is generally assumed that whatever decisions I make will be the wrong ones, that I will leave defenseless babies in the homes of monsters while tearing hysterical children from the loving arms of their innocent parents.

1

Thus, I never know what to expect when I knock on people's doors. Their reactions range from shock, to anxiety, fear, or outrage, and I'm just as likely to be greeted with angry threats as with hysterical tears. I'm entrusted with one of the most important responsibilities society can confer; as a result, I'm continually called upon to defend my actions, not only in the homes of my clients, but in the offices of my superiors, as well as in courts of law. I must sense whether someone is telling the truth or covering up, lying or reciting practiced lines. I visit precinct houses, day care centers, hospitals, and schools, to help me reach a decision that I alone can make. Wherever I go I'm feared and resented, because of who I work for, and because of what I do.

I'm the Simon LeGree of social work, the Bogeyman with a clipboard; I'm a child abuse investigator, and people always think I'm going to take their kids away.

In dire circumstances, I can.

■   ■   ■

I've been trained to judge a situation quickly to assess the degree of risk a child faces; I must determine the quality of a lifetime of parenting in an hour or less. I must find credible evidence to back up my contentions, and must always justify the decisions I make, regardless of what they are. I've had to learn to trust my own judgment, especially when it seems no one else around me does. I need to be authoritative without compromising compassion; purposeful without losing sympathy. I see endless human suffering and pain, yet I'm expected to be sensitive and caring without allowing emotions to muddle my objectivity. I often wade through dozens of unfounded accusations, but must stay alert for those that bear substance. I must be mindful of the rights of parents while enforcing the rights of children. And no matter how emotional a situation I've dealt with, once I'm back in my car, I must put it all behind me, and be ready to dive into the next case.

There's always a next case waiting.

I've taken children from parents who would kill to stop me; I've allowed children to remain while "concerned citizens" scream incredulously in my ear. If a child is hurt I should have been there sooner; if there are no marks or bruises I'm overreacting. I work in a system created for noble purposes that allows itself to be manipulated by persons with less-than-noble motives. And the only ones who understand are other protective workers, when I can find time to seek one out before going to my next case.

There's always a next case waiting.

They can train me for many things, yet at times I feel totally unprepared. I'm told, "Don't worry, you're not alone out there," but it often feels that way. We seldom work in pairs, and though support is but a phone call away, I'm the one on the scene, clutching onto calm and reason, trying to stay afloat in a maelstrom of swirling emotions.

I find myself questioning my own feelings, my upbringing, my parenting, while struggling to keep my personal beliefs and biases in check. I'm often called upon to enforce, instruct, and even demonstrate practices with which I may not agree. I expect adherence to a value system defined by law, from people who may never have been taught any values at all. I look for parenting skills in persons whose only guidelines are often the manner in which their parents raised them.

Nearly half of all male sex offenders were sexually abused as children themselves. It is my role to break the cancerous cycle of abused-child-becomes-abusing-parent, regardless of whether the abuse is physical or sexual. It is also my job to save a child from further suffering, and I'm called upon in every case to decide whether the trauma of being ripped from the arms of one's family will have less effect on a child than allowing him or her to stay in a situation with a high potential for physical and emotional scarring.

I work for Child Protective Services (CPS), the primary government agency dealing with child abuse or neglect, at least at the county level. Though the agency has been around almost twenty years, it will take another generation or two to realize the full effect CPS is having on children today. I seldom learn whether or not I've done the right thing for the child in the long run, and I carry the extra burden of knowing that whatever I decide today will have a profound impact tomorrow, regardless of the decision. It's harder to learn from my mistakes, since it might be years before I realize I've made one. And of course, by then, the damage has already been done.

I'm not supposed to take the cases home with me; I'm not supposed to get emotionally involved. Yet there are people's lives I touch that touch me right back. Now and then a case rears up that I can't stop thinking about, coiling itself around me like a boa, refusing to let go, squeezing me until I stagger. For these cases especially, I go the extra yard and make sacrifices because I see the potential for positive change in my hands, and I know that I can make a difference that may still be felt long after I'm gone.

Still, it all comes back to the family's first shock at my first knock. I remove children from their families only as a last resort, yet everyone assumes that's why I'm at their door. I do not wear a cloak of doom, yet people dress me in it just the same, case after case after case.

And there's always another case waiting.

They tell me they couldn't do my job, while inside they're hoping I won't have to.

I'm a child abuse investigator, and people always think I'm going to take their kids away.

CHAPTER TWO

The doorbell button was cracked and painted over, so I didn't bother with it, and I didn't expect my hearty knock on the battered aluminum screen door to prompt an answer either. So, like I'd done a few thousand times before, I wrote my name and phone number on a yellow sticky-note I kept on my clipboard. I was looking for a place to stick it when a muffled voice floated out, telling me to wait a minute. If they'd known who was standing outside their door, I wonder if they'd have answered at all.

It gave me a moment to survey the none-too-friendly environs.

A piece of each side of the mat by the door was missing, so that I and anyone else who ventured up the cracked and crumbling redbrick-and-mortar steps was greeted with the message "LCOM." The place needed a paint job desperately, and the weeds in the yard needed mowing. A window on the first floor had a hole in the glass pane the size of a fist, and two others upstairs radiated aster-shaped cracks from the point of impact caused by a thrown rock or maybe a BB. A tattered, ratty-looking brown sofa lay upturned amongst the weeds, three legs kicking upwards at the sky, dirty-white stuffing spilling out of several holes, like some large, furry animal that had lost a race to get across a road.

I'd visited enough of these houses to know that as bad as

the outside looked, the inside would be no better. Assuming I got past the front door.

The white woman who answered was older than I'd expected, or maybe she was just tired.

"Amanda MacAvoy?"

"Yes?"

Dry, wispy hair the color of dead, faded leaves splayed around her head, and I wasn't sure whether her chin or nose was pointier. She was thin-lipped, although her lower one was cracked and swollen, and she sported a pretty nasty mouse under one eye. Her complexion had been ravaged by acne, yet it was her eyes that held the key to the woman's personality; gray, listless, washed-out eyes from which the zest of life had long ago departed regarded me from the other side of the torn screen door. If anything remained at all in those eyes, it was resignation; seeing the bruises all over her arms, the baby those arms held, and the brood of dirt-covered, runny-nosed children clinging to her skirts, I could understand why.

I flashed my ID. "I'm Mr. Richards from Child Protective Services. Can I speak to you a moment?"

Though her eyes grew wider at the mention of CPS, she shrugged and pushed the screen door open toward me with her foot. I stepped inside and surveyed the interior with an internal grimace; it was every bit as bad as I'd anticipated.

When a client offers you a seat on a piece of furniture even more decrepit than the one in Amanda's front yard, for the sake of propriety you gingerly lower yourself onto the front edge, squatting more than sitting, ready to jump up quickly should you notice anything crawling or scuttling nearby. Sometimes you just out-and-out fib and complain of an old war wound or explain that you'd rather stand because you're sitting in the office all day as it is. But in this case, she did not offer me a seat nor did I take one.

"Is Mr. MacAvoy home?" I stood near the door, thankful it was still warm enough outside to leave the door open; the stench of rotting garbage, unwashed bodies, and days-old diapers assaulted my nose and dared me to keep down my breakfast.

"No," she answered, shifting the baby to her other shoulder. "He in trouble again?"

"That's what I need to determine. We've received a report alleging child abuse, and I had hoped to speak to both of you about it together. But if he's not around, you and I can talk anyway."

I saw the uncertainty creep into her eyes as her jaw muscles twitched. She clutched her baby a little tighter, defensively yet defiantly, as if to tacitly inform me that some things would not be stripped from her. Like her children and her dignity, for example.

I took as deep a breath as I could under the circumstances and read from the photocopy pinched on my clipboard: "'Reporting party alleges father burned child's arm as punishment by immersing it in scalding hot water. RP did not witness incident, but saw blisters on child's fingers. Child never received any medical treatment for this injury.'"

"Who they talking about?"

"Your daughter Jenny."

"That's a lie. Who made that report?"

"I'm afraid that's confidential."

A hard edge of annoyance crept into her voice."Well, Confidential had better get their facts straight! First of all, I ain't no child abuser. Second, she only burned a couple of fingers, not her whole arm, and that was an accident. Third—"

"What sort of accident?" I interrupted.

"She pulled a cup of hot coffee down on herself off the counter, and some got on her fingers. That's the truth, I don't care *what* Confidential said. You can even ask Jenny yourself."

"Is she here?"

"Yeah, she's here. JENNY! Get out here and talk to this man!" The baby in her arms startled awake with a jerking motion of its arms, opened its eyes, and promptly burped up milk all over its mother's chest.

"Can you tell me why she's home from school today?"

The woman gave her best impression of a smile, failed utterly, and turned her back to me as she headed down the hall, calling over her shoulder, "Lemme go get Jenny out here."

She turned into the last room at the end of the hall, and I heard, but could not make out, her urgent whisperings as she prodded a young child out to talk to me.

"Go on, tell 'im. Tell 'im how you burned your hand when you pulled that hot coffee down on yourself. You'll see, mister, it's just like I told you. Go on, Jenny, don't be afraid."

By her chin-on-shoulder posture and small, slow steps I could tell this child was probably terrified of me. As I knelt down in front of her to get my face even with her eye level, I tried to show empathy in my eyes. Long, straggly blonde hair framed a round, dirty face. A turned-up nose was lightly seasoned with tan freckles. Golden bangs covered most of her forehead, and the one direct glance she ventured at me revealed eyes the color of robin eggs. But it was her expression, innocent and confused, that seared its way through my memory, straight into my heart. I'd seen that expression before, in countless other children I'd interviewed. An expression that seemed to ask for help, but simultaneously feared what changes in her life my presence might create.

She held up four fingers for me to see, and I handled them as though they were rare coins. They were uniformly puffy and blistered, though some of the blisters had already broken and were starting to heal. I grimaced as I asked, "Does it hurt much?" to those limpid, azure eyes, which darted to the woman's face before the mouth answered me.

"No-o," she said tentatively, eyes now cast at the floor.

"What happened?"

Another glance at her mother.

"Go ahead, tell him you got burned."

"I got burned."

Although Mrs. MacAvoy apparently could ignore the baby's regurgitated milk on her chest, she couldn't ignore the intrusive ringing of the telephone, and she and the baby disappeared to answer it, which was fine with me. It gave me a chance to speak to the child without her mother being there, and I realized that this might be the only shot I'd get at such an exclusive interview.

Little did I know how right I'd be.

"So how did your poor fingers get burned?"

With still another glance at the doorway through which her mother had departed, the child wore a worried, puzzled expression, as though some internal question was being debated, and after a moment, a decision reached.

"Are you the man who's going to take me to my new home?"

I smiled. This was a common fear among children, especially the younger ones, who often have been threatened by parents or other children that "CPS will come take you away and put you in foster care if you don't behave." This is a major reason why the reputation of a CPS investigator ranks somewhat lower than that of the Bogeyman; while both of us can snatch you away from home and family whenever we want, the Bogeyman only comes at night.

"No, precious, not unless you want me to. I'm here to find out more about how your hand got burned."

Despite the feeling that time was slipping away, I let her mull this over in silence while I continued observing her facial expressions. She looked at me, looked at the doorway, looked at the floor. Then she looked at me again, returned her gaze to the floor, and said softly, "I was bad."

"What did you do that was bad?"

"I spilled. I reach-ted for a cup on the counter and it got spilled."

"And that's what burned you? Hot coffee?"

"Hot *water*." Her little jaw was set firmly; her statement was adamant, intractable. I, however, was becoming confused.

"Hot water splashed you when you spilled the cup?"

She tilted her jaw towards me, regressing to cover her anxiety as she said in a baby voice, "No, silly, the hot water didn't splash me, it burned my hand 'cause I was bad."

My gut reaction told me I had enough already to indicate that the report was probably true, but the state of New York would want more, so I tried to come right to the point. "Did your hand get burned by accident, or did someone help you to burn it?"

Fear returned to her face as she looked past me, then resumed her staring contest with the floor. I'd run out of time; mother was back.

"What kind of question is *that*?" I don't know if the phone call she'd received had anything to do with it, but the mother suddenly seemed as nervous and frightened as the child. Her voice took on the edge of someone who's fighting to keep her world from caving in, and feels herself slowly losing ground. "You . . . you got no right to come in here accusin' folks of doin's you got no proof for."

"I'm accusing no one, ma'am, I'm just trying to investigate—"

"I think you done enough 'vestigatin'. You seen the child, she's okay, we both told you what happened. There ain't no abuse goin' on here, and I ain't answerin' any more questions until I have my husband here and I can talk to my lawyer. So I'm gonna have to ask you to leave."

I answered, "As you wish, ma'am. I'd like to set up an appointment to speak with your husband anyway." I handed her my business card, along with her copy of the rights letter (explaining her options as an alleged perpetrator in a CPS report). "Please have him call me to set up a convenient time." I turned to the child again and extended my hand to shake hands goodbye, which she did reluctantly. It was a pleasant way to exit, and gave me one last look up close at her injury. "Bye-bye, Jenny. It was very nice talking with you."

"'Bye," she said, her eyes making contact with mine for only a brief second.

I would have bet a month's wages that before my key found its way into my car ignition, my card had found its way into the MacAvoy garbage pail.

CHAPTER THREE

For as many times as I've done this, I can never get over that look, that expression I saw in Jenny's face, the one that lies just beyond the defensive wall children often erect between themselves and strangers. It was a haunted look, and it haunted me. It made me feel that there was more that the child wanted to tell me, but she had been afraid to. I could still see those large, sorrowful eyes, behind which lurked a sadness that spoke of adult burdens prematurely shouldered, pain uncomprehended but felt all the same. And there was something else—a glimpse, a trace of familiarity I couldn't quite identify, dancing and teasing along the muted edges of my memory. I'd seen her before, or someone like her, but then again, after seventeen years as a social worker, a good many of the faces I'd encountered had melted one into another.

I knew I'd need to see Jenny again. But I wanted something more concrete to go on next time out, so upon my return to the office I telephoned a doctor friend of mine who'd helped me out with medical advice in the past.

Though I hadn't spoken to him in over a year, Dr. Irving Bronson's voice had not changed one iota, and I found that reassuring; the older we get, the more the constancy of little things seems to matter.

"Keith! Good to hear from you. How's your latest concert tour coming along?" This reference to the Rolling Stones rock group member with the same name as mine was Irv's attempt

11

at a joke, one that many people make in an attempt at clever-
ness, but one that I've heard so often I usually just try to ignore.
Yes, it's my real name; no, we're not related; and if I made the
kind of money he does, this book would be about the music in-
dustry, not child protection.

"Listen, Doc, I got a burn case I'm not real comfortable
with. The story is that the child pulled some hot coff—" the
small, adamant face popped into my mind, and I corrected myself "—hot water down on herself about two weeks ago, but the
injury looks more like the hand was immersed than splattered.
Can you judge time of onset just by looking at the injury?" I
was grasping at a straw, hoping this might lead to some sort of
time inconsistency.

"I can make a rough guess, but after two weeks, I'll only be
accurate to within a few days." So much for that gambit.

"Are you available to testify as to splatter or immersion
pattern of the burn after you've examined her?"

"Sure, but I'll be in the Bahamas all next month, so you
don't have a lot of time."

"You still accepting Medicaid?"

"Not as a general rule, but if you can get the child here,
we'll work something out. Parents cooperative?"

"Not especially." That's one of the catch-22s I'm caught in
half the time. I can only force a physical exam by court order,
but without the findings a medical exam might give me, I probably don't have a strong enough case to show imminent risk,
especially when the parents are so vague on what happened.
"Maybe I can bluff them into cooperating, but if they don't go
for it, I can't force it. I guess I'll have to get back to you."

"I'm glad I don't have your job," he said.

I rang off, a vague uneasiness gnawing in the pit of my
stomach. There was more to this case, there had to be. You
didn't have to be a medical expert to tell the difference between an immersion burn and a splatter burn; you only did if
you wanted to testify to it in court. Yet I had little hope that
Jenny's parents were going to let her be examined.

How I hate dead ends!

■   ■   ■

Despite the frenzied craziness a CPS caseload engenders (especially one as large as mine), I thought about Jenny more than any of my other cases. Usually, I try to put the cases behind me and think about other things, but MacAvoy was one of those that stays with you despite your best efforts to forget it. After three days had passed and I'd heard nothing from the MacAvoys or their lawyer, I decided to initiate a little follow-up action on my own.

Knowing where the family lived, I called the local school district to determine whether or not Jenny had been enrolled. Though able to pinpoint which school she should be attending based on the MacAvoys' address, they had no record of the child ever having been registered.

I checked the identity of the reporting party from the only copy of the report that contained such information. I'd assumed it was the school, but I'd assumed wrong; the word "Anonymous" glared back at me. No one to call for additional or more specific information.

I checked another number in the phone book, calling the diocesan offices to check whether Jenny may have been enrolled in a private, Catholic school. This was admittedly a long shot—people on Public Assistance seldom have that kind of money. Once again, there was no record of Jenny's enrollment.

It occurred to me I hadn't asked for the actual date of birth for the child—information I usually request on a first visit. The report stated she was five, and I felt that to be fairly accurate. This was another dead end of sorts, since in New York State, children are not required to be enrolled in school until the age of six.

I resolved to make another visit to ask the mother for Jenny's date of birth, and assuming my estimate was correct, to suggest that Jenny get a checkup and up-to-date immunizations preparatory to her enrollment. Of course, I would recommend a particular doctor I knew to be terrific with children!

Once again I found myself ignoring that cracked doorbell button and knocking on the torn screen-door. This time there was purpose and authority to my knock, so of course this time it went unanswered.

A narrow concrete walkway led around the small house, and I followed it to what I hoped would be a side or back door. I took in the dingy, grime-enshrouded windows on the side of the house; barren dirt patches interspersed with clumps of crabgrass that hadn't been cut in months, if ever; a days-old bag of garbage that had split and spilled its guts against the house and was being preyed upon by large, arrogant black crows who ignored me as I walked past.

The backyard was even more neglected-looking than the rest of the property, with more trash and a rusting car body sitting on cinder blocks, totally stripped of anything worth salvaging. A reddish-brown swing-set frame, as rusted as the car body, stood in a far corner, an unsightly testimony to the forgotten time when it had been shiny and new, the center of that most precious and delightful of human sounds, children's laughter.

There was no more response to my knock at the back door than there had been at the front door, but I determined it best not to leave any sort of message. As I walked around to my car, I was approached by a woman who definitively stated what was already obvious: "There ain't nobody home."

I smiled and acknowledged the comment, continuing to slide into my car, but the woman's curiosity was too strong to let me go that easily. "You some kinda insurance guy?" she asked, noting my clipboard. I shook my head no. "Police?" No, but I asked the woman if she had any idea when the MacAvoys might be returning. She didn't, but she took one more guess. "Child abuse, right?"

"Social Services," I conceded, starting my engine as she launched into a gossipy rendition of the family's reputation in the neighborhood; Amanda MacAvoy watched children for some of the neighbors (although this informer said she wouldn't trust the woman to burn if she were on fire), and the whole street had been treated to periodic episodes of thumping and screaming as Jud was in the habit of coming home drunk and practicing his shadow-boxing, using his wife as the shadow. I heard about every injury any child had ever suffered on the premises, as well as speculations concerning everything from sexual abuse to drug dealing, prostitution, and black-marketeering.

I'd learned more from this negative visit than I probably would have had somebody been home, but it was all hearsay, and couldn't be used in court, if the case ever got that far. Still, this woman's assertions helped confirm my uneasy feeling that there was much more going on in the case.

About the only things she couldn't tell me were whether or not Jenny was going to school, or when I could catch the family home. After thanking her, I drove away with the woman's caution still ringing in my ears: Jud MacAvoy was just no good, and I'd do best to steer clear of him.

CHAPTER FOUR

I fell into it.

Or rather, I was "sort of shoved."

That's the true answer to a question I'm often asked: namely, "How'd you get this job?"

I tell those who do the asking that I always wanted to be a social worker, I tell them I always liked children and decided to help protect them, and sometimes, depending on who they are and how I think they'll take it, I tell them I really wanted to be a teacher but couldn't stand the thought of whole summers and two weeks at Christmas away from my job.

But the honest truth is, I graduated from college, needed a job, took a battery of civil service tests, and the Department of Social Services made me an offer before anyone else did. A bachelor's degree and a valid New York State driver's license were the only prerequisites, and I qualified. It was later, after I had been a caseworker for a few years, that I was assigned to be a Child Protective Services worker.

Almost nobody volunteers to work CPS.

There are those who do, usually because they either feel a desire to make the world a better place (remember that 1960s slogan that says "If you're not part of the solution, you're part of the problem"?); or because their present assignment becomes intolerable; or, sometimes, because it's the only way they can effect a promotion.

Otherwise, unless administration is desperate for warm bodies and hires brand new people right off the street, experienced workers are transferred in, kicking, screaming, or otherwise protesting, and plotting from day one possible ways of getting out. I was in the latter category, although I didn't protest too much. Personality conflicts with the bosses in my prior assignment (dealing with day care providers) made it easier for me to go, and the assignment was thrust on me somewhat unexpectedly, so that I had no other job options at the time. People can only change when they have another job to change to.

Most states have a central training facility; some cities, like New York City, have set up CPS Academies; but the rest of the CPS workers in New York State are trained by the staff of Family Life Extension Center, Cornell University, and usually are treated to a two-week, expense-paid trip to Ithaca, Cornell's home town. The training is excellent, combining textbook theory with what an individual worker is likely to encounter in the field—but since each county runs its own bureau for child protection, methods and systems are varied and diverse. There's no way to fully learn the job other than doing it, although talking with experienced workers can sometimes produce insightful tips. Most new CPS people are given about a month to sort of get their feet wet before they are sent for training.

Because it's a job nobody wants, many people adopt an I-don't-know-and-I-don't-want-to-know attitude toward CPS work, almost as though they are afraid that anyone showing even the slightest interest will automatically be earmarked for transfer in by administration. ("You're curious as to what CPS is all about? We'd like to help you find out. Here's your first case!") CPS thus carries a kind of stigma, which often can cause problems when misunderstood. I had to admit that my image of the job before I was forced to do it differed greatly from the reality of what the work actually entails.

Surprisingly, once in the job, I found a lot of reasons to stay; one reason was the feeling that, although every job has its down side, there were pluses to this one that somehow made it worthwhile. After I'd been doing it for a while, people would ask me whether or not I liked it. I couldn't answer that at first, so I always said that one thing was for sure—whereas other jobs and other assignments may have been construed as jokes, working in CPS was no joke. Now, eight years later, I simply say there must be something about it I like very much, because I'm still doing it. Just don't ask me what that something is. I've been too busy to take the time to figure it out.

I am, however, in a vast minority, being a male; my department is made up of approximately 75 percent women, not counting secretaries. While supervisory staff runs about 50-50, two-thirds of our senior workers are female, although, understandably, most of our night/emergency staff are male. I'm also somewhat of a minority by way of experience; although approximately 63 percent of our staff have at least one year's experience on the job, only 46 percent have at least two years experience. Thus, well over a third of our investigations are being done by "rookies," and over half our people can be expected to leave the job within two years, frightening statistics for a job dealing with so serious a social ill as child maltreatment. I shudder to think how low the figure is for workers, such as I, who have five or more years of experience.

An interesting phenomenon occurs when comparing single and married people who do this job. Marrieds, for example, don't know how single people manage to get through each week with no one to lean on. If not for an understanding spouse, many co-workers say they would have been committed to a rest home long ago. Personally, it's made me go home many a night and hug my own children a little longer than I might have were I working in another profession, and I've come to realize what great kids they are. Having to know the state guidelines for what is and is not appropriate parenting also has me constantly questioning my own methods. On occasion, I tell my own children about some of the unfortunate people I encounter, just so they'll appreciate how good their situation really is.

Yet, many single or currently unattached workers say that they're glad they don't have spouses and kids, after visiting some of the strange and twisted families they have to work with. I don't know how our single-parent CPS workers manage it at all, especially when their own ex-spouses may likewise be sitting like snipers in a tree, waiting to shoot them down by playing the same games with their custodial and visitation rights that the workers see their clients suffering from. Having been raised by two loving and caring parents who stayed married until death did them part, I also can't know what it's like to be a child trying to grow up in such an embittered environment. Thus, I do try to be a little more empathetic and understanding with single-parent families, since many people really are good parents, trying their best to raise children under difficult circumstances.

Most of the cases we receive deal with neglect, poor guidance, or inadequate supervision issues. As of this writing, the figures for cases in this county that are ultimately determined to be unfounded (untrue) are running between 60-70 percent, and the number of "indicated" cases (some credible evidence supports the allegations) has actually declined over the past two years. This means that if I entered someone's home with the assumption that they must be guilty of abuse or neglect simply because a report has been filed against them, I'd be absolutely wrong about two-thirds of the time.

This is why it is essential that we investigate each case on its own merits and faults; this is why, although everyone has a horror tale to tell about some friend or relative who had dealings with CPS, similar cases are not always handled the same way, and the results don't necessarily turn out the same.

What does seem to remain constant is the degree of professionalism found in most workers, who themselves are just people juggling tremendous internal and external pressures, both within the agency and within themselves. For myself, I've found the best way to alleviate such pressures is to talk about them. Though there have occasionally been conflicts at the dinner table when I'm trying to relate case specifics to my wife Gloria (without mentioning any names, of course—client confidentiality must be maintained), while my children are being their usual selves, interrupting inappropriately and making what seem like a million trivial demands, Gloria has been very good about letting me vent my frustrations after a rough day.

She has also seen what stress and tension can do to me. During one particularly rough stretch, she gave me a small, pink, polished piece of rose quartz, which I carry in my pocket every day. This crystal is said to send and receive on the universal frequency of unconditional love; it can send both health and love in any form to anyone. I believe it helps me to maintain both love of self and compassion for others; to see opportunities for positive growth (to make lemonade when all I'm given is lemons, to paraphrase a popular poster gracing the walls of social workers everywhere), and to keep things in perspective, reminding me that no matter what happens, I am loved and have a loving household to go home to when my day is done. Not bad for a stone the size of a small gumball.

Gloria works in an elementary school, so she hears not only what goes on with the children, but also what school personnel have to say about CPS workers and what they do or don't do. Sometimes she'll pass certain stories or comments she's heard along to me, and if I can, I'll try to explain (without naming names) why cases were handled in certain ways. Thus, she has an "inside track," and I receive feedback that I try to use constructively. She also clips articles out of the newspaper for me that she feels will be relevant to my job. (For example, she has given me articles about a Wyoming woman prosecuted for alcoholism during pregnancy, a bill proposed in the New York State legislature to make ongoing CPS investigations inadmissible evidence in custody hearings, and an update on the sex abuse trial of a California child care provider.)

No one, however, can understand what I do as well as someone who is also doing it. Co-workers empathize best because they might have dealt with the same situation yesterday, or may find themselves in the same boat tomorrow. Unfortunately, we are so busy scurrying around, trying to get the work done, that we don't afford ourselves the chance to discuss the case situations and our feelings about them as often as perhaps we should.

We formed a lunchtime worker support group, the Child Protective Worker's Association (CPWA), several years back, that has been very helpful to me personally, but that only includes a core of fifteen to twenty workers in a bureau of over a hundred; as far as I know, it is the only such organized group existing in the state, if not the nation. Perhaps rapid turnover is part of the reason our group isn't larger; people aren't around long enough to get involved. Perhaps people feel put upon enough each day, without having to give up what little time they have to themselves. There also may be a feeling that we are some sort of militant political activist group (which we're not) and that association with us will only invite some sort of retribution from superiors. But as far as I'm concerned, I often paraphrase a common saying heard from military personnel during the Vietnam era: "What are they going to do, send me to CPS?"

One of the hardest aspects of the work is seeing such misery suffered by undeserving people, innocent parents as well as maltreated children. I also feel for other workers who succumb to the pressures, are blamed when something goes wrong, or are scapegoated by media, community, and/or their own administration.

Don't get me wrong. Workers who continually mess up on the job or who aren't carrying their weight have no business in this type of work, but the vast majority I see are just people trying to get a difficult job done, for one of the noblest reasons on earth. Putting their personal feelings on hold while on duty, they are left to resolve professional and emotional conflicts in their own way, on their own time, without any guidance as to how that might be accomplished.

That's one pretty tall order for a group of people who more than likely won't be around long enough to develop ways, other than leaving, of keeping the job from destroying them.

CHAPTER FIVE

The temperature was higher than usual for autumn, owing in part to the few days of Indian summer we'd enjoyed. This day was overcast with an early morning mist, which I hoped would burn off before lunchtime. It gave the MacAvoy neighborhood an eerie, surreal quality, and also made visibility impossible beyond fifteen feet; thus, when I heard the children's voices, they were disembodied, floating out of the fog like something you'd see on "The Twilight Zone."

The voices were squabbling, as children will do while waiting for a school bus, and they grew louder and more agitated until finally, the sound of a little girl crying out for her mommy reached my ears. The crying grew louder, as though the child were approaching my position near the front porch, but then receded as the child must have run around the other side of the house. I followed the sound through the fog, and thought how representative this dreamlike scenario was of the challenge a child abuse investigator faces on each case— following the sound of a crying, unseen child through fog, not sure if the child is in danger but knowing with a growing sense of urgency that it is your job to protect her, if you can find her.

The crying stopped abruptly, so unless a worse tragedy had befallen the girl, the child had either found her mother and was snuffling into her chest, or had simply entered that messy, reeking house. When the backyard fog dissolved around me and I came upon Mrs. MacAvoy hanging laundry on a rope stretched between two elm trees, I was thankful for the chance to speak to her without having to go inside. There was no sign of the girl.

"Mrs. MacAvoy?"

The woman did not stop her clothes-pinning, but dropped one as she jumped at the sound of my voice. She must have heard the crying through the mist, as I had, but was making no move to investigate; all her energy seemed to be focused on appearing calm.

Maybe this was a dream, after all.

"Did I hear a child crying?"

The woman shrugged. "Kids're always crying someplace."

"But it seemed to be coming from back here."

"Fog like this can play some nasty tricks." She had not yet turned to face me.

"I wonder if you'd help me refresh my memory," I said, not convinced by her fog explanation but deciding not to press it further. "Did you say that after Jenny's hand was burned, you took her to a doctor?"

"I never said that."

"*Did* you take her to a doctor?"

"No, she... wasn't burned all that bad." She dropped another clothespin, barely keeping hold of the wrinkled, damp shirt she was trying to hang. Off-balance was how I needed her to be, but since she was answering my questions I tried not to push too hard.

"Mrs. MacAvoy, you've been very cooperative with me, and I want to thank you. It can only help Jenny in the long run." That seemed to relax her just a bit, and I continued. "Since we're all interested in Jenny's well-being, I wonder if you'd consent to having her examined by one of our local pediatricians."

"I don't think so," she answered, much too quickly to have given the idea any serious consideration.

"It'll be free, if you're worried about the cost."

"That ain't it," she said, stealing her first glance at me since my arrival. She opened her mouth to say something, then decided against it, apparently wrestling with some inner conflict. I allowed a moment of silence, during which she dropped two more clothespins; there hadn't been a single one on the ground when I'd first arrived, and now there were five.

"Then what's stopping you?" I finally prompted.

"Ain't nothing stoppin' me. Just don't see the need, is all."

"Jenny'll be starting school pretty soon, right? She's going to have to have a physical checkup and get her shots up-to-date anyway. Don't you want to be absolutely positive everything's okay with her?"

"I'm already positive. 'Sides . . . ," she trailed off, getting the last item in her basket hung and retrieving the fallen clothespins from the soft, damp, ground.

"Besides what?"

"Nuthin'."

"Please, ma'am, if there's something else I should know. . . ."

She drew a deep breath, holding the now-empty laundry basket with both hands in front of her, like a shield, and looked me in the eye. I noted that she was sporting a new, purple shiner under the eye she'd kept turned away from me. "Jenny ain't here no more," she said, and then walked past me toward the house.

"What do you mean? Where is she?" I asked, following her brisk pace.

The woman never broke stride, nor looked at me again, but just before she entered the house she said, "Jenny's upstate visiting her other father's family. Now please leave us alone."

"You mean Mr. MacAvoy's not her real fa—"

The back door slammed in my face, leaving me with more questions and less answers than I'd had at the end of my first visit. Suspecting a child is abused can be distressing enough; when that same child suddenly and inexplicably disappears, your emotional instinct shrieks at you to do something, yet past experience reminds you that there's nothing you can do.

There were no more sounds of children on the street; the bus must have arrived and loaded up its charges. I returned to my car and sat there for a few moments, composing my thoughts and jotting down a few notes.

Suddenly, Jenny appeared out of the fog, startling me as she peered through my curbside passenger window. She was wearing a dirty pink jacket, unzipped, with nothing on her hands or head. Her hair was just as blonde, her eyes as blue as I remembered, and her expression nearly as sad.

So much for her being upstate.

I could see her burned hand had healed somewhat as she held it to her eyes to look in my window. I quickly scooted across the seat and rolled it down so she wouldn't have to come around to my side and stand in the street as we spoke.

"Hi, sweetheart! Was that you I heard crying just a little while ago?"

She nodded yes, slowly and only once.

"What made you cry?"

"Peter hit me with a book, right on my sore place on my poor head." She said it as a pouting indictment, no trace of tears now. This was a child not given to prolonged crying jags, as evidenced by a certain roll-with-the-punches toughness I'd seen in other children who'd had to learn to curtail their tears quickly. These children had acquired the abilities to comfort themselves and to keep emotionally distant from others in order to survive; the fact that Jenny had sought me out in such a fashion meant that she still possessed the capacity to trust, and that whatever emotional bruising she'd borne might not yet be irreversible.

"Can I kiss where it hurts?" I asked, and after a moment's deliberation, she nodded yes, turning to afford me access to the right rear part of her skull. As I bestowed a brief-but-gentle smooch, more noise than contact, I noticed the area was swollen, like a bump from a fall. I noticed something else, too, but first I asked, "What made your poor head so sore?"

"I bonked my head after Da—," she started, then dropped her eyes to the ground. A quick glance up at me, then back to the ground. "I fell down," she murmured, after another short pause.

Calmly, gently, I reached through the window and cupped her chin in my palm, lifting to direct her eyes back to mine. "What made you fall, sweetheart?"

She tried to look behind her, towards the house, but between my grip on her chin, and the fog's obscurity, it was more of a sidelong glance, which apparently did not reassure her, for she remained silent. I pulled my arm back through the window.

"Were you going to tell me that your daddy made you fall?" The eyes shot up immediately, and after another glance at the house, she nodded yes, more affirmatively this time.

"How?"

"He pushed me down after I yelled at him for hitting Mommy," she said, showing more of her ability to hold back tears while venturing a few glances at me to note my reaction. I made sure that if she read anything in my face, it was sympathy.

"You saw him hit Mommy?"

She nodded yes.

"Did this happen when you spilled the hot water?" I asked, trying to direct our talk back to her burn.

"No," she said quickly, redirecting the conversation in a new direction of her own. "Are you going to take me to my new home now?"

Our interview was abruptly terminated by the arrival of her mother. "Jenny! What are you doin' talkin' to that man? Get away from there!" Mrs. MacAvoy appeared out of the lifting fog, the baby on her shoulder, and grabbed Jenny's arm, pulled her away from the car, and started to march her inside.

"Didn't you say she was with her father upstate?" I called to their receding backs.

"She's gonna be," yelled the woman over her shoulder before the fog that still lingered between my car and their doorway swallowed them up.

CHAPTER SIX

Once again I drove away knowing there was much more beneath the surface of this case and feeling helpless at my inability to uncover it, or to do anything about what I had seen. While Amanda MacAvoy was not the first client who'd ever lied to me, and certainly wouldn't be the last, it was the matter-of-fact way she'd done it that rankled. Jenny's trepidation at discussing her injuries, the new information she'd given me, and all those glances at the house combined to worry me as though Jenny were my own child. I could never imagine raising children in such an atmosphere, let alone that slovenly environment.

My alarm was tempered somewhat by revulsion at what I'd noticed as I'd leaned through the window and kissed her head. In many of my cases, I hear all sorts of allegations about food on the walls, feces on the floor, roaches in the home, environments so unhealthy that the Board of Health deems them unfit for human habitation. While some houses might well deserve such criticisms, I don't usually find things to be as bad as alleged.

Despite not having noticed them on my first visit, there was no mistaking the tiny, milky white, pencil point-sized scalp-scuttlers that had hopped about in Jenny's scraggly blonde hair—she had fallen prey to head lice. As usually happens when I've come into contact with vermin, my skin began to crawl, and I craved nothing in this world so much as a hot

29

shower. While I'd never yet carried any infestations to my family, once I got home I'd take the precaution of laundering both the clothes I had on and the car's seat covers—after my shower.

This would be as much psychological purge as hygienic practice; unfortunately, my date with soap and hot water was still hours away. Once or twice in the past, I'd taken personal time in order to run right home and cleanse myself; however, this practice was frowned upon for the simple reason that on certain days I'm inside enough infested houses that a shower after each visit would result in half my day being spent in the bathroom.

My only option, as I drove to the office, was to try to put it out of my mind until I could get home, chalking it up to one more of those little hazards they never seem to mention in the job description.

■   ■   ■

Though the parking lot at the office was not always a reliable indicator of what sort of day it would be, today I could have bet the ranch on it. We get paid every other Thursday, and when the lot is full on a non-payday Thursday, it usually means only one thing: Hectic!

It means there will be too many people trying to use one of too few telephone lines, a lot of noise and smoke, and more chance of someone presenting an unexpected problem in person (thereby necessitating immediate action and keeping you from whatever you had planned to do). There's a good chance you'll have to wait in line to talk to anyone you need to talk to, usually your supervisor (especially my supervisor—when he's around), and if you need information from the computer system, odds are that somebody else will be sitting at whatever terminal you want to use.

Still, there was at least one car in the lot I was glad to see— a pale yellow Honda Civic that belonged to a fellow caseworker named Cathy Whiting. Best of all, Cathy was still in it as I walked past.

She rolled down her window; her soft, not quite shoulder length brown hair bounced around her head; her green eyes squinted up at me as she shielded them with her hand.

"Hi, stranger," she said, "how's the job treating you?"

"SOS. You know. How's my favorite foster care worker to-day?" She'd earned this unofficial title by being intelligent, trustworthy, and one of the few people in the agency around whom I felt totally at ease.

"I'm okay. Think we can do lunch later?"

"I'd love to," I answered sheepishly, "if nothing comes up." We had made a similar arrangement last week, and I'd been forced to cancel because of an unexpected emergency on one of my cases. I'd been meaning to get back to her, but hadn't had the chance.

Even though Cathy and I understood that our relationship was strictly platonic, chatty co-workers loved to speculate on what an attractive divorced woman was doing eating lunch with a married man. Truth is, as with most jobs, those who don't do it can't really understand what you go through, and in order to help get you through some days, you need to form your own support group. Cathy and one or two others constituted mine, especially during the times between the monthly CPWA meetings.

"Listen," she said, raising her voice as she started her engine, "I overheard Roxanne pass a comment to someone on the phone about the 'inferior quality' of your work, and how she hopes it 'doesn't establish a pattern'. I'd make sure my rear end was protected if I were you, Keith."

"I will. Thanks for the tip. One o'clock in the lobby, right?"

"Right." She backed the car out of her spot, shifted gears, and the sun glinted off her retreating windshield.

As I watched her drive away, I tried to find a plus side to this. After all, it wasn't every day I could manage a lunch break, let alone take a full hour. My lunchtime is normally spent either catching up on paperwork at my desk, or wolfing down a quick bite as I'm driving to my next appointment. It would be refreshing to worry only about keeping food stains off my clothes for a change, instead of off my papers or off my car floor.

Lynne, our efficient, young-but-matronly unit clerk, was holding the phone out to me as I walked in the door and deposited my briefcase on my drab gray desk.

"Keith? Mrs. Rodriguez for you. This is her third call." I noted the time on the big clock on the wall; it was 10:57. I slipped one arm free of my coat and cradled the receiver between shoulder and jaw as Lynne traced circles around her ear with her forefinger. I flashed her a what-can-I-tell-you look and adopted my professional voice.

"This is Mr. Richards."

Mrs. Rodriguez had called before, alleging that her husband had beaten her. We'd checked her case out thoroughly with the school, the local emergency room, and the police, and no one had ever seen so much as a scratch on her or any of her children, so we'd "unfounded" the case, referred her to a local battered spouse hotline, and closed the case. Yet despite our long and lengthy explanations (including one session with a Spanish-speaking worker) that a finding of "unfounded" meant expungement—destruction of all records and references pertaining to the case—calls continued.

We'd referred her to a mental health clinic, and also to a therapist for marital counseling, and tried many times to instruct her not to call unless something was seriously wrong with the children. She called anyway. I'd found that letting her speak her piece was a faster way to get her off the phone than giving her any more long explanations, so I let her babble as I examined my incoming mail.

I'd received a school report on a girl who had a chronic attendance problem, and this would probably give me enough to file a petition against the parents for educational neglect, thereby using the court to apply pressure to get the child in school regularly. There was a psychological report on a different case, which verified that a handicapped child's only behavioral problem was hyperactivity and that the parents had sought help in a timely fashion for the child, which would allow me to unfound the allegations of medical neglect as long as the parents continued his therapy and administered his medication on a regular basis.

There were also internal reports due on how much time I'd taken off last month, how many cases I'd been assigned last month, why so many of my cases were overdue, how many children I'd placed in foster care last month, why I'd been so late in getting these reports done last month, and all sorts of other bureaucratic necessities, which I'd get to once my caseload was squared away. There were no subsequent maltreatment reports, no emergencies, and nothing requiring my immediate attention, so I figured I was ahead of the game and turned my attention back to dispatching Mrs. Rodriguez's call.

By now she was used to being told we had another call waiting, and she'd spoken most of her piece for this morning, so she allowed me to ring off. No sooner had I slurped a sip of hastily prepared coffee than the phone jangled at my elbow again.

It was a client who had received the appointment letter Lynne sends out on all new cases. Only two in five usually respond to it, which is okay with me, since whatever I find when I go into the home is much more representative of actual conditions when my visit is unannounced. The clients can't clean the house, make sure there's food in the fridge, dress the children in clean clothes, coach them on what to say, etc., if they don't know ahead of time that you're coming. (Unannounced visit findings also seem to carry more weight in court testimony.) Still, you can only do so much, and whenever these new clients do call, I almost always set an appointment.

While I was doing that and writing it down in my appointment book, in walked Tricia Smollins, a worker in the Home-finding and Resource Certification unit. She had done the certification on the emergency boarding home in which another handicapped child had been placed, and was probably here to press me into getting this boy a more permanent, more appropriate placement. I hung up and started to explain to Tricia that I'd only just received the paperwork from the child's school's Committee on the Handicapped (COH), thereby paving the way for a referral to the Hyde Park Children's Center, a facility operated for the purpose of helping troubled teens and preteens. COH findings in writing were a prerequisite to admission consideration.

Lynne interrupted. "Roxanne wants to see you in her office ASAP."

"Did she say what about?"

"No, but she got huffy when I told her you were busy on the phone."

Roxanne was known to get huffy if her lighter didn't light on the first flick, but it was best to try to placate her. I said to Tricia, "Sorry, I really have nothing more to tell you right now. As soon as I can get some movement on that case, I'll get back to you."

"Okay, Keith. I hate pestering you, but we all have our bosses to appease."

"At least yours can be appeased once in a while." I stood to escort her out of the room on my way to Roxanne's office, but before I could take a step, the phone rang again.

Lynne was on another line, so I answered the phone, praying it wasn't for me.

But it was, and it placed me smack in the middle of a no-win situation: risk angering a long-winded, short-tempered client by cutting him off; most certainly anger my Assistant Director if I didn't.

I breathed a heavy sigh as I looked heavenward for help and forgiveness for the lie I was about to tell.

"Mr. Brandt? I'm afraid I have to cut this short. I'm just on my way out on an emergency sex abuse case. I've got the police waiting for me and I really have to go. Could you call me back tomorrow morning and we'll discuss this further?"

The slam of the phone on the other end gave no indication of whether he would or wouldn't.

With another heavy sigh, I thrust my hands in my pockets (feeling the rose quartz crystal in my left one and smiling a private smile) and proceeded to find out what my impatient, harping office mother wanted.

■   ■   ■

To be promoted from casework supervisor to assistant director is to take a quantum leap from upper-level line staff to lower-level administration, sort of like a master sergeant being promoted to second lieutenant. Rank *does* have its privileges, and walking into Roxanne D'Angelis's office reminded me again of that fact, from the carpeting on the floor, to the paneled walls, to the oversize desk and swivel chair in which she sat, to the amount of space afforded her for bookcases, plants, and extra chairs. (I found this all to be particularly galling, knowing that the same amount of space would be used in another area for anywhere from three to five workers, all crammed in like sardines, forced to share phones, breathing air, personal space, and, sometimes, even desks.

The only benefit anyone else might have derived from this arrangement was that it kept her and her daily three packs of cigarette smoke confined to this one small area. Her compulsive habit also explained why Roxanne's teeth stayed a permanent, dingy yellow, and why her breath, like her office, perpetually smelled like humanity's ashtray.

Roxanne is a classic case of someone who decided to go into administration after a brief dabble with social work and thinks she knows all there is to know. What she lacks in case assessment skills, social work training, or CPS experience, she makes up for with catlike qualities that have helped her survive within the bureaucracy: cunning, caution, and an ability to always land on her feet. The tragedy of Roxanne is that she probably could learn to be a quality administrator without sacrificing her compassion, but she doesn't feel it's worth the effort, thus withering whatever potential she has. One can't learn from mistakes one won't acknowledge, and Roxanne is too insecure to allow herself to admit she is as fallible as the rest of us.

She was talking on the phone when I entered, and gestured with a half-smoked cigarette at an empty, upholstered seat in front of her desk. I took it, thinking not for the first time how nice it is that at least you get to sit in a soft chair when you're going to get your butt chewed out.

This particular summons, however, had been issued for case assignment, not reprimand.

"Yes, I'm assigning it to the worker right now. I'll be certain to get back to you as soon as we have an assessment of the situation. Yes, I will. Good-bye now." As soon as she hung up, her Mary Poppins facade floated away as on a change of the wind, and Roxanne returned to being my AD.

"That," she said officiously, "was the commissioner."

"Herself, or someone from her office?"

"Herself. And she wants you out on this case I'm about to give you as quickly as possible."

"Wants *me* out on it? Asked for me personally? I'll tell you, administration knows a top-notch worker when they see one."

She ignored that and pushed a thin folder in front of me. "ZIFARELLI, DENISE" was typed on a label adhering to the folder's tab, and inside was a photocopy of the New York State 2221 form, the one that is telexed to our registry unit on every new case coming in (or new report on an existing case). Included on this form are the date and time of referral, responsible county, names and addresses of the subjects of the report (though often it initially comes through with faulty or incomplete information, and family members are often listed as "unknown"), and the specific allegations. On the bottom, the reporting party is identified with an address and phone number if such information is available—sometimes, all that is written is the word "Anonymous." In all cases, as I had informed Mrs. MacAvoy earlier, we keep the identity of the RP strictly confidential, despite the fact that sometimes the RP admits to the client that he or she made the report. Other times it's not very hard for the alleged perpetrators (those against whom the charges are made) to figure out who turned them in.

(To all those who have asked in the past, and will no doubt ask in the future, yes, this is America, and yes, a basic principle of our justice system is that you have the right to face your accuser; but, no, in CPS proceedings you are not necessarily guaranteed that right. This systemic quirk was forged from the fact that our legal powers derive from family court, not criminal, and has been further tempered by all the emphasis placed on preserving reporter confidentiality. Yes, it stinks, and no, there's not a whole lot you can do about it.)

"RP states that she has three small children home who cannot care for themselves properly," the report read, "and has claimed she can no longer handle the pressures of 'being a Zifarelli'. RP claims to have taken a large dose of sleeping pills, and someone should come out to check on kids."

The RP was listed as being Marianne Zifarelli, who was also listed as the mother of the children in question; this was a case in which a desperate client, in seeking immediate help, had called in a referral on herself.

"Additional Info," the report continued, "Mother is the ex-daughter-in-law of Legislator Anthony Zifarelli, having married and divorced his son Michael. RP claims to have made similar referrals on herself in the past, but claims 'this time I really did it, this time I'm serious.'"

The case record so far contained a single sheet of paper. Since there were no accompanying volumes, odds were that any prior referrals were determined to be unfounded, which would have caused any case materials to be destroyed in the name of confidentiality. "No prior records?" I asked, to make sure.

"None on file."

I gave a low whistle. "Sounds like this lady likes the attention." I'd read about this case in the papers. Marianne had walked into their bedroom one night to find Michael engaged in some extramarital gymnastics with a svelte secretary, and she could no longer deny the rumors she'd heard for years. A nasty divorce ensued, followed by a nastier custody battle, which wasn't quite over yet. Now some families like to keep this sort of thing quiet and discreet, but this family felt the newspapers were their playground, and the papers obliged by giving the case a lot of exposure. "He never used any positions like that with me," Marianne had been quoted as saying in court.

Roxanne pulled out another cigarette, lit it with a gold butane lighter, and exhaled as she spoke, her eyes squinting through the smoke, the cigarette bobbing on her lips. "I was involved in the last threat she called in. Apparently, Legislator Zifarelli was made aware of it and asked to be notified if it happened again. Seems like he's trying to make a case for her emotional instability in order to get custody of the children transferred to his son."

"Should we be getting into the middle of their custody battle?"

"No," Roxanne answered, "but it shows why the commis-

sioner is so interested in the case. Keep that in mind as you investigate, and watch what you say."

"I intend to. But why the sudden advice? Why now?" I decided to ask, just to see what her answer would be in light of
what Cathy had told me; I didn't for one second believe it was
out of Roxanne's genuine concern for me.

She gave what she probably intended as a condescending
smile, but it came out more like a grimace.

"Because we're short on staff today, and because I was specifically instructed to."

"Well, it's nice to see somebody still worries about me," I
said as I slipped the record under my arm and rose from the
chair.

Social workers are people who deal with people, and they
can burn out simply from dealing with other people's problems
for too long. At one time, Roxanne might have cared about her
co-workers, but after sitting for so many years behind her desk,
she'd lost her perspective, and her empathy along with it.

"Don't flatter yourself," she called after me, "they're
much more worried about our liability than your competence,
or relative lack thereof. And by the way, since your supervisor
is going to be out indefinitely, you will be reporting directly to
me."

My immediate supervisor, Garwood Taylor ("Woody to
my friends," he'd always say), had been in a car accident and
would not be back to work for quite some time. Speculation
was that this would, after thirty-odd years with the agency, finally force him to retire; Roxanne was going to delight in keeping me right under her thumb in the meantime.

At least I could escape the craziness of the office for a little
while.

I grabbed my briefcase and was wrestling into my jacket
when the phone rang again. Lynne was away from her desk,
and there was no one else around, so I answered it, hoping it
wasn't for me so I could take a quick message and get going on
Zifarelli.

"Child Protective, Mr. Richards."

"Is this Mr. Richardson? I was told you were the man to
call about a case you got on Amanda MacAvoy?"

"May I ask your name, please?" I answered, neither confirming nor denying anything about MacAvoy until I knew to
whom I was speaking.

"Oh, I'm sorry, Mr. Richardson, my name is Carla Simmons. I'm Amanda's mother and Carlotta's grandmother. She
was named after me!" the woman said proudly.

"How can I help you, ma'am?"

"Well, I was told you were the man who was gonna take
the baby away from Mandy, and I just wanted to ask if you
could place the baby here with family rather than put her in
some foster home with strangers."

I glanced at my watch with a growing sense of urgency;
not only was time running out for Mrs. Zifarelli, but if Rox
anne walked by and saw me still here on the phone instead of
out on the case, there would be hell to pay.

"Thank you for sharing all this with me, ma'am, we'll
keep you in mind as a possible resource. Is there a number
where we can reach you so we can discuss this in detail when I
have more time? I'm afraid you caught me right in the middle
of an emergency." This felt like having cried wolf for years and
now actually having the beast sniffing at the door; but it was
obvious the woman had heard it all before.

"Oh, I know how you people work. You're always in the
middle of one emergency or another. I ain't got no phone, I'm
callin' from a friend's. Just let me speak my piece and then you
can get on to your 'emergency'."

She then began briefing me about how neither the
MacAvoy nor the Simmons families were particularly fond of
one another; the fact that "them chil' abuse people was always
involved, not because of Mandy, oh no, Lord knows she always
tries her best, it's that scumbucket Jud MacAvoy what's the
cause of all the misery"; and finished by complaining that it
wasn't fair that grandparents had no rights, because poor little
baby Carlotta belonged with family.

"How's little Jenny taking all this?"

From the sudden silence on the other end, I might as well
have asked her a question about quantum mechanics. "Jenny?
What's she got to do with anything? Don't you mean Carlotta,
the baby?"

"Well, yes, of course, but it was Jenny I was called out to see. I just assumed you were concerned about both children."

"Sounds like you assumed wrong, young man. Jenny is Charlie's little girl, not Mandy's, and we ain't spoken to Charlie in years."

"Who's Charlie?"

"My other daughter."

"Then I'm all confused," I said, as I imagined sand granules inexorably sifting downward in some universal hourglass. "Wasn't Jenny supposed to go and live with her grandmother upstate? I thought that was you."

""I ain't seen Jenny in months. Don't seem like I'm gonna see the baby for a long time, neither. I'm the only grandparent that poor li'l baby's got, and I can't even get to see her. Ain't right, just ain't right, her livin' with strangers. And by the way, I don't live upstate, I live right here in Selden."

"Oh. Then maybe I've confused you with Jud's mother, I apologize."

"You *must* be confused, young man. Jud's folks are dead. Serves 'em right for bringin' that piece of dogmeat into this world. My daughter woulda been better off if she'd never met him. That weasel never put in an honest day's work in his life. Knocked up my little girl, took her off to live in some hole, brought her nothin' but grief and shame—"

"I'm sorry, Miz Simmons, but I really have to go," I cut in, risking rudeness to effect a necessary outcome. "Perhaps you can call me again tomorrow and we'll continue this conver—"

The line went dead, and if slamming the phone down is an art influenced by individual style, then Ms. Simmons's sounded very similar to what Mr. Brandt's had been, even though I'd been telling her the truth. I was standing there, literally holding the phone, figuratively holding the bag. I had a lot of questions and a couple of legitimate concerns, but no time to address either right now.

Still, I found myself mulling the MacAvoy case over as I drove to the Zifarelli home. Questions about Jenny flew through my mind before I could even try to figure out how to go about answering them; as so often happens in this job, I had to put all my concerns about one case on a back burner to concentrate on another case. Jenny would just have to wait for the time being so I could try and keep the Zifarelli children from being motherless by morning. It was asking a lot, especially since I could feel myself making an emotional investment in Jenny, but I've always prided myself on my professionalism, and besides, that's why the county treasurer issues me a check every other Thursday.

■   ■   ■

The Zifarelli home was located in a neighborhood of upscale wage-earners, including doctors, dentists, corporate lawyers, computer store owners, and technicians from the nearby Shoreham Nuclear Plant, all people earning enough to pay someone else to tend their homes. The houses had all been constructed within the last fifteen years, and not one had been sold for less than $400,000, then or now. Yet the Zifarelli place was conspicuous by the look of negligence which bespoke Mrs. Zifarelli's living situation and emotional state: tall, thin, fronded grass stems and tough, dark green weeds that hadn't been mowed in months; shutters missing slats and in need of a paint job. A look similar to that of the MacAvoys, only this place had been much nicer to start with.

The report on my clipboard gave me little more information than what Roxanne had told me; Mrs. Zifarelli was in her forties, had three children, and had been divorced by her husband. She had retained custody of the children after the hotly contested battle in family court, another lead story for the local news media.

The judge had been caught between a rock and a hard place in his decision; had he ruled in favor of the father, he would have been accused of a political buy-off, and by granting custody to the mother—which he ultimately did—he risked the countersuit that was promptly filed by Mr. Zifarelli's outraged family, charging both reverse discrimination and having allowed the news media to improperly influence his decision.

At any rate, the case had a very volatile history, and as

soon as I'd seen the name and address, I had planned to proceed carefully, even before the administrative caveats relayed by Roxanne.

As soon as my foot hit the walk the front door opened, and a dark-haired, round-faced girl of about six peered through the upper glass panel of a two-panel storm door. I held up my ID for her to see.

"Hi, I'm Mr. Richards from Social Services. Is your mommy home?"

The face disappeared and was replaced a moment later by the larger, narrower, more Latin-featured face of her brother, who looked to be a few years older.

"Our mother's lying down inside," he explained as I ascended the steps. "She doesn't feel very well."

"Can I ask her a few questions? She should be expecting me."

"You have to show me something to prove who you are."

After I did, I was ushered upstairs to find Mrs. Zifarelli lying on a ruptured Naugahyde sofa in the spacious living room, her head positioned so she could see who came and went from the room. It took me only a few seconds to determine that her eyes were seeing precious little, though, and her brain was registering even less. Between her half-closed eyelids I could see her pupils lolling about like canoes in a monsoon; her breathing was labored and sporadic. I tried not to let panic creep into my voice as I asked the boy, "Does your grandmother or another relative live close by?"

He shook his head no.

"Do you know a phone number where your father can be reached?"

He again shook his head no.

"Does your mom keep a book with important telephone numbers in it?"

He nodded yes, but when I asked him if he knew where it was, he shook his head no.

"Where's your phone?"

He pointed to a spot on the kitchen wall. As I dialed 911 for an ambulance, both children sat on the couch next to their mother, hands clasped in lap, faces devoid of expression, patiently waiting. Well-behaved kids, I thought to myself as my call clicked through, though I couldn't help feeling that this was nothing new to them.

Once the ambulance was dispatched (they promised to send a police car right over, as well), I dialed my office to report back to Roxanne. Plans would have to be made for the children, and I couldn't make them myself.

Of course, Roxanne would want to conference this immediately with Brandon Ericsson, Child Protective Services Director and Roxanne's immediate superior, and he'd probably have to discuss it with the commissioner's office before I would receive any answer. Even if it was decided that we would have to take custody of the children, we would need verbal approval from whichever family court judge was on call today. (This approval would give us seventy-two hours to prepare a proper custody petition and submit it before the court. If the judge felt the facts warranted, the children would be remanded to the custody of the Commissioner of the Department of Social Services and thus continued in the agency's care; if not, the children would be returned to their parents, or a responsible relative.)

In this case there would be no surprises. Odds were that if the father could be contacted, the children would be given over to him. If we couldn't locate him, we would have to place them in an emergency boarding home for the time being. Then, too, a lot would depend on how Mrs. Zifarelli fared once we got her to a hospital.

I felt useless. I walked over to her, placed my hand on her forehead, felt her pulse at the wrist. It was weak and erratic, and her breathing seemed to be getting shallower, too.

I wished the ambulance would hurry up and arrive. This woman was slipping fast, her kids seemed to sense it, and I had no answers to the questions they were going to start asking. Almost on cue, the youngest child, a girl, came out of a room off the hallway. "Is my mommy gonna die?" she asked, in a calm, tiny voice, her innocent brown eyes cutting through my professional facade and pinning me to the wall.

"We'll do our best to take good care of her," I said, trying to answer honestly without alarming anybody further. "Some men are coming in an ambulance to take her to the hospital."

"In a what?"

"An am-bu-lance. It's like a special truck for rushing people to the hospital when they need to see a doctor right away."

"She knows what an ambulance is," said the boy. "This isn't the first time we've needed one."

Stephanie, the six-year-old, looked me straight in the eye and asked, "Are you going to put us into the foster care?"

"I don't know, sweetheart. Right now we're trying to find your daddy or your grandma."

"Please don't let our mother die," she said, breaking down and sobbing into my pants leg as she hugged it.

I smoothed her hair and patted her back. Though I normally try to be careful about touching any of my clients, my heart told me it was the right thing to do. "We'll do our best, but it really isn't up to us."

Those would be the truest words I'd speak all day.

CHAPTER SEVEN

Marianne Zifarelli was still breathing when the ambulance took her away. The two oldest children just stood there watching, as stoic as the bluestone pebbles in the driveway; but Denise, the youngest, began sniffling, then gave in to a full-fledged cry. I tried to comfort her, but she sobbed out that she was scared for her mother and was afraid her family was going to be split up, so I held her, but said nothing. Better to be silent than to give her false assurances; I try not to make promises I may have to break later on, especially if there are a number of factors beyond my control.

I waited until one-thirty, then called the office again.

Roxanne had gone to lunch and wasn't expected back until about two-fifteen, so after leaving a message as to where we'd be, I seat-belted the kids in my car and drove to the nearest fast food joint, where I treated them to lunch. Admittedly, it wasn't Disneyland and none of them had much in the way of appetites, but every now and then, we social workers like to do something kind to offset the cold, rigid, bureaucratic image so readily bestowed upon us by television, movies, and the news media. Despite all our bad press, most of us really do care.

I was in the middle of a hamburger when I remembered what I'd originally planned to do for lunch today. I hoped Cathy would understand; what she couldn't know is how disappointed and frustrated I felt. One gets tired of making personal plans and having the job elbow them aside. It's nice to be

45

able to keep those plans once in a while; it makes one feel less owned.

When we returned to the Zifarelli house, I called in once more and was placed on hold. When a voice finally clicked on the line it was Roxanne's, and her tone wasn't exactly cordial.

"Where the hell have you been? There was no answer at the Zifarellis, we checked the hospital but they said you hadn't gone with the ambulance, you never showed up here at the office, we didn't know what the hell happened to you! The commissioner called again to find out what was going on, and I couldn't tell her because nobody told me. So she called Brandon and started giving *him* a hard time. I was just dialing the police to call in a missing persons report when you called; we're going to have to have a little talk when you get back here. Where are you now?"

Through the phone I heard the click of a lighter and understood at once that what made her pause was not the need to breathe, but rather the need to puff. One of the things I so loved about Roxanne's style was how she always acted so low-key, calm, and tolerant of others' feelings when embroiled in a crisis; it made things much, much easier for me to handle now, knowing I had "a little talk" to look forward to once I got back to the office.

"Yes, the children are fine, thank you for asking," I said. "When I called in earlier, I was told both you and Brandon were out to lunch, so I took the kids for a burger and a soda. I left a message; didn't you get it?"

"No, nobody gave me any messages, and I've been much too busy to check for any myself."

I just shook my head, amazed but not surprised. "Well, we're all back here at their home now, and the children are very worried about both their mother's condition and where they're going to have to spend the night. Has anybody been able to contact their father yet?"

"No. There's no answer at the number listed for their father in the case record, and Legislator Zifarelli is up in Albany this week. Can the children supply any names or numbers for relatives?"

"No luck."

"Well, if worst comes to worst, Judge Sullivan has already approved temporary custody in the event no family member can be located."

"So what do I do now?"

"Stay put. Better they wait in their own home than here in the office."

"Wait for what?"

"A decision on what to do with them. We must make a concerted effort to contact the father."

I glanced at my watch. 2:55. In addition to a concerted effort, they were going to have to make some concrete decisions, too, and pretty soon.

▪   ▪   ▪

The yellow touch-tone continued to hang on the kitchen wall, maddeningly silent. Three games of Parcheesi and two more of Uno helped pass the time, but did little to ease the tension. Finally, at a quarter of five, I called back; I normally only work until five o'clock. Under the circumstances I had figured to be working overtime tonight, but overtime is supposed to be approved in advance, just one more niggling detail that hadn't yet been addressed. More importantly, the children were asking questions that deserved honest, informative answers, and I had none to give, although dinnertime was fast approaching.

Roxanne was in a meeting; there was no message for me.

I asked Lynne if she could interrupt Roxanne's meeting. I held for a few minutes, then Lynne came back on. "Roxanne says they're trying to decide what to do right now, and she'll get back to you in a few minutes. Try to stay calm and be patient. Brandon said you're already approved for whatever overtime you need."

"A few minutes" turned out to be three-quarters of an hour (during which time I was able to sneak in a quick call to my wife to tell her I wouldn't be home for dinner tonight); the phone finally rang back at 5:35, with Roxanne's voice barking out orders immediately. "You'd better cancel any plans you had for this evening. We need you to transport those children to the Mitchell emergency home in Commack."

"Was there a problem in finding a home? I mean, we've been waiting all afternoon, and they're getting kind of antsy."

"Couldn't be helped. We had to see if the father would return our calls." She gave me the exact street address and directions, then told me she would approve an hour's overtime.

"I was told Brandon approved whatever time I needed."

"You should be able to get the children there within the next twenty minutes. And don't forget to bring their clothing."

I was about to point out that to gather clothing together for three children, load the clothes and the children in my car, drive to Commack and find this place, introduce myself and the children to the foster parents, sign them into the home, get them settled, and answer any questions the foster parents might have was going to take a lot longer than twenty minutes, but the children didn't need to hear me arguing on the phone with my boss, and it could all be hashed out tomorrow, anyway. So instead I just said, "Okay."

"Um, there's one other thing you should know. Mrs. Zifarelli was DOA at University Hospital. Try to break it to the children as gently as you can."

The older boy seemed like he would try to take the news stoically, almost as a confirmation of his expectations, though bottling up his emotions would probably be more damaging to him in the long run. It was the younger children's reactions I didn't want to face—if they broke down and started crying, I feared I would, too.

"Wouldn't that be better done in a day or two, instead of hitting them with everything all at once?"

"They have a right to know; it's better not to withhold that information."

Easy for her to say. She didn't have to explain to those expectant faces that their mother had "taken a little something to help her get to sleep" and it had helped too much, or that we didn't know where their father was, or that they would be spending the night in a strange bed in a stranger's home. Roxanne was right about not hiding it from them, but she didn't have to see their expressions, or answer the questions such information would prompt, or struggle to keep a lid on her own internal desire to rant and rail at the injustices in this world.

All she had to do was order me to do it, and hang up the phone, which she did.

Not for the first time, I found myself wishing I'd chosen as my profession something, anything, other than social work.

■   ■   ■

The long day was over at last.

Mrs. Zifarelli reposed in the University Hospital morgue, and her three children were spending the night with the Mitchells. Mrs. Mitchell was one of the best at warming up newly placed, inconsolable children, and she really helped ease the shock of sudden placement and the sting of whatever had caused it. Would that we had two dozen more like her! So, although the conditions weren't exactly optimum for the children, they were the best we had to offer for this night. If only we'd been able to contact the father.

In fact, my last duty had been to drive by Mr. Zifarelli's home and affix a copy of the court order to his door, informing him in writing that we had custody of his children and leaving word as to how he could contact us. A second copy would be sent to him via certified mail tomorrow; this double notification procedure, the omission of which meant certain reprimand in court, was known as the "Nail and Mail," although modern technology now allows us to use tape on the door instead of a nail.

It was after eight before I accomplished all this and headed for home. I drove slowly, small translucent drops spattering the windshield, slicking down the streets, and making the world look like a Leroy Nieman painting. Fortunately, there weren't many cars on the road, and the steady, sloppy, snick-snick-snick of the windshield wipers had a calming, tranquilizing effect on me as I tried to put the last fifteen hours in perspective.

Parts of the day had seemed to move swiftly, like a fast-forwarding videotape in a VCR; others had ground to a screeching halt, most notably, the afternoon spent waiting around. You would have thought they would have moved more quickly in such a case; after all, what I liked to call the Major Maxim applied here—What We Are Doing Is For The Protection Of Children (making all other considerations secondary). I supposed everyone was afraid to make a decision, due to the political overtones involved.

Was it better that we hadn't known whether or not the woman was dead before the ambulance carted her away? Better for me, certainly, because it was easier to hope along with the children than to have to console their grief. Mrs. Mitchell would be very comforting, certainly much better at it than I, and it gave me a chance to get a handle on the feelings I'd shoved aside all day, but with which I was wrestling now—like disappointment and frustration. One of the hardest things for me about working overtime is the feeling I get that the job owns me, that I have no control over my own life anymore. It now occurred to me that I'd missed two meals today—lunch with my friend and dinner with my family.

My labors this day had earned me the right to a shower, a warmed-over meal, and a few hours sleep before I could get up tomorrow and do it all again, though hopefully, this would be the only suicide and only foster care placement I'd have to deal with this week. As usually happens when I work through until after my children's bedtime, I also felt pangs of guilt and resentment; the job had once again deprived me of spending what few hours I have after work with my own children.

As I always do when I finally arrive home on such occasions, I headed straight for their bedrooms, tucked them in, and kissed them goodnight while they slept. Tomorrow night, they'll ask me to tell them the whole story, and I will (albeit a somewhat pared-down version), but although it makes us all thankful for how fortunate we are to be an intact family with no major problems, it always seems like a meager payback to them for doing without their father for the night because he's out helping someone else's family.

Just as I'd been stuck with answering the Zifarelli children's questions about a situation over which I had no control, my wife Gloria had been saddled with a similar scenario with Morgan and Will, in addition to having to prepare and clean up dinner by herself. Certainly there are plenty of single-parent families where the mother or father works full-time and must provide dinner by themselves every night; still, it's an imposition Gloria has never enjoyed having thrust upon her. While she tries her best not to take it out on me when I finally do arrive home, if she seems less than enthusiastic and not as comforting toward me as I'd like her to be, I try to reserve for her some of the understanding and empathy I automatically afford my clients all day long.

I'm not the only one upon whom this job places demands.

CHAPTER EIGHT

The next day continued the rainy, misty weather of the day before. The sky was a morose gray, the drizzle just heavy enough to keep the streets slick and slippery. It was fine with me, though; my mood was anything but sunny, and why waste a gorgeous day on a rotten mood? Besides, my first phone conversation of the day would have destroyed any traces I might have had of a good mood, if I'd been in one.

"This is Mr. MacAvoy. You the clown who was out to my house, upsettin' my wife?"

"I am the worker assigned to the case, yes. How may I help you?"

"You can help us by not comin' around here no more, making false accusations and causin' trouble. That's harassment, and any more of it and my lawyer'll have your ass in court so fast you won't know what hit you."

I knew it would be important to the case to wear down this man's hostility, but that would take time I didn't have. "It all boils down to a matter of rights, sir. I have the right to investigate these allegations; you have the right to talk to me about it, in person. So I'd like to make an appointment with you —"

"Don't need no appointment. The allegations are lies, my wife done told you that. Besides, the case is over now."

"Actually, sir, the case isn't over until I make my report back to the state."

"Then make your report now, 'cause you ain't got no more case."

"How do you mean?"

"No kid. You ain't got a kid, you ain't got a case."

"I don't understand."

"Jenny has gone to live with her aunt in North Carolina."

"Her aunt? But I was told she went to live with her father upstate, which I didn't understand either because I thought you were her father."

"Well, you were told wrong, my wife shouldn't have said that."

"Can you give me a forwarding address?"

"I got nothing more to say. You got any more questions, talk to my lawyer!"

If the man was going to hide behind his lawyer, why call me at all? Sometimes people want bragging rights, as in "I really gave those CPS people a piece of my mind," or they just want to let off some steam, or they can't scream and curse at whoever called them in, so they take it out on me. At such times, I fall back on an old public speaker's trick—I imagine the audience/caller stark naked except for a pair of argyle socks, and somehow the ridiculousness of it all helps keep things in perspective.

But I wasn't in a laughing mood now. I was tired of hearing receivers slammed down on the other end of the phone (though I was getting better at anticipating it soon enough to pull the receiver away from my own ear first).

After a quick trip to the computer to access information from our Public Assistance records, I requested and received approval for a long-distance phone call to the North Carolina Department of Social Services. After a half-dozen transfers to various departments, I gave the worker to whom I was ultimately connected the names, birthdays, and social security numbers for each of the MacAvoys. The woman ran them through their master computer and came up empty. No record of anybody by that name receiving any type of Public Assistance in the state. She invited me to try back in a week or two to see if anyone had applied in the meantime, and I thanked her and dutifully jotted down the number, knowing full well I'd probably never use it. If I didn't find out what had happened to Jenny within the next two weeks, I probably never would.

Three phone calls then came in from various people concerning the Zifarelli family; one from a school social worker to confirm the rumor making the rounds about Mrs. Zifarelli's overdose, one from a foster care worker who was charged with completing the paperwork the children's placement with Mrs. Mitchell had generated, and one from a newspaper reporter who wanted information I was not at liberty to provide. Instead, I referred this last call to our Central Office public relations liaison and earned another haughty phone-slam for my troubles.

I needed to hear a friendly voice and tried to call Cathy to apologize for yesterday, but was told she was in a meeting.

Another day of exciting, challenging CPS work was off to a flying start, and I hadn't even gotten my fatality yet.

■ ■ ■

The coffee in my mug was as cold as pond water, the hour was already closer to lunchtime than breakfast, and I still hadn't gotten through to Cathy. I figured that today was probably her turn to be tied up by the job.

There are days where no matter who I go to see, they're not home; days where despite setting firm appointments with people, they stand me up. This was one of those days when everybody I needed to speak with was either not available, speaking with someone else, or unable to help me. It was a good thing I didn't hold the future of the free world in my hands; the president's line would probably have been busy, too.

I contented myself with writing up my report on the Zifarelli case and catching up on paperwork on about four others. I couldn't concentrate, though, and found myself sitting with pen in hand at ten to twelve, a half-finished sentence in front of me, with no idea of what I would write next. My thoughts kept returning to MacAvoy, not Zifarelli.

I'd gotten almost no cooperation from the parents, had found out next to nothing about how Jenny had gotten burned, and to a certain extent, what Mr. MacAvoy had said was correct—Jenny's departure would bring the case to a screeching halt. True, I was still responsible for making a determination to the State Central Registry (SCR), but that would be the end of it. The other children were not seen to be at risk, and any suspicions I'd had centered around a child who, as far as we knew, was no longer in the home.

New York State gives us up to ninety days to complete an investigation on each report we receive. We then must determine whether we will "indicate" a case (in some states they label this "generally felt to be true," or some similar self-doubting terminology) or "unfound" it ("generally felt to be false"). To convict a murderer, you need to prove the case "beyond a reasonable doubt"; but in a CPS investigation, you only need to show "some credible evidence" in order to indicate it. Should the decision be appealed, a higher level—"a preponderance of evidence"—is required to keep the case on record.

Trouble was, I didn't have any. Though I suspected abuse, I'd uncovered no credible evidence to show that Jenny's burns were anything other than accidental, and without a medical exam or further interviews, I wasn't likely to find any. In frustration as much as anything, I was suddenly hit with the desire to unfound the case, close it out, and be done with it. Forget about the ninety-day deadline. Though I didn't like the idea of all the records being destroyed and having to treat the case as though the report had never been made, I couldn't see letting the thing sit for another eleven weeks, when I knew full well I'd already seen all I was going to see of the child.

On impulse, I grabbed the DSS-2223 form and started writing my (abbreviated) report to the SCR. I didn't include the change in Mrs. MacAvoy's story once she'd conferred with her husband, nor the discrepancy as to how Jenny was burned (and whether it was hot water or coffee). She hadn't simply gotten the story wrong; something was going on, but I had no proof and, thus, no reason for further investigation.

Someone came through the room and announced the lunch truck had arrived. I made a quick perusal of his wares and decided that my sumptuous noontime repast this day would be a mayonnaise-loaded tuna fish sandwich washed down with a can of diet soda. I continued writing up the paper as I ate at my desk. Sure, I was entitled to leave the building for an hour, and sometimes I went and sat in my car just to get away; today, staying in was worth it to get some of this work done.

As I ate it occurred to me that I hadn't yet seen a newspaper; it would be interesting to note how the press would sensationalize the Zifarelli suicide. One thing was certain: it sure wouldn't read like my case notes.

I couldn't help but shudder when I glanced at the continually growing pile of new case records overflowing my IN basket. I knew there were eight or nine new cases there that I hadn't even read yet, because MacAvoy and Zifarelli had monopolized so much of my time over the past week. Added to my existing load of forty-five cases, they put me over the fifty mark, more than two-and-one-half times the state-recommended per-worker caseload. It always rankled that for all the strict mandates and procedures the state set down for us to follow, for violations of which the agency could be sanctioned, the caseload size was only "recommended," and seemingly ignored when reasons were given—or blame placed— for not getting the work done.

I found I was only able to wrap up our investigations within the ninety day period in maybe a third of my cases, which meant that thirty to forty of my families were not getting benefit of the timely investigation to which they were entitled. Outsiders who complained of this to administration would, of course, be told that the caseworker was overloaded, but the implication was that caseworker fault, not lack of staff, was the real reason. All in all, it was a lame but convenient way of explaining a problem that should not exist.

As I washed down the last of my lunch and turned back to the MacAvoy write-up, Cecil Perry, our senior-worker-cum-covering-supervisor, came out of Woody's cubicle, a single case folder in hand. Normally, he would have just plopped it down on the pile in my bin, but obviously this one demanded immediate or special attention. "Got a fatality for you here, Rich."

When you opened the case folder and looked for the State Central Registry (SCR) report on such a case, the first thing you noticed was that word "FATALITY" stamped in fuzzy red letters. This immediately kicked into gear a special set of procedures not necessary on most other cases. The family name was "Browne," and they had been a family of six—until the death of fourteen-year-old Michael. But this wasn't your usual "parents-abused-him-so-severely-that-he-died" type of fatality—this was a family, previously indicated several times in the past, whose case had been closed at the time of Michael's death, which had occurred some seven months ago!

Apparently, there was a problem in ascertaining exactly what the boy had died from, and the final, official medical examiner's report was somewhat vague. Still, someone in the district attorney's office, whose job it was to review such cases, decided that reporting was done better late than never and called it in, demanding an immediate investigation from us as to whether the parents had been negligent in seeking medical care for this child. The past history showed that the family had not been the most conscientious in securing medical care for the children ("they're healthy kids, they never get sick!" explained Mrs. Browne), and the school had had to get CPS involved in the past to get the children's immunizations up-to-date. The parents were originally reported for educational neglect, because, by law, the school couldn't allow the children to attend until they'd been properly inoculated—the parents argued that it was thus the school's fault the kids weren't attending. However, we'd never been able to show that the children had suffered any ill effects as a result of lack of medical care.

The concern here, of course, was not for Michael (someone asked me how I was doing with this case, and in a moment of black humor, I replied "He's still dead." If this seems sick or callous, perhaps it is, but sometimes a little callousness is what makes you able to function at all), but that if the parents were found to be at fault, a record should be made of it, as possible ammunition to use in the future should the remaining children's health and well-being start to decline.

The first order of business was to write to the county medical examiner for a copy of the autopsy report. Once that request was on its way, we could proceed with interviews of the family, and attempts to secure the child's medical and school records. (The parents normally had to sign papers allowing release of this information.)

Procedure mandates an attempt at contact with the family within twenty-four hours of receipt of a new or subsequent referral. Swamped as I was with three or four such mandated visits today, I asked Cecil if we could seek a waiver on the twenty-four-hour contact for Browne, something administration sometimes authorizes, though hesitantly. I knew what Roxanne's answer would be, but I wanted to make a point, as well as remind her that other cases would have to be put on hold to cover this one.

The Browne referral was a classic case of PYP—Protect Your Posterior—albeit one that had to be taken seriously due to the child's death and the district attorney's involvement. Although it was going to make CPS look rather foolish to be pursuing this investigation so long after the fact, when it was the DA's posterior that needed protecting, you jumped through whatever hoops were held in front of you. The only thing I resented was, as the case now stood, the competency question would be conveniently forgotten and emphasis placed on a quick, thorough resolution; had this been an open CPS case at the time of Michael's demise, the fur would have flown like a mink in a mower, the implication (or direct accusation) being that *we* hadn't been doing our job properly.

I went ahead and made the visit. As it turned out, after all my concerns, there was no answer to my knock upon the Browne door. I shook my head at the irony, unaware of how fortuitous this negative attempt would wind up being. It would necessitate a follow-up visit the next day, which would keep me from being assigned a case that was unfolding right this moment three blocks away.

Though we wouldn't hear about it until the morning news, a young girl was giving birth at home to a baby she didn't want (and didn't want anyone to know about), and later tonight, she would wrap it in newspaper and rags and, under cover of darkness, try to drop it from her third-story apartment window directly into the trash dumpster below. She would miss, and two schoolgirls on their way to cheerleading practice would find the bloody mess on the pavement early tomorrow morning. Police would be called, and within an hour, Joe Picante, another worker in my unit, would be wishing he'd taken time off to have his car worked on, as he'd originally planned, instead of coming in and being the only worker in the office when the telex came down from Albany.

Fate and Irony can be whimsical fellows, and this time they had decided to give Keith Richards a break.

CHAPTER NINE

I was born a Libra, meaning that my October birthday is influenced by the sign of the scales. Though this may sound silly to some, I believe it tends to make me generally low-key, congenial, charming, compassionate, and able to look discerningly at both sides of an issue, all traits that are helpful in this job. Being a Libra makes me strive for the harmonious balance of things, to try to find good out of evil, happiness out of sadness, an optimistic outlook from a depressing situation.

One such example was Corrado Martinez, a personable thirteen-year-old Hispanic youth with whom I was involved for nearly six months. Corrie was a classic example of a case that stays with you after you go home at night, the kind of person you still wonder about years after you're no longer involved. Although we're supposed to arrive at a case determination within ninety days, it had been impossible to wrap up this one in less time. Originally referred to us on an abandonment/educational neglect charge by a school attendance officer who had done all he could for the boy, Corrie grabbed me by the heart the moment I met him.

Several years before, Corrie's mother had died what I thought was a noble but meaningless death. As Corrie and his brother Emilio watched in horror, she stepped in front of a shotgun blast discharged at Corrie's stepfather by an irate drug customer who felt Raoul Martinez had ripped him off. Theresa's last sacrificial act in this life was to take the buck-

61

shot meant for the father of five of her seven children (she had never been married to either man), leaving Raoul, thirty-eight, with a carload of kids to care for—when he wasn't in jail for one thing or another.

Raoul had always left the child-rearing to Theresa. Rather than turning him away from drug-dealing, the sudden responsibility of caring for the children nudged Raoul deeper and deeper into it, because now he had to pay a cousin to help him with the kids, and he could not prove himself eligible for a welfare check as Theresa had done. The older boys drifted away and never saw their father again until they reunited years later in Rahway State Prison. One of his sisters, Corrie told me, became "a high-class *puta en La Ciudad*" ("whore in the City"). A second sister was pregnant at fifteen, ran away, and never came back. There weren't any rumors about what had happened to her; she was simply never heard from again.

That left Corrie and two brothers. Emilio, nineteen when I first met Corrie, had let the boy stay with him in a condemned house he'd renovated, hoping to save it from a wrecker's ball, counting on bureaucratic lethargy to keep it standing, at least through the coming winter. Emilio supplemented his meager income any way he could, which included applying as payee for a welfare grant for Corrie.

The other brother, Jorge, had embraced the fellowship of a group of young gay Hispanics and had attained the highest educational degree of anyone in the family when he graduated from vocational beautician's school. He had yet to pass the licensing tests, though, making him not quite legally employable, and we never were sure what he did for a living, though Corrie suspected he turned to the same vocation as his sister in the city.

Corrie, for his part, had bounced around. The youngest of the family, he'd spent his childhood being shuffled between his natural father, who lived in Florida, his stepfather Raoul, his mother's sister (whom he called *Tia Incy*, or Aunt Incy, for her given name of Incarnation), and his two brothers. When I first met Corrie, he was staying with his aunt, who seemed genuinely interested in the boy, and who was asking my help to get medical coverage for him (she said the money wasn't all that important to her, and I believed her, at least in the beginning). This would be the first major step toward getting Corrie medical and dental care he'd never received.

Corrie was extremely insecure. He always carried about two dozen wallet-sized photos of girls who had written on the backs how much they liked him, how they wanted him to keep in touch, etc. "These," he would say, letting the picture-sleeve insert of his wallet unfold like an accordion to the floor with a yo-yo-like flip of his wrist, "are my dollies." He would then name each one, reminisce about what made his relationship with her special, and then either smack his lips or blow kisses to his favorites.

The largest part of his need to convince himself (and everyone else) of his success with his "dollies" was the gruesome cruelty life and ignorance had inflicted upon his face. When he was seven, he was involved in a fight with a nine-year-old youngster in a tough Miami barrio. The nine-year-old was embarrassed that this skinny punk, two years his junior, could defend himself so well, and had pulled a knife when Corrie wasn't looking. The end result was a stab wound to Corrie's left eye that had never been properly treated. Corrie said his father's girlfriend at the time cleaned the wound out and put a patch on it; but soon thereafter his father beat the woman up in a drunken rage, she was taken away in an ambulance, and Corrie never saw her again.

The wound healed itself over time, but not properly. Of course, Corrie could no longer see from that eye. But the entire cornea turned a milky white, covering the sclera, iris, and pupil with a dull ivory jelly, and making his eye like that of an ancient god in a piece of statuary, except that Corrie's eye continually wept a clear, viscous exudate, which he was perpetually wiping away. He said that some mornings, he awoke to find a glob had dried in the corner of his eye like a puddle of cement which had been left to harden. Though generally a pretty upbeat person, Corrie complained often of headaches, especially when his teeth weren't bothering him.

Once we were able to get medical coverage for him, I took him to an ophthalmologist who advised surgical removal of the eye and insertion of a removable prosthesis—a glass eye. Talk of surgery scared Corrie, but the doctor explained that his headaches would only get worse, and there was also fear that if left without treatment too much longer, the infected eye would start to endanger the vision in his healthy one. Corrie said he would cooperate, but was relieved when I told him that CPS procedure dictated we get a second opinion. In the meantime, we were going to the dentist.

It was funny watching this child in a developing man's body regress to being about five years old while in the dentist's chair. Never having been to, seen, or heard stories of the dentist, he had no idea what to expect, and enjoyed himself by playing with the equipment, looking at himself in the mouth-mirrors, "shooting" me with the air hose, spitting water into the spit receptacle, etc. The first visit was pleasant enough, but only entailed the taking of X-rays and the cleaning of his teeth by a cute dental hygienist. One minute, with the innocence of a five-year-old, he asked about what she was going to do with this pick, or where she was going to place that gob of tooth-polish; and in the next he adopted the grin of a practiced lecher, trying to say things like, "I wanna make you tingle, too, honey, and it ain't your gums I'm talking about" while the suction hose and rotary tooth-buffer sprouted from his mouth.

It wasn't until his second visit, when he'd been complaining of a toothache for nearly a week and needed emergency root-canal, that he learned why people hate going to the dentist. The look on his face as he tried to ask what the dentist was "going to do with that needle," and felt the dentist demonstrating the answer, was a classic expression of lost innocence. "If I'da known the answer was gonna hurt so much," he later mumbled out the side of his mouth as the novocain was wearing off, "I never woulda asked."

It took me nearly all of the ninety days just to get his medical coverage established and his dental needs attended to. Corrie was re-examined, and the recommendation of his second doctor echoed the first—the bad eye had to be removed and the socket fitted with a prosthesis. The next two-and-one-half months were spent getting medical documentation of need, a step-by-step explanation of exactly what the surgery would entail, approval for financing the procedure through our Medicaid administration, and the special approval required by the governing board at the medical center to enable him to be treated there.

Meanwhile, my relationship with the boy grew. I was glad to see him staying at his aunt's, because his stepfather's house was rough, dirty, and rumors were that Raoul had continued his drug trade unmolested by police. According to Corrie, although Raoul dealt drugs as a livelihood, he forbade their usage by anyone in his family, and threatened to "beat the living shit" out of anyone who touched them.

Corrie's aunt seemed to care for him, but the longer Corrie stayed there, the more I started to hear complaints from Aunt Incy that she couldn't make it with another mouth to feed without help from DSS. Though the case was being processed, it took some time (it was difficult acquiring necessary documentation), and at one point, mistakenly thinking that the Public Assistance/Medicaid case was within my power to approve, she threatened that he couldn't stay through Christmas, knowing how fond of Corrie I'd grown and hoping that would be the final inducement to get me to open the case.

Unfortunately, Corrie took this as the message he'd known was coming, because he'd heard it most of his life—once again it was time for Corrie to move on, to find another place for himself to live. I had no knowledge of any of this until I showed up the Monday before Christmas with a knit hat, a pair of gloves, and a brand new soccer ball in my hands, all boxed and wrapped for Corrie. I had finally cut through a lot of red tape only the week before to get him enrolled in the local school district and was full of the joy of the season and the feeling that I was really making a mark on this young man's life. This was going to be the best Christmas he'd ever known.

Except that there was no Corrie. He'd taken off over the weekend, the aunt explained (through a neighborhood girl who spoke English), and they didn't know where he was. Just as well, she rationalized, because after all she'd gone through with getting him in school, on Public Assistance (PA), and making room for him in her home, when he ran away she said she couldn't take that kind of ungratefulness. Maybe he really was as bad as his family said, after all.

The woman shrugged at me after her interpreter had finished this explanation, again reinforcing my suspicion that Aunt Incy could understand the language just fine when it suited her purposes. When I'd explained to her on an earlier visit (in English and without an interpreter) the necessary procedures to establish a PA case, she had never so much as asked me to repeat anything. But now she looked at me with a what-can-you-do expression on her face, self-righteousness rising like steam from her chunky body. I resented both the ignorance she feigned and the game she was playing. Corrie was out there somewhere, his Christmas in ruins, having been once more rejected at a time when he needed most to feel love, compassion, and a sense of belonging, all because of his aunt's impatience. I later learned that Raoul also had hoped some PA money would come to his household for Corrie, and threatened Aunt Incy with all sorts of unspeakable acts if she didn't bring the boy back to his home. This, too, may have made it easier for her to let him go.

I checked with both his brothers, and neither one had seen him; I prayed that he wound up in a better household for the holidays than either of them could provide for him. As it turned out, he'd stayed with a friend and had not attended school after the first three days following his enrollment. I'd left the presents I'd brought for him at Aunt Incy's, believing he'd show up there on Christmas Day or something, though he never did. Thus, her children wore the gloves and hat; her children played with the soccer ball; Corrie had missed out again.

I felt cheated out of the joy of giving him something he really wanted, as well as something he really needed, and resented both his aunt and Corrie himself for having deprived me of that tiny bit of satisfaction I'd hoped to derive from the job. When I finally ran into Corrie on the streets about two weeks later, and learned all of this, I yelled at him more than I should have, about his being labeled a runaway and screwing his life up when I was trying so hard to help him, more out of my own disappointment than anything else. He took it as a further rejection, and cursed me out, knocking me off balance as he shoved his way past me.

I called his name, asking forgiveness of a thirteen-year-old unused to having the power to bestow it. When he turned around and saw me there, sitting in the mud and snow, my clipboard in a puddle and my papers blowing all around, he laughed harder than I'd ever seen him laugh before. He extended his hand to pull me up, forgiving me with the gesture, and I pulled him to me, hugging him and further muddying his filthy jacket in the process. Then we started laughing again, tears rolling down our cheeks as we pointed to one another, two sorry sights each convulsed with laughter at the other's appearance while totally oblivious to our own. I always felt, in retrospect, that that belly laugh was probably the best present Corrie could have received that year, and ultimately found great satisfaction in watching him enjoy it.

I managed to get him placed temporarily in a teen group home on Super Bowl Sunday. He liked it there, though he complained about chore responsibilities, like every other teen in America. In March, his dental work was completed. By Easter, he'd been placed in a residential school for boys, and he liked it there even better than the group home, except that there "aren't any dollies here."

On May 1st, I was instructed to write the case up and transfer it to the institutional unit by the end of the day, a deadline based not on expediency or case need, but on the simple fact that Roxanne feared economic sanction of the agency for any case held in an investigative unit more than six months. Besides, she'd known how close I'd grown to the boy and felt it was time for me to terminate my involvement.

Roxanne had warned me in no uncertain terms about having any contact with the boy once the case was transferred. Though Corrie's new worker was kind enough to give me periodic updates of Corrie's progress, it wasn't until weeks after the fact that he told me Corrie had finally undergone his eye surgery. If I'd known when and where, I would have visited him at the hospital anyway, and I'm sure Roxanne knew it.

Maybe she did Corrie and me both a favor by ordering me to move the case on, but with any of my dealings with Roxanne, I always felt spite lurking about in the shadows. The

hardest part was not being able to help Corrie through his surgery, not being able to explain to him what was happening.
One minute I was his worker, his brother, his father, and his
best friend all rolled up into one; the next, I'd abruptly disappeared from his life without so much as a goodbye.

CHAPTER TEN

When the civil service test results for probation officer are published, there's always a mass exodus of many of our trained, experienced people, and who can blame them? The pay is higher, the job is easier and less threatening, and you get to carry a gun.

Things are also more cut-and-dried as a PO. Call somebody an addict, or a criminal, or a coward, and you pretty much know what his reaction will be and can deal with it. Call somebody a bad parent, or a child abuser, and you don't know whether to expect tears or violence, apologies or anger.

One of the sorriest reactions, from the child's standpoint, is the parent who stares at you dully, not comprehending what you're telling them, because they just don't have the capacity to understand parental responsibility, let alone improve their parenting skills. They simply don't know any better, and in a sense, are merely children themselves, concerned not so much with what harm may befall their offspring as they are with what trouble they may be in because of it. There must be potential if there's going to be improvement.

Although the county has not made clipboards standard issue, everybody has one. They serve as a combination desk, workplace, and shield, a visual symbol of our vested authority, and in the case of snarling dogs, a great "snout-bopper." (This was not just mere theory; on three occasions, I'd had to defend myself against attacking dogs, including one time when a father who feared my removal of his daughter actually sicced his pit bull on me. Fortunately, I've only been bitten once on the job, not seriously enough to penetrate my skin, and that was by a child!)

When workers get together to talk shop, there are more than a few war stories of violence encountered on the job that make the rounds. Self-defense is something we are not trained for as Child Protective Services workers, despite some common-sense training the police gives us (stand at arm's distance, keep oblique body angle, don't turn your back on a hostile client, etc.), so that if we are unable to defuse a hostile situation by "talking the person down" or other crisis intervention techniques, we're left to our own devices to find an effective resolution. After all, we're dealing with a very emotional aspect of people's lives, and are often intervening at a time when the parents, if not the whole family, are undergoing some sort of crisis. When people allow their judgment to be ruled by emotion rather than by intellect, rationality and logic no longer exist.

Fortunately, for all the rude, provocative, and downright hostile behavior I've encountered at people's doors when I first identify myself, I usually manage to appeal to most people's sensibility and fairness and accomplish what I'm there to do, often eliciting apologies by the time I'm ready to leave. You differentiate between yourself and the job, and let people know you're just looking for answers, that you have no personal ax to grind. I've been very fortunate so far; still, I sometimes feel like it's just a matter of time before I, too, will be physically attacked by a client.

■　　■　　■

While Joe Picante was out chasing down police and medical people on what we were beginning to call his "bathwater case" (the mother hadn't meant any harm, kidded the black-humorists, she'd just proverbially thrown her baby out with the bathwater, and forgotten the bathwater), I made a second negative visit on Browne and returned to the office. Before I had taken my coat off, there was a phone call waiting for me and a message that Roxanne wanted to see me.

I took the call first, but found myself wishing I'd asked Lynne to take a message; an irate school nurse wanted to take me and all of CPS to task for responding so slowly to a referral she'd made personally over six weeks ago. In truth, I'd barely had time to read the case over, and had not felt it to be of monumental urgency; continual emergencies and priorities set for me by my superiors on other cases had kept me from following up on it as soon as I would have liked—i.e., at all.

The case name was Hart, and Nurse Redmond was alarmed at the steadily-worsening demeanor of eight-year-old Monica. Always a shy, withdrawn child, Monica was an underachiever who of late would only speak in monosyllables, barely above a whisper, and who gave Nurse Redmond an "unsatisfactory" explanation for the three days she'd been out of school the previous week. Though it certainly sounded like things were deteriorating at home, there was nothing physically observable on the child, and before I could press the nurse for more specific information, Roxanne's secretary tapped me on the shoulder, made a slashing motion across her throat after pointing to the phone, and jerked her thumb in the direction of Roxanne's office.

I explained as politely as I could that I would have to get off the phone now, and I requested the nurse's number so I could call her back later. "I'm sure you'll be much too busy," she snapped, slamming down the receiver.

"At least I'm free to go in and get yelled at by Roxanne," I murmured to myself. On my way out of the room, Lynne asked me one question that needed answering so she could complete a report she needed to submit this morning: of the fifty-three cases listed on my caseload, eleven were past the ninety-day state-recommended deadline for completing each investigation; for six of those eleven, that deadline was ninety days ago (meaning it had been six months since the initial call was made to the State Central Registry); and Lynne's report required a reason on each overdue case as to why things had taken so long.

"If they want these cases wrapped up in the state-recommended time period, then tell them to give me a state-recommended caseload," I replied, and headed for Roxanne's office. In the background I heard a phone ring, and another worker answered it and asked Lynne where I was. I picked up my pace.

Some days, though, it just isn't worth the effort. I knew the last time I'd been summoned (to be assigned the Zifarelli case) I'd sort of dodged a bullet. If Roxanne had questions and/or minor issues to resolve, she'd speak to a worker at his or her desk; a summons usually meant some sort of trouble. So although I was temporarily escaping the sizzling skillet that was my office, I knew I was most likely walking into a roaring blaze in Roxanne's smoky sanctum, and as soon as she saw me enter, she turned up the flames.

"I'm so glad you could see your way clear to join us," she mumbled around a fresh cigarette, lighting it up and waving smoke away from the two impeccably groomed gentlemen seated at her desk. As she made introductions, I eyed them warily. Both men were dressed like they'd just come from a photo session for the fashion issue of *Gentlemen's Quarterly*: three-piece navy pinstripe suits, designer shirts and ties, black two-tone wing tips; nails perfectly manicured, not a single, jet-black hair out of place; pungent cologne not quite strong enough to mask the nicotine stink of the room. Though I'd never actually met either man, I knew the one to be Michael Zifarelli, son of the county legislator. The other was probably his lawyer.

"...and this is Mr. Richards, who is the caseworker assigned to the case." Roxanne turned to face me, full of importance and loving being center stage. "Mr. Zifarelli is requesting, through Mr. Aiello here, that his children be allowed to return to him, and I was just explaining his rights in terms of a 1028 dispositional hearing—"

"*You're* the stupid sonofabitch who put my kids in a foster home?" he said, in a quiet, controlled tone of voice. He looked to be in his late thirties or early forties, and he regarded me with cold grey eyes that emanated the message that this was a man used to having his questions answered. I looked to Roxanne in the wild hope that at least some minimal support would be forthcoming but there was none; she merely puffed away and let me flounder on my own.

"I made the placement, yes." My voice came out steady and confident, and I intended to keep it that way. This meeting had already begun to have the feel of testifying in court, and experienced workers know that perhaps the single most important thing you can do when testifying is to maintain your professional image. Besides, we had made a diligent effort to contact this man and include him in the planning for his children, but he'd been unavailable, and we'd had no choice. We were on firm ground here and should have had nothing to fear. Still, a little backup from Roxanne about who'd made the ultimate decision to place the children would have been nice; after all, I was only following the orders she had passed on to me.

The lawyer spoke next. "You made no attempt to contact any of Mr. Zifarelli's relatives?"

I took this as a tacit concession that the father himself had been unreachable. "I had no way of knowing who they were or how to contact them. The children were unable to provide me with any such information. Didn't Mrs. D'Angelis explain any of this to you?"

"No."

I turned to Roxanne with a questioning look on my face. "I thought they should hear it from you," she shrugged.

"Since there appeared to be no familial resources available to us, we considered the children destitute under Section 396 of the Social Services Law and, accordingly, made the best plan we could for them."

The two men pondered this. Though I figured this lawyer must have had vast experience, I was equally as certain he knew next to nothing about matters pertaining to family court (other than, perhaps, divorce proceedings). It was he who broke what was becoming an uncomfortable silence.

"How soon can the children be ready to go home with their father?"

Roxanne managed a weak smile. "I was about to explain that when Mr. Richards arrived." She plastered a smile on her face, struggling to remain in control of both herself and the interview, and for the first time I realized just how intimidated by these men she really was. "I'm afraid any further action taken with regard to the children must be handled through family court." Though she bravely gazed right into the father's eyes as she spoke, he returned it with such intensity that she finally felt compelled to find something interesting about her desk blotter.

"Rudy," he said, continuing to glare at Roxanne, "she tryin' to tell me I can't have my kids back today?"

Rudy answered him, though he, too, was staring directly at Roxanne. "Oh, no, Mr. Z., I don't think that's what she meant. *Or is it?*"

Her fingers trembled as she lit another cigarette off the one already in her mouth. "I apologize for any inconvenience this may cause you, Mr. Zifarelli, but New York State law is pretty clear on this." She snuffed the old butt out as though she were trying to stab a hole through the ashtray, then took a deep drag before continuing, "The children at this point can only be returned by the decision of the court, after conducting a 1028 hearing, which you must apply for. Once the court is satisfied that there is no imminent danger or risk to them, arrangements can then be made for their return."

"How long's all this gonna take?"

"Once the application is made, the hearing must be held within three court days. Then, if the court so decides, arrangements can be made to—"

"Three days? *THREE DAYS?* There's no fucking way I'm waiting three days to get my kids back, Rudy!"

"It's okay, Mr. Z., I'm sure we can make things happen much faster than that. Right now we gotta get over to family court." The attorney stood and held the father's custom-tailored raincoat for him. He slipped into it and allowed himself to be soothed, but just before they left he whirled around to face Roxanne.

"You haven't heard the last of this, understand? Nobody grabs my kids away from me and gets away with it. *NO-BODY!*" Then he turned on me, and stuck a well-manicured forefinger two inches from my nose.

"And if you ever set foot on my property again, it'll be the sorriest day of your life—if not the end of it!"

It was obvious the man was more concerned about retaining possession of what was his than he was about the well-being of his children. Not once during the entire interview did either man inquire as to how the children were doing.

"Thanks for all your support," I said to Roxanne once we were alone.

She stubbed out her half-smoked cigarette after lighting up yet another from it. "I thought I handled things extremely well," she replied.

The pity was, she really believed it.

■ ■ ■

Two aspirin skidded drily down my throat as the phone rang. I was the only one in the office at the moment, and I nearly coughed the pills back up as I answered. "'Lo? Chil' Pertekiff."

I looked to my IN basket where three new case records had magically appeared, and noted that even on my desk other records were nearly burying the MacAvoy record I had left on top only yesterday. It peeked out from under, patiently awaiting whatever I would ultimately do with it. Despite my intended plan of action then, things had changed, and now I wasn't so sure about anything.

The caller was Cathy, who asked if I could meet her at her car in about fifteen minutes; what she had to say was for my ears only. I agreed, giving no explanation to my officemates other than that I'd be right back.

■ ■ ■

The day was warming up, returning to the balmy, Indian summer weather we'd enjoyed last week. Cathy sat in her car, and I climbed in next to her. I was really glad to see Cathy, and began trading amenities, but she was here for a reason, and she got to it right away.

"Remember how I warned you yesterday about your assistant director? Well, I have an update. As you know, I'm pretty good friends with Brandon Ericsson's secretary, and she told me she overheard him telling Roxanne about a formal complaint being made by the Indian Tribes School District. Seems they're not pleased with the handling of that case last month involving the little girl who was nearly scalded to death in the bathtub by her mother. Wasn't that your case?"

"Right. The Bouchet case. The mother was Haitian and said angels told her to purge the demons from the child's soul with boiling water, or some crazy thing like that. The papers had a field day with it."

"Well, some hot-shot city lawyer has picked up on the case and is going to represent the family in a couple of multi-million dollar lawsuits against the school, the agency, and the worker involved. Seems the family is suing because we didn't take protective action soon enough to save this child from her mother. The school is also bringing a suit against the agency and worker, claiming that the identity of their reporting party was revealed to the family, thereby breaching confidentiality laws."

"Just in case the judge shoots them down, they don't go down alone."

"Something like that. It means the agency is going to be doing some scrambling, and they're going to be all over you to find out what happened, what you did, what you said, all that stuff."

"So? I did my job properly, I'm sure the agency will back me up."

"Maybe. And maybe not. Just watch what you tell people, and be even more careful about any reports you write. Roxanne didn't have a whole lot to say in your defense."

"I stand you up, yet you still take the trouble to warn me like this," I marvelled. "You've got to be about the only friend I've got in this place."

"I'm not blaming you. We'll just have to set something up for a time when the job won't get in the way, say . . . two weeks after we both retire?"

We both grinned. "Thanks, Cathy. I appreciate the advance warning."

"What are friends for?" She winked at me. "Now get the hell out of my car before people start talking."

CHAPTER ELEVEN

When I returned to my office, I automatically checked my IN basket, a reflex I'd acquired after only a few weeks on the job. Two new cases had magically appeared. In my message envelope there were also three half-slips of green or pink message paper. The first noted that an attorney had returned my return of his return of my return of his call. The second concerned a doctor who had received a release of information form signed by our client/his patient and wanted to give us whatever information we needed over the phone. This would save him the time and expense of photocopying records, or having to write up some sort of report, but would thus put the burden on me of writing down what he said in my dictation notes, nowhere near as official—nor as convincing in court—as a report from him, in his words, on his stationery.

There was also a message from a reporting party, a grandmother who had called almost every day for updates on our investigation of the referral she had phoned in against her daughter, who, in turn, had denied everything. Her five-year-old granddaughter was being spanked too hard, shaken, and emotionally abused by Brad, the mother's live-in boyfriend (we usually would call such a person a "parent substitute" if he lived in the home, a "paramour" if he didn't). The child had looked fine, no marks or bruises, and had seemed credible in denying that Mom or Brad had ever beaten her. Grandma, of course, was incredulous that we "weren't doing anything about this terrible situation, and after all, a child is involved here." Of course, the crux of the situation seemed to be this parent's decision not to let her mother see her daughter anymore, because Grandma had bad-mouthed Brad once too often to the child.

The new cases didn't look too bad—a lack of supervision (LOS) case involving a mother leaving her six-year-old alone after school, phoned in by her ex-husband; and an anonymous referral about two parents doing drugs and not caring adequately for their two-year-old. New York State mandated I go out on these within seven working days; Pelham County wanted me to attempt contact on each within twenty-four hours of the time they were called in. The LOS had to be seen today, the other could wait until tomorrow, if necessary.

I set about phoning back the RP in the first case, another contact they liked us to attempt within twenty-four hours of receipt of a case. There was no answer; the ex-husband was probably at work himself.

I then returned calls on the phone messages that had been waiting for me. I finally was able to speak to the attorney; the doctor proved most helpful, but I convinced him to follow up our conversation with a short note in writing (entire medical histories, scrawled in illegible handwriting, didn't really help as much as a summary and current diagnosis/prognosis); I didn't call the grandmother back because I'd been out on the case just last week, had seen nothing, (and had told her so in one of her subsequent calls) and had nothing new to tell her now. Besides, she'd wasted a lot of time accusing us of not doing our job—why do people get so obnoxious when you tell them something they don't want to hear?

I began to try to catch up on some paperwork that was overdue. The Uniform Case Record (UCR) is a nine-page standardized form that must be filled out within thirty days of opening an indicated case; a second follow-up form is due within ninety days; and thereafter, one must be done at least every six months for as long as the case remains active for services. Nobody likes UCRs except auditors; they're cumbersome, always seem to be overdue, and many of the sections don't apply to your particular case. Plus, they're almost always hand-written, and people looking through a particular record will tend to skip the UCR and read the typed dictation instead.

Still, the due dates are computer-tracked, and woe betide a worker with too many outstanding UCRs due. As with many county jobs, if the paperwork isn't done, the agency loses state reimbursement funds, which means administrative heads roll; thus, one is constantly caught between staying in the office to write paper, thereby not visiting the ongoing cases in a timely fashion, and making the field contacts to the exclusion of an up-to-date case record. There are too many cases and not enough workers to satisfy both criteria, just another added pressure in an already stress-filled job.

"Look at this pile of work," I said aloud to no one in particular, "it's like trying to plug up a dozen holes in a dike all by yourself."

"During a flood," said Joe Picante from behind a mound of case records, himself having just returned from an exasperating, time-devouring morning.

"Using only one hand," added Ophelia Jeffries, known to us all as "O.J." Liked and respected by her co-workers, she was a savvy, thirtyish, woman working in her hometown with people she'd grown up with, and while she could be painfully blunt about some things, she was also remarkably insightful, and her impressions of people were seldom wrong.

A divorced mother of three, she was probably the best choice for the next provisional senior caseworker appointment, but though she'd hoped to be promoted with the contingency that she score well on the senior worker exam given several months ago, the county executive had imposed a freeze on hiring and advancement (currently being challenged by the union), and so qualified, competent people like O.J. stayed mired in lower-paying positions than what they deserved, so the politicians could claim they were doing all they could to balance an already overspent budget. In fact, several were proposing a freeze on any new wage increases for county employees over the next two years, which, if passed, would mean we'd have to shoulder whatever tax increases the legislature imposed without benefit of any raise to offset them.

"What would you do with your other hand?" asked Buddy

Hollister, allowing himself a small break from the paperwork he'd been completing to effect a removal he'd done two days ago.

"You don't really want me to show you now, do you?" O.J. said, pushing her glasses up her nose using only her middle finger.

"Hey, everybody, O.J.'s gonna show us what she does with her free hand in her free time!"

"I'm afraid nobody's gonna have much free time today," announced Cecil, emerging from the supervisor's cubicle and stopping next to my desk. "Especially you, Keith. In addition to those two I gave you this morning, we have a sex abuse case you have to get out on. Six-year-old girl told somebody at school, but was vague about it all. Coordinate your visit with Sex Crimes."

"The girl is six? Should I take the dolls?" I asked.

"Probably a good idea. Read it over first and see what you think," he said, placing my field copy (the one with the RP notation obscured) on my desk and dropping the rest of the case record into Lynne's IN basket for processing.

The report read as follows: "Cindy has disclosed that her ftr. has 'done sex' with her, playing 'the grown-up game.' Specific details unknown. Ch. has faded bruises on her thighs and genital area. Ch. is afraid because her ftr. told her they'd both be in trouble if she told anyone. She does not want him to go to jail.

"Additional Info—Mtr. and ftr. are in process of divorce, though they live in same house. Unk(nown) if ch.'s brother abused also. Source requests immediate contact."

The report was called in by the school nurse, whom I called back immediately. She confirmed the allegations, saying the child's bruises were noted by a teacher's aide when Cindy went to the bathroom. Mrs. Riordan, Cindy's mother, had also contacted the nurse, asking to be notified if there was anything untoward or unusual about Cindy's toileting behavior.

Her principal wanted to know whether or not to release the child home. I replied that I'd have to see what the availability of the Sex Crimes detectives was before I could say whether we would interview the child in school or later at home, but promised to let the school know either way.

The Sex Crimes bureau of the Pelham County Police Department had struck an agreement with Child Protective Services years ago; both agencies would make every effort to coordinate their time and personnel so that alleged victims would be interviewed together, saving them retelling their stories over and over again. The police would share with us a copy of any written statements made by victims or spouses of alleged abusers; we would share with them our impressions, pictures, and information, and allow them to sit in on our interviews.

This arrangement usually worked beneficially for all parties concerned, as long as everyone kept in mind that we each had our own job to do, and they could be done without stepping on one another's toes (remembering, of course, the Major Maxim—We Are Doing This For The Protection Of A Child, and all other considerations are secondary). Sometimes the detectives worked in pairs, often a male and a female, especially helpful when the victims were girls who felt more comfortable talking with a woman.

There were other times when the detective would speak to the parent (the mother in any case I'd ever been assigned), while I spoke to the child, and we would compare notes later, after the interview was over. Once you'd been out on a dozen or so of these interviews, you got to know the detectives on a first-name basis, knew their differences in style, and could structure your interview accordingly. Sometimes, they don't have enough staff to cover, and you find yourself conducting the interview alone and sharing details with them later, especially if the alleged perpetrator was not living in the home or would no longer have ready access to the child.

On this particular occasion, I set up an interview at the home with the mother and child while the eight-year-old brother was still in school. I was to be accompanied by Walt Reese, a nineteen-year veteran who was great when it came to standing up to alleged "perps" and showing compassion to the spouses, but who was, I suspected, a bit squeamish when talking to kids (having none of his own), and who usually covered

up for it by asking the children if they had told their mother everything. As the answer was invariably yes, he'd then simply
take the statement from the mother as to what the child had
told her.

The rest of Reese's involvement would usually consist of
either letting me do the talking, which was fine with me, or
justifying his competence by telling the child about how many
other children he'd dealt with in this situation. This was fine
for making the child understand that he or she was not the
only one ever victimized this way, an important concept to get
across, but not the only issue to be dealt with. I'd found that
sometimes there was other information the child had not yet
disclosed to anyone, not even the mother, that only my interview and/or the child's doll-play would uncover. There's always the fear that they're not telling you everything, either,
especially in cases where the child is particularly close-
mouthed.

Thus, I knew going in that I would have to establish an
early rapport with Cindy, perhaps using the dolls while Reese
was taking the mother's statement in another room, and I
hoped that whatever had happened to her had not obliterated
her trust in men entirely.

I had arranged to meet with Mrs. Riordan at 2:15, about fifteen minutes before Cindy would arrive home from school.
Jody, her eight-year-old brother, would not be home until
about 3:15, all of which was fortunate timing to structure this
visit. Mrs. Riordan sounded genial, if nervous, and her anxiety
rose when I told her we'd have to interview the boy as well, but
she was anxious to cooperate, another plus. Sometimes you get
a mother who is tied to the abusing spouse/boyfriend/
paramour both emotionally and financially, and who sweeps
the whole thing under the carpet by denying anything happened. Thus, they don't have to deal with the problem, because
by not recognizing its existence, there's no problem to deal
with.

These mothers usually swear their abused children are
"lying," and are the toughest to deal with, because acceptance
of the problem is the first step toward getting it all out in the
open, ugly as it may be, and allowing the healing process to be-

gin. In these cases, I often wonder whether the mother or the child will have a harder time dealing with what has happened, and whether there will thus be a rivalry set up between them as to who has been victimized worse, who is suffering the most. This kind of rivalry is also quite common among siblings who have been abused.

It sounded, however, as though Mrs. Riordan would go about things properly, and that would start everything off on the right foot.

I waited in my car outside the house until Reese pulled up in his dark blue Pontiac with the short police radio antenna rising from the trunk like a hornet stinger. We entered together, introduced ourselves, and were invited by Mrs. Riordan to have a seat at her kitchen table.

I wondered whether the Riordans had enjoyed a healthy sexual relationship or not. As with rapists, sexual abuse of children is usually more of a power/innocence game than a sexual one; the gratification of the abuser is more psychological than physical. Thus the timeworn excuse that "if my wife had slept with me more often, or at all, I wouldn't have done this" didn't really hold water. I was just wondering if I should expect to hear it from Mr. Riordan.

In truth, Mrs. Riordan was not unattractive under her wide-frame glasses, with short, straight hair the color of bittersweet chocolate. Though my report said she was thirtyish, she looked to be five to seven years younger than that, with a slim, boyish figure. Her smile was pixie-like when she chose to bestow it, and I suspected there was more warmth behind her tired, pained expression than present circumstances moved her to show.

I wondered how soon Reese would start trying to put her at ease, and I didn't have long to wait. Though he never actually touched her, his body English was clearly focused on her, emanating the message that here was a shoulder she could cry on, if she needed to.

For her part, though, Mrs. Riordan impressed me. She sat demurely, clearly trying to get control of her emotions, being as cooperative as she could with the two strangers who had entered her home to make official inquiry into a matter that one part of her was probably still hoping was all a terrible dream, some giant misunderstanding that would be quickly and easily cleared up.

"How are you doing?" I asked, focusing a bit of attention and compassion on her for the moment, before the children arrived home.

"I'm a little shaky," she conceded.

"Are you up to giving us a statement now, or would you rather wait until after we talk to your children?" asked Reese.

"You have to talk to both of them?"

"I'm supposed to," I said, "just to be sure we know the full extent of what we're dealing with. If Jody has also been abused, and we ignore him, he could wind up with even worse problems down the road, including hating his sister for getting all the attention. We really need to be sure."

"Of course." She lit a cigarette with trembling fingers, and calmed herself with a few deep drags. "I just gave these damned things up last week, too," she said wistfully. After taking a moment or two to collect her thoughts, she said, "Okay, I can give you my statement now." I sat and listened while Reese wrote.

Born Margaret Myrtleson, Mrs. Riordan had been married at nineteen and widowed at twenty-one, after an auto accident claimed her husband and robbed her of the physical ability to ever have children, or so she was told. She met Jack Riordan at her husband's funeral several weeks later, and they were married within two years. Jack was eight years older than she, but always maintained that her age didn't matter. Jack not only seemed wonderful, supportive, and caring, but within six months she was pregnant, and less than two years later, she'd gotten pregnant again. However, after Cindy was born, having found that pregnancy and child-bearing weren't as much fun as she'd thought they'd be, she'd willingly had her tubes tied.

"We still practiced love-making, mind you, but while I wanted to more than ever, Jack's interest seemed to fade after my ligation. I just chalked it up to the pressures of parenthood, earning a living, and growing older, but now that I think about it. . . ."

They fell on hard financial times. Jack lost his job, couldn't seem to hold another one. He began to drink, coming home soused and picking fights with her. He beat her on two separate occasions, though to the best of her knowledge, he never beat the children, nor did he beat her in front of them. This alarmed her, of course, but afterwards he'd offer to make love with her, to make it all better, and since this was about the only interest he'd shown in such matters, she'd always given in. He was surprisingly gentle, and very apologetic, so she accepted it, even came to look forward to his tipping a few, in hopes they could skip the beating and get right to the love-making.

He seemed like a marvelous father to the children, although like many men, his interest in the children escalated only after they were out of diapers. His drinking problem worsened, though, and eventually got in the way of his ability to get a job, let alone hold one. To help supplement the family's income, Mrs. Riordan took a part-time job working as a "housekeeper" in a local hospital. She worked the midnight-to-8:00-A.M. shift so it would bring in a little more money.

"I'd get home about eight-thirty or so, and Jack already had the kids up, dressed, fed, and ready for school. I thought this arrangement was working out well—if Jack wasn't going to hold down a job, at least he was helping around the house. The only problem he mentioned was that Jody was waking up too early and not letting him sleep, and so finally, he . . . he—oh, that filthy sonofabitch!"

Her face turned red again, her jaw set tightly, both the result of the war within her as to whether tears or anger would escape from her eyes. Ultimately, both did.

"Ma'am?"

"I'm sorry." She swabbed her damp cheeks with the heels of her hands. "I just realized the real reason why Jack wouldn't let Jody out of his bedroom until eight o'clock—and why there'd be times when Cindy was bathed and Jody wasn't. God-*damn* him!"

"How'd you find out about what was going on?"

"Last Friday, Cindy tripped and fell on her way to the bus stop, and skinned her knee. I brought her back home to clean her up and noticed some red marks on her legs. I didn't think she'd gotten them from the fall, so I asked her about them. She wouldn't say anything at first, then said she didn't know how she got them, but I know that look she gets when there's something she's not telling me. We'd just had this big talk last week about lying and not telling me everything, and—well, she told me it was from the game."

"I asked her what game was that, and she said, 'the grown-up game.' When I asked her to show me how to play, she just sat there, hands folded in her lap, looking at the floor. She wouldn't even look me in the eye. I asked her who she was playing it with, thinking maybe some of the kids in the neighborhood were playing "doctor" or something. She still wouldn't answer, so I started running down a list of all her little friends. She shook her head no after each one. I asked her if it was Jody. She shook her head no.

"Finally, I asked her if it was a grown-up, and she nodded yes. By process of elimination, I eventually asked her if it was Jack, and she finally looked me in the eyes. Then she just stared at the floor again and wouldn't say anything else. She seemed so terrified I was afraid to keep badgering her with questions, but I had to know.

"I asked her again if it was Jack, and it was like a dam burst. She started crying, burying her head in my chest, and kept saying things like how she'd be in trouble now for telling, and how she didn't want to go to jail, and didn't want Jack to go to jail, either."

"Where *was* Jack during all this?"

"He said he was going out on a job interview. He'd been on job interviews before, but he'd always come back smelling of beer. Sometimes, with the kids off to school, we'd, you know, fool around a little ourselves, but as I said, that was only after he'd been drinking, and . . . well, even that wasn't happening very much anymore. Now I know why."

"Were you ever able to find out exactly what he did?"

"No, but the marks I saw looked like finger marks, and I—I think he may have . . . fondled her." More tears welled up in her eyes, and I felt my heart going out to this woman. Somehow, I wished I could just reach out and comfort her, make her pain go away and let her know somebody cared, but under the circumstances, it was probably the worst thing to do.

Instead, I offered her a tissue, trying to be helpful though the gesture seemed vastly inadequate. I allowed her a moment or two to compose herself, and got no complaint from Reese, who'd been scribbling furiously to get it all down. I jotted a few notes myself, then said, "Mrs. Riordan, it's important for us to find out exactly what's happened to Cindy, right down to graphic details. I apologize for any embarrassment this may cause, and for having to put Cindy through this whole process, but this is the only way we can get the abuse to stop. Plus, Cindy's going to need professional counseling, and the therapist will need to know precisely how Cindy's been traumatized. You also should consider counseling for yourself as well, ma'am. This is not an easy thing for anyone to deal with, especially at a time when you're apt to feel all alone."

"Cindy and I both have a screening appointment at the mental health clinic on Thursday," said Mrs. Riordan, "although they said we may have to be put on a waiting list to actually begin regular sessions."

"Good for you, ma'am. That's absolutely the right move to make."

"Is your husband still living here, Mrs. Riordan?" asked Reese, "and where is he at the moment?"

"I expect he'd be at work. He only just got this job last week. When Cindy first told me, I just wanted to cut the bastard's heart out. But I figured, no, I ought to discuss it with him first, hear his side of the story. He admitted that he'd 'messed with her', but he apologized so much, swore it'd never happen again, swore he'd get help for himself. He sounded so sincere, I really wanted to believe him, but how can you trust a man who's done something sexual with his own daughter?

"Anyway, he begged me for a chance to make amends. We agreed that he would move out, and live with his parents in Nassau County for a while. I wanted to see if he'd really go for help, if maybe this was something we could work through. Meanwhile, a friend of mine who works in the records room in police headquarters ran a check on him. It turned out he had a prior conviction for child molestation before I ever knew him, which he never told me about. That's when I filed for this."

She handed me a temporary order of protection, dated yes-

terday, which barred him from the premises or from any violent acts or threats against his wife or children. There would be
another hearing in a few weeks, but the courts had not set the
date on their calendar as yet. She'd had to divulge these facts to
the intake officer at probation when she applied for this OP,
and she supposed that was how the report came to be made to
CPS.

Though I could not confirm or deny this to her, she was absolutely correct but since the school had already made a report,
probation's report was listed as a duplicate.

For a lady in emotional turmoil herself, Mrs. Riordan was
making all the right moves, especially for her children, and I
admired her for it. Too bad there weren't more mothers like
her.

"Will Jack be arrested?" she asked Reese.

"Depending on what your daughter has to say, he probably
will, although odds are he'll be out on bail the next day."

"Even with the priors?" I asked.

"Yeah," Reese said, "they'll just jack up the bail, as long as
he agrees to stay away pending the outcome of the investigation. He doesn't work with children in his job, does he?"

The sound of a bus horn honking in front of the house
drifted to our ears. "No, he just started working in a convenience store, about four days ago," said Mrs. Riordan. "Excuse
me, I think that's Cindy."

CHAPTER TWELVE

While Mrs. Riordan was escorting her daughter inside, Reese nudged me. "It's going pretty well, so far," he said. "I'll get a statement from the mother now while you talk to the kid?"

"If you like," I said, eyeing him amusedly. We were now entering waters deeper and less familiar to him, and Reese was preferring to stay in the shallows.

The girl had inherited her mother's good looks, and her smile was a heart-melter. Innocence shone from a round face framed by long, fine hair the color of cashew nuts. When she saw the two strangers sitting at the kitchen table, though, that smile faded faster than yesterday's news.

"Who're they?" she asked, as though she'd discovered two new fish in an aquarium.

"These nice men have come here to ask you some questions, Cindy, about . . . you know, what we talked about?" Her carefree, home-from-school-at-last look was replaced by uncertainty, nervousness, and suspicion—the kind of look children get when the doctor tells them they may have to get a shot.

It was time for me to focus the interview. "Cindy, I'm Mr. Richards, and this is Detective Reese. Like your mom said, we wanted to meet you and ask you some questions."

"Are you the police?" she asked.

"Well, he is. I'm a social worker. Don't worry, sweetheart, all we want to do is to talk. And maybe play a little bit."

"Play?"

"Yes. Cindy, we talk to lots of little boys and girls, just like you, to make sure their parents are doing a good job of taking care of them. If their parents *are* doing a good job, we just go away. But if their parents aren't, then we try to teach them how to do a better job. Understand?"

She nodded yes.

Reese interrupted to offer to take Mrs. Riordan's statement in another room, but she declined when Cindy said she wanted her mother to stay with her.

"Now Cindy, has Mommy ever talked to you about good touches and bad touches?"

She nodded yes.

"Can you tell me a kind of good touch?"

"Hugs," she said, as her mother gave her one.

"Very good! And can you tell me what a bad touch is?"

"If someone touches my 'jyna."

"That's right, sweetheart. You're a very smart little girl." I smiled my warmest smile, to try to put her at ease as much as possible before the first big question.

"Has anybody ever given you a bad touch, Cindy?"

She looked at Reese, curled deeper into her mother's arms, and looked at the floor, saying nothing.

"Sweetheart, if Mommy has told you about bad touches, then she probably also told you that the first thing you must do when that happens to you is to tell someone, right? If someone is doing that to you, it's wrong; they're doing a bad thing, and we want to make it stop happening. That's why we need you to tell us who it is, and what they did."

Still nothing.

Reese gave it a try. "Honey, it's a crime to do things like this to children like yourself, and whoever did this to you committed a crime. We need to know who it is so they can be pun—"

I put a restraining hand on his forearm and shook my head no. Fear of punishment, both for herself and the perpetrator, could be a major reason why she might not tell, especially if it was her father.

"Cindy, if someone is bad-touching you," I said, leaning over to look up into her face, "then you're probably feeling mixed-up, or yucky, or maybe even scared. But the worst part is that it's going to happen to other children and make them feel yucky and scared too, unless you help us stop the bad-toucher. That's why it's so important that you tell us, yes or no: is someone giving you any bad touches?"

A tentative eye glance was followed by an even more scared look, then, reluctantly, a single nod. Yes.

Mrs. Riordan tightened her arms around her daughter.

"Can you tell us how it happened?"

More floor-staring and silence.

Reese was about to say something else, and again I caught his eye and shook my head no.

"Cindy, I apologize to you," I said, "I told you before we might play, and when you asked me about it, I didn't answer you. We're going to play right now; but first, I have some friends I want you to meet."

I went to my car, took out the large, electric blue athletic bag, and returned to the kitchen. "Why don't we go into the living room," I suggested, "we'll have a little more room there."

We settled ourselves, Mrs. Riordan on the sofa, Cindy on the floor at her feet, me on the floor next to Cindy, Reese in an easy chair across the room and out of Cindy's range of vision for the moment. I unzipped the bag and laid out the contents, piece by piece, on the floor. I said nothing and looked to Reese while putting my finger to my lips. Mrs. Riordan also picked up my lead.

When Cindy saw the dolls, she immediately brightened, curiosity supplanting some of her fear and suspicion. Still clutching her mother's legs, she let go with one hand, to point.

"What're those?"

"They're my friends," I said, continuing to lay out the last ones. There were eight in all: a male adult, a female adult, a male child, and a female child, all with white skin; the other four were identical, except they had dark brown skin, and their hair was shorter, curlier, made out of black Velcro. They were all clothed, and were soft and cuddly, like rag dolls, with blank expressions on their faces. The mouths were all in the shape of an "O", and large enough to insert the first joint of my pinky finger. Their hands were represented not by fist-like lumps, but with each finger of each hand represented separately.

"I don't think you've seen dollies like these before," I continued. With her free, pointing hand, she reached out and took the adult female doll, checking it out before giving it a hug. That's when she noticed two of the reasons these dolls were so special. Pulling the loose-fitting blouse down, she exposed the small breasts of the adult female.

"Look, Mommy, she has boobies, just like you!"

Reese pretended to find something fascinating about a cob-web in a far corner while Mrs. Riordan turned the color of a to-mato. Cindy began to revel in the joy of discovery, however. She pulled the rest of the clothes off the doll, discovering both the anal and vaginal openings, as well as the patch of simulated pubic hair. "And a 'jyna, too!"

She grabbed the next doll, the male child, undressed it, and discovered its penis, a proportionately-sized cloth digit, which stuck up and out as though erect. "This one has a peenie! Mommy, look!"

Mommy did, tentatively touching the pubic hair, turning the doll over to observe its anal opening, handling the doll the same way as her daughter did with the adult male she was now inspecting. If Mrs. Riordan blushed any more, her eyes would be swollen shut.

"We have a little problem, though, Cindy," I said. "My friends don't have any names yet, and I was hoping you could help us name them."

Cindy mulled this over for about a tenth of a second, then held up the adult female and proclaimed her to be "Mommy." The adult male she named "Daddy." The female child she named "Stephanie," and the male child, strangely enough, was "Bryan," perhaps an idealized version of her brother, with a name she preferred over Jody.

So far, so good. The naming isn't as important as the child's identification with them and especially the one that most closely resembles him or her; Cindy's naming the adults after family members made her identification even stronger. With that marvelously clear vision children have of the world, uncluttered by the burdens of tact or social nicety, Cindy continued to name the black dolls with the names of some of her classmates—Tyrone, Keisha, and Tyrone's and Keisha's Mommy and Daddy. (This gave Mrs. Riordan a moment or two to recover her composure, as well; it's important that the parents show as little of whatever discomfort they may be feeling as possible, since the children will pick up on it.)

"Now that we know who our friends are, Cindy, maybe they'll help us to tell a story."

They did, and Cindy's story was roughly as follows:

Once upon a time, Stephanie and Bryan's family lived next door to Tyrone and Keisha's family. Stephanie and Bryan were good children, except that Bryan was always getting in trouble for bothering Stephanie and Daddy. Daddy got mad and made Bryan stay in his room, especially when Mommy had to work. Daddy was a good daddy, but sometimes he'd make Stephanie do things she didn't want to.

"What kinds of things?" I asked. "Like work around the house?"

"No," answered Cindy. "Like play the grown-up game."

"How do you play that?"

Cindy got quiet again, so I offered some encouragement. "Maybe Stephanie and Bryan could show us how to play."

"Not Bryan, silly. He's not allowed."

"Oh, okay. How do Daddy and Stephanie play the game?"

Cindy turned around and looked at her mother for a long moment. Then she said, "If Stephanie tells, she'll be in a lot of trouble, and Daddy may have to go to jail."

"Well," I said, "since it's only a made-up story, we won't let anybody get in trouble. We just want to find out how to play the game. How does it start?"

"Daddy calls Stephanie into his room and makes her sit on the bed. Then Daddy goes to the bathroom and comes out with his magic wand."

"His magic wand?" I echoed.

"Yeah," she said, grabbing the daddy doll's penis and wiggling it. "Like this. Only it's out of his pants."

I heard a sharp rush of breath from Mrs. Riordan as she tried to keep a gasp from becoming obvious.

"The daddy's wand only works when it's awake," Cindy continued, "and Stephanie has to wake it up."

"How does she do that?"

Cindy took the Stephanie doll and placed its mouth on the daddy doll's penis. "Like this."

"Does Stephanie like to wake it up?"

"No."

"Why?"

"Because it smells awful."

"What happens once Daddy's wand is awake?" Out of the corner of my eye I saw Reese shift uncomfortably in his chair, his writing hand scribbling furiously nonetheless.

"It has the power, like She-Ra's sword."

"Does Stephanie use this power to fight evil, like She-Ra does?"

"No. You have to use the wand to open the magic box."

"Where is this magic box?"

"In Cindy's 'jyna."

The use of her own name did not go unnoticed by me, nor by Mrs. Riordan, who was breathing hard now, her color pale, her jaw set, and her lips pressed tightly together, trying not to communicate her feelings to her child.

"How do you open the magic box?"

"Daddy puts grease on his wand to turn it into a key," she said. "Then Cind—I mean, Stephanie, has to lie on her back. Then he puts the key into her 'jyna and the magic box opens."

"Can the Stephanie doll and the Bryan doll show us?" I asked. Cindy positioned the dolls to demonstrate an act of co-itus, the daddy doll on top. She even stuffed the cloth penis into the other doll's vaginal opening.

"Does it hurt?"

"Sometimes."

"Then what happens?"

"Then Daddy moves the key in and out of the box until he has to make wee-wee all over Cindy's tummy."

"Wee-wee?"

"Um-hmm. Only it's magic wee-wee."

"What makes it magic?"

"Well, it doesn't smell like wee-wee. And it's like milk, not yellow."

"Does anything else happen?"

"Daddy takes a tissue and wipes it all off, and when he's all done, he takes a dollar out of the magic box and gives it to her."

Shock and outrage were turning Mrs. Riordan's face ugly during Cindy's story. She stiffened, and the child sensed this, but to her credit, by the time Cindy turned around, Mrs. Riordan had plastered a smile on her face.

"What do you—I mean, what does Stephanie do with the dollar?"

"Save it in my jewelry box."

I paused a moment, continuing after Reese's nod indicated he'd caught up his note-taking.

"Do Stephanie and Bryan have any other stories to tell us?" I asked.

"No."

"Do Daddy and Cindy play any other grown-up games?"

"No."

"Do Daddy and Cindy play this game the same way every time?"

She nodded yes. Then, realizing her mother was upset, she said, "Mommy? Am I in trouble?"

I answered. "No, sweetheart, you're not. You're doing the right thing telling us, and if anybody ever bad-touches you again, you'll tell us that, too, won't you?"

She nodded yes.

"Has anyone else bad-touched you, Cindy? Anyone else played the grown-up game with you?"

She nodded no and no.

"How many times did you play this game?" asked Reese.

Cindy shrugged. "Lots."

"When was the last time?"

"A couple days ago." She curled back into her mother's arms for reassurance, now that we were talking about her in the first person again. Mrs. Riordan helped us to set the date of the last incident, then asked Cindy for permission to look inside her jewelry box. The child agreed, and after Cindy stated that she had saved no other money in it, Mrs. Riordan opened it and counted the contents; all single dollar bills, fourteen dollars in all.

"Cindy," I said gently, "isn't it amazing that Stephanie and Bryan are playing the grown-up game too? And there are many, many more children that I see every day, who are forced to play this game by grown-ups who are being bad when they make their children play it. It's not nice, not a good game for children to play with anybody, but when a grown-up makes you play it, or gives you money or candy or presents to play it, they're being bad and the children should tell them 'No!' I'll bet Stephanie and Bryan don't like to play the grown-up game, either, do they?"

She shook her head no.

"And their daddy did wrong by playing it with them, just like your daddy did wrong by playing it with you."

"Am I going to go to jail?"

"No, sweetheart, it's not your fault."

Reese finished writing out their statements, instructed mother and child each to read their statement over and initial certain parts, then sign at the end to certify that this was an accurate and true representation of their version of what happened. Finally, Reese notarized them.

Meanwhile, I enlisted Cindy's help to redress the dolls, say goodbye, and put them away. "Can you bring them over to play with me again? Please? Please, Mommy, can he?"

"I don't think so, Cindy," said her mother. "Mr. Richards needs the dolls to meet other little children who are waiting their turn to play with them." Her involuntary shudder at the end of this explanation betrayed the turmoil she must have been feeling.

"I may have to come back, Cindy, but Stephanie and Bryan and their friends do have lots more children to meet, so I don't know if they can come back soon or not. But I want to thank you, Cindy, for being such a good girl and answering all our questions. You did the right thing telling us the truth, and we're going to make sure Daddy doesn't play the grown-up game with you anymore."

"Are you going to lock my daddy up?" she asked Reese.

"Maybe for a little while," the detective responded, "just to teach him he did wrong and to punish him for that."

"But why? He's not a bad daddy."

"He may be a very good daddy," I said, "and I'm sure he still loves you very much. But what he did was wrong. For any adult to play the grown-up game with any child is a crime, Cindy, and your daddy should have known that. "

I had my doubts about Jack Riordan; I didn't see how anyone could commit such a heinous act against a child and still profess to love them, but it was important that Cindy be made to feel as loved and secure as possible, to help her face the major changes that would be made in her and her family's lives in the coming months.

I was very impressed with the way Mrs. Riordan had handled herself and interacted with her daughter and doubted whether I could have handled things so well were I in her shoes. At least Cindy had that going for her; many parents are too overwhelmed by the whole situation to be able to deal with their own pain, and their own feelings, let alone to be able to deal with their children's. She deserved a word of recognition, and I made a mental note to tell her so before I left.

Jody arrived home just as Cindy was asking her mother if this was all over now, and if she could have permission to play at a friend's. Mrs. Riordan said okay, and while she sent Cindy to her room to change into playclothes, I briefly interviewed her son.

He acknowledged he knew what good and bad touches were; he answered that if anyone bad-touched him he would tell someone; and he totally denied anyone had done anything like that to him. After some other questions to corroborate his sister's situation with regards to him (being made to stay in his room while mother was working, being aware that their father sometimes called Cindy into their parent's bedroom and he wasn't allowed to go, etc.), I was certain he had not been abused and quietly told both Reese and Mrs. Riordan so. She expressed appreciation that we didn't tell him everything that was going on, preferring to handle that herself if and when she felt he needed to know.

"So, what happens now?" she asked, scooting her son off to change his clothes and check on his sister.

"Well, I would imagine that the good detective here will make arrangements to pick Mr. Riordan up and book him on rape and sodomy charges," I said, getting a nod of assent from Reese. "We also will need to speak with your husband about the allegations, but we'll defer to the police. I'll either talk to him in jail, after he's brought in, or at home if he's able to make bail."

"You mean he may stay locked up?"

Reese was much more comfortable now. This was his area of expertise, his bailiwick, and he reveled in the spotlight of his vested authority. "Yes. We'll seek a warrant immediately. Only thing is the timing. This is my case, but I'm off for the next three days and then I start a week of night shifts, so I'm not sure exactly when we can pick him up. I have to ask for your cooperation, ma'am, that neither you nor the kids let on that you've spoken to anybody about this. If he finds out, he might get spooked and run."

"But what do I do when he calls? He called last night, and I got him thinking everything's all right, that he'll just go to counselling, and I'll let him back in the house. But I don't know how long I can keep him thinking that way. Just talking to him, knowing what he's done, makes my skin crawl. And that was before I knew . . ."

Her voice cracked, and she was fighting off tears again. "I . . . I mean, I just thought . . . he was fondling her, and now I find out. . . ." Her trembling hands covered her face, and I couldn't help but place my steadying hand on her shoulder. She made no move to turn away.

"I'm sorry," she said, "it's just that I . . . I'm worried about how this will affect Cindy; I want to cut his privates off and feed them to him; I don't know what's going to happen with the house and the bills if he isn't part of the family anymore; I don't know how long I can hide the fact that you're after him; and . . . well . . . I feel so . . . foolish."

"Don't, ma'am," I said. "Just about anything we could have suggested, you've already done, or at least started the process. Did I mention that it might be a good idea that Cindy have an internal gynecological exam?"

"We have an appointment tonight with her pediatrician."

I smiled in sheer admiration. "See? You've anticipated your children's needs and have already started dealing with this problem, even though you had no idea of its magnitude until a few minutes ago. In that respect, Cindy's very lucky. A lot of mothers find it easier to just deny the whole thing. But you've got the perpetrator kicked out of the house, Cindy's medical exam set, a screening appointment with a counselor, the police and CPS working on the case—all by yourself, and in a short period of time. You deserve a lot of credit."

"Oh, yeah. I'm sure I'll make Mother of the Year."

I tried to look her straight in the eye. "Mrs. Riordan—Meg—it won't serve any purpose to start heaping guilt on yourself. You've been great with your kids, and you should go easy on Meg Riordan, too. The worst is over, you've put your fears behind you and have gotten past the disclosure. Now that you at least know what you're dealing with, you and your children can bind up your wounds, and let the healing begin."

I turned to Reese. "Isn't there any way someone else can pick up the father? I mean, I have to talk to him, and this means I have to wait to be able to do my job, too."

"I know," Reese conceded, "but it can't be helped. We've been down-staffed since the county exec decided to trim the budget. I mean, how's he going to approve replacements for our people when he has all those county cars to maintain for his hand-picked assistants to drive around in?"

"All that doesn't help Mrs. Riordan's situation much."

"I know, and I'm sorry. I'll do what I can."

We shook hands, thanked everyone for their cooperation, said our goodbyes. I made sure Mrs. Riordan had my number and told her to call if she had any other questions or problems. I also gave Reese our fax number so he could transmit copies of the mother's and child's statements to us. We'd need them to support the petition we'd be filing in family court within the next two or three days, depending on the volume of cases already on the court calendar.

As I drove away, I saw Mrs. Riordan standing in the doorway, an arm around each of her children, steadfast in her resolve to protect them.

Your ordinary, all-American, single-parent family.

That has just had its emotional insides ripped out by the roots.

CHAPTER THIRTEEN

Gloria's cousin was getting married. The wedding was to be held on Saturday afternoon, with the reception immediately following. As for most married couples with children, Saturday had lost that "must-go-out" urgency, and was usually spent home relaxing, watching television, or renting a video, recharging our batteries for the coming week. Tonight would be an exception, and I was looking forward to it. Gloria and I didn't get out together without the kids all that much, and once the babysitter had arrived and we were actually in the car headed for the church, I allowed myself to start enjoying the time away from being either a parent or a Child Protective Services worker.

I found myself wondering about Gloria's cousin preparing for her wedding right now, which led me to wonder about all those people preparing for dates at this moment, which led me to wonder about how many other couples whose relationships had grown rocky or destructive might have started out this way. This led me to wonder how many alcoholics would be getting tanked up right about now, laying the foundation for some incident of domestic violence later tonight, or what new stories ex-spouses would be pumping out of their children while on their weekend visitation, or how many single parents would be making inappropriate child care plans for their kids while they, too, tried to escape the pressures of parenting for a few hours, all of which might be prompting reports that would end up on my desk on Monday morning.

"Penny for your thoughts?" Gloria's voice broke the silence in the car, as well as my train of thought, God bless her.

"Just thinking about everybody else getting ready for this wedding, as we are," I covered, vowing to try to put the job out of my mind for the rest of this night, anyway.

But it was not to be.

The ceremony was lovely, with typical sartorial finery, ceremonial solemnity, nervous smiling faces, and salvos of flashbulbs. Before I knew it, we were at the reception hall, mingling away with Gloria's family. Cocktails, plates of food, and glasses of champagne kept appearing in my hand, and surprisingly, they kept emptying. Gloria excused herself to talk with relatives I didn't particularly like.

"Keith? Keith Richards! What are you doing here?" said a voice belonging to Norma Vezey, a twice-divorced CPS undercare worker to whom I'd passed any number of indicated cases for ongoing services. I explained my wife's relationship to the bride, and as it turned out, the groom was Norma's nephew. Standing with her was a tall, slim woman with auburn hair and smoky-gray, plastic-framed glasses. "Keith, this is my friend Sam. Sam Bishop, Keith Richards."

A small, firm hand slipped itself into mine, as the woman smiled amiably. "Nice to meet you, Keith. Isn't that the name of one of the Rolling Stones?" A nice smile. Warm, like her handshake. She wore a midnight-blue, satiny pants suit, with a red paisley scarf draped down from her left shoulder. She shouldn't be hiding behind those glasses, though; they did nothing for her.

"Yes. No relation," I answered, automatically pasting a tolerant smile onto my face.

Norma said, "It's really funny you should happen to be here. We were discussing the woeful lack of foster care resources, and how CPS referrals were shooting through the roof. Sam was curious as to how much child abuse we're really finding out there." She sipped her drink, something with a small, pink plastic stirrer sticking out of it. "I was just telling Sam that the only reason I was able to get three children into a foster home yesterday was because your Zifarelli kids were returned to their father."

"I hadn't heard about that."

"Sure. I had to wait all afternoon for an answer, then finally Tricia Smollins called me at four-thirty to tell me the slots were available. You know how things like this always come down to the last minute."

"That's been my experience," I agreed, dazzled but not surprised by how quickly two "connected" gentlemen in three-piece suits had been able to negotiate the bobsled-run of family court.

Norma turned to her friend. "Keith is in investigations. He gets the referrals when they first come in, sees the families, assesses the risk to the children, and reports his findings to the state. He also helps set up a service plan for indicated families, then passes it on to an undercare worker like me for ongoing involvement."

"So you're sort of on the front lines, then?" Sam leanedd close to me as she spoke into my ear, surrounding me with a perfume scent too pungent for my tastes.

"It feels more like being in the trenches."

She smiled at that, a little longer and broader than necessary. She'd turned her body to face me full, showing Norma her back. "I'll bet you see some really tough cases."

"Yes, I do, and that's not just limited to my clientele." She raised her eyebrows and cocked her head slightly, not getting my meager joke, as if she wanted me to elaborate. "But nobody wants to hear all the gory details."

"No, please go on, I find it . . . ," she rested her teeth on her lower lip as she searched for the right word, "fascinating."

Even a sponge can only soak up so much before it reaches its saturation point and needs to be wrung out, and I guess I'd reached mine. Sam Bishop was an excellent audience, and for some reason, I didn't mind that she was doing the wringing.

"We really don't have the staff to cover all the cases adequately, especially when they get to the stage where someone like Norma would inherit them. Thank God so many of the referrals turn out to be utter bullshit," I said, internally rationalizing my use of such language by blaming the booze.

"I want to say hello to somebody," Norma excused herself, "you two go on and chat."

"You were saying that all of your referrals are bullshit," Sam said, turning her attention full on me and ignoring everyone else in the place, making me feel like some kind of honored guest.

"No," I said, after I took a moment to register what she'd said, "they're not *all* bullshit, just a lot of them. People try to manipulate the CPS system all the time. You know, schools and hospitals calling to protect their behinds when a kid has a hangnail, neighbors harassing neighbors, estranged spouses trying to zap it to their ex. We shouldn't be doing school attendance officers' work, nor that of the probation department, but they often get us involved so that maybe *we'll* write the petitions and force families to cooperate.

"I also hate the referrals that come in stating 'an older sibling is beating on a younger one and mother allows it to happen. No bruises or harm to child. Reporting party is anonymous.' Those are just busywork, if you ask me. Sometimes it does more damage to a child for their family to have to go through the investigation. People under investigation aren't automatically guilty, you know; thanks to the governor, at least the fact that you're under investigation can't be admitted as evidence in a custody hearing anymore in New York State. Yet at times it still feels like I'm being made to conduct some kind of damned witch-hunt."

I paused for a breath, marvelling at how easily this was all pouring out. For some reason, it was becoming important to make her like me, and maybe, just a little, to empathize with me, too.

"You don't feel as though what you're doing is worthwhile? Protecting children? Saving lives and injuries of those who are defenseless and innocent?" she said, a gleam in her eye I couldn't read.

"Of course that part is worthwhile. But why should two-thirds of the reported families have to go through all this rigmarole to save the children in the other one-third? Seems to me that that two-thirds become the 'defenseless and innocent,' yet they're often treated as lepers and criminals by self-righteous fools. We've done a great job alerting people that the tiniest suspicion is grounds for referral. What we haven't made clear is that that same suspicion does not automatically give people the right to treat those they suspect like shit."

"You sound pretty angry."

"It's just tough to swallow day after day. I mean, you feel good about the kids you do save, the families where you make a positive impact. But by the year 2000, every parent in America will have been referred at least once, I'm sure, and it just doesn't seem right. That's an incredible waste of time, tax dollars, and manpower. There's got to be a better way."

I helped myself to two refills from a tray of cocktails that floated by, handed one to Sam, and lapsed into silence while my thoughts drifted.

Once you hit your thirties, you start to believe in your own mortality, start to question your own existence, start to realize you're looking for answers you may never find. I've come to understand my lot in life is to shoulder the irony of having to toil each day at the emotionally demanding task of trying to help children and their families stay together by improving the quality of their lives, while at the same time wrestling with all the same problems, and searching for proper solutions, in my own family, with my own children.

After another moment or two, Sam said, "If you feel your job is so worthless, why do you do it? Why don't you quit?"

I shrugged. "I'm good at it, I need the paycheck, and maybe, just maybe, I can make a difference. Still, I often go home at night asking myself if we really accomplish anything with our reports and our petitions, with all the paperwork we do. Are we really helping people, or just adding to the chaos of life? Perhaps when we remove children from abusive parents we're protecting them physically, but do we cause more damage emotionally? In those cases where a child is brutalized so severely that they need hospitalization, or in sex abuse cases, or in other cases involving chronic domestic violence, I know our influence brings about some positive changes, but I have to wonder about all the other 'lesser' cases.

"Is it worth it to summon a child to the principal's office in school, and put them through an official interview, just to see their bruises and give their parents a lecture? Because, in those cases, we really don't have strong enough evidence to remove the child, and outside of perhaps effecting an order of protection, all we can do is make a notation of the "abuse" in the State Central Registry, recommend counseling, maybe keep an eye on the situation, and hope for the best.

"When grandparents call out of frustration at their legal powerlessness in matters pertaining to their grandchildren, or a family member tries to use CPS to get their relative into a substance-abuse rehab program, or a disgruntled neighbor makes an anonymous referral because the mother never returned her toaster, are those investigations and interviews really helping the children of those families, or adding fuel to the fire of situations that are hard enough to cope with already?"

"You seem to have a real problem with this whole system. Is it possible you've been at it too long? Do you think maybe you're burning out?"

I grinned a small, "who knows?" kind of smile while I shrugged my shoulders. "A lot of people burn out at this job before they've fully learned it. That's why we have such a high turnover rate among staff. Have I burned out? Could be. But burnout is an entity not recognized by our administration. I'm in my seventeenth year with Social Services, eighth in CPS. Six years ago, the commissioner at that time was asked about burnout, and do you know what she said? Not that it's a problem that has no answer save to change jobs. Not that she was authorizing any studies to generate ideas to counter burnout. Not that we were doing all we could to fight it. She stated, 'There is no burnout in Pelham County.' Period. Isn't that a marvelous standpoint? She's the commish, she says it ain't so, and thus she sweeps the problem under the rug. If it doesn't exist, she doesn't have to address it, let alone do anything about it. Not her problem. She's on top of this progressive department, in charge of all these employees, and with one simple denial, she thinks she's asserted her authority and wiped out a problem she really doesn't want to deal with.

"If one of my clients ever denied a drinking problem that way," I continued, "we'd write them off, because until they recognize the problem and want help with it, there's nothing we can do except see to it they don't drag their family down with them. Not the case in DSS. They treat their employees like chattel, then wonder why so many people walk, why they lose so much money training folks who are gone a year later. Then they have to train all the replacements, who also don't stay."

"You're still at it."

I nodded and sipped my drink. "That's because one of the tactics they sometimes use is to assign employees to CPS who've been with the agency long enough to be thinking about a pension, employees who don't want to throw away whatever longevity they've invested, say eight to ten years. After that point, if the person doesn't quit within the first six months, they know that employee is in for the duration. No matter how bad it gets, that poor slob is trapped into working for the pension. So you wind up with people who have either been around so long they don't give a shit or who have just started so they don't know shit. Over 50 percent of our staff have been at it two years or less, and it's worse in the city.

"Then everybody wonders how a Joel Steinberg is able to do what he did? Not me, I don't wonder. It's fortunate that we haven't lost more kids like Lisa than we have, while we're running around checking out three dozen other referrals concerning dirty households and tiny bruises."

I drained my glass, and started to hunt for another round for us both, but Sam declined. "Do you find yourself turning to alcohol like this very often?" she asked, sounding as casual as if she were asking for phone change.

"Whattaya, writing a book?" I said, then laughed. "No, not very often. It's . . . it's been a long week, and I have to keep all this pent up inside of me. I'm sorry, it's nice of you to sit here and listen to all this venom spew forth from a total stranger. I'm usually much more upbeat."

Gloria, having been alerted, no doubt, by observant family that her husband's attentions were being monopolized by an attractive young woman, returned to my side and slipped her arm through mine. "Would you introduce us, sweetheart?" she asked. I did, and Gloria asked, "Not the Samantha Bishop who writes for *Newsday?*"

Samantha smiled sheepishly and answered, "Yes, I am." She looked at her watch, and put down her half-full glass. "Well, thanks for the chat, Keith, it was most interesting. Nice meeting you, Gloria." She melted away into the crowd as easily as she and Norma had materialized from it.

"A reporter, just what I needed," I grumbled as Gloria and I began a slow dance together. "It might have been nice for Norma Vezey to make note of that fact when she introduced us."

"Is that what you were talking about, your job?" Gloria asked, and I realized how powerful her curiosity must have been to prompt her to dance to "We've Only Just Begun," a song she abhorred.

"Yeah. Between the champagne and my need to bitch, I guess I sort of got on my soapbox a little bit. Well, listen, even CPS workers are entitled to their opinions, right?"

"You ought to watch whom you give your opinions to, okay?"

"Okay. But it must get tiresome for you, hearing me sing the same old song day after day." I inhaled the sweet, familiar scent of her perfume, and it was like changing out of new, stiff boots into a pair of warm, fuzzy slippers.

"It does, but at least it keeps you out of trouble. Honestly, I can't leave you alone for five minutes."

"Sure you can, but you won't," I grinned devilishly, "because you're such a possessive wench." This earned me a hard but surreptitious pinch on the buttocks, which I deserved. "You know, this is the first time we've danced together in I don't know how long."

"Probably since the last wedding we attended," she agreed. The song ended, and as the band swung into a reggae version of "Proud Mary," we headed back to our table. Two hateful, overplayed songs in a row was just too much to bear. "Think I can trust you to behave yourself while I go to the ladies room?" she asked.

We stayed until the reception ended, dancing, laughing, and having a good time. I didn't spot Norma or Sam Bishop anywhere for the rest of the night, though, and I couldn't help but feel that despite my right to express them, my opinions would come back to haunt me somehow.

CHAPTER FOURTEEN

From the Monday morning mail bin of worker Keith Richards:

Three new cases. Four phone messages. A survey about on-the-job hazards, including violence directed towards us in the course of our duties. A report about delinquent and/or overdue cases. A memo reminding us not to reveal reporting parties and to honor client confidentiality whenever possible. Another memo asking for volunteers to work Emergency Services (ES) shifts at night or on weekends (pure overtime, but I need the break from the job more than I need the extra money—plus, it's hell on people with families). A note from Cathy asking me to give her a call. A reminder from Cecil that my attendance is expected at a unit meeting to take place in approximately thirty minutes.

I filed the two memos and the reminder in the circular file, then started looking through the cases. An inadequate guardianship/educational neglect for poor school attendance, another IG for alleged drug abuse and lack of supervision, and a subsequent report on a case I had indicated only three weeks ago. The latter two had been visited by Emergency Services last night, and the RP on the ed. neglect had stated that the family was out of town until tomorrow, so none of these new cases required my immediate attention. I resolved to see the subsequent the next day, however, especially after the RP from the school, unaware of ES's attempt last night, called to ask when someone would be out on it. The child, nine years old, was saying that his father (who had blackened his eye and bruised his arm in the past—the reasons why I'd indicated the case) had threatened him with "the beating of his life," because the child was failing two subjects in school; no bruises seen at this time. Unfortunately, without any marks or bruises, there wouldn't be a whole lot of credible evidence to substantiate anything other than tension in the home.

I tried calling Cathy, but her phone was busy. Last week's events started running through my mind, like some out-of-sequence instant replay, and it occurred to me that despite the conflicting explanations Jenny MacAvoy's parents had given about her current location, I had evidence that the child wasn't where either parent said she was. Thus, a missing persons report was in order, especially since the weekend had passed. (Police usually won't take such a report unless the person is missing at least 48 hours.) I wanted one more try at locating her, so I dialed Mrs. MacAvoy, expecting either that the ring would go unanswered or that she would hang up as soon as she recognized my voice.

I was very nearly right.

"Mrs. MacAvoy? Mr. Richards, CPS. I spoke to your husband the other day and he said Jenny went to live with her aunt in North Carolina . . . ?"

"Er . . . yes, that's right. Look, I really can't talk to you anymore—"

"But you told me she was with her father upstate, and North Carolina DSS has no record of her. If you could give me a name and address, maybe I could close the case out *wherever* she is."

Silence crept through the receiver as the woman mulled this over. When she next spoke, her voice trembled. "I'm sorry, Mr. Richards. Whatever my husband told you is the truth, and I can't talk about it any more. He wants you to call our lawyer and leave us alone."

"But the lawyer won't know the address. If you could just—"

There was the soft click of the receiver being placed almost apologetically back in its cradle on the other end.

Though the urge to close the case out and be done with it still ran strong, it was important to be sure I'd done a thorough job first. Besides, I couldn't very well close out a case listing a child's current whereabouts as unknown when we knew exactly where the child's family lives. I decided to run a check on our computerized Welfare Management System (WMS) to see if the Services or Public Assistance records might have updated info.

I found a couple of interesting facts. Approximately four years ago, Jenny was known as Jennifer Simmons and was listed as daughter in a PA grant payable to a Charlene Simmons, of Farmingdale. But the most recent screen on Charlene showed her as having three children, not four. A search of the other screens revealed that Jenny had been removed from Charlene's grant last March, although she never did appear in Amanda MacAvoy's. On my first visit, Jenny had definitely referred to Amanda as "Mommy" (indicating the child had been with them for some time), yet Jenny had never been added to the grant. This was most odd because people receiving PA as long as the MacAvoys wouldn't bypass such a golden opportunity to increase their monthly income.

At least it seemed the MacAvoys were being up front about Jenny's being gone, even if they couldn't agree on where.

Before I could follow this through any further, the word went around the room—Cecil was starting the unit meeting. Once again, the Jenny MacAvoy mystery would have to return to a back burner.

We all dragged our chairs into the smallish cubicle where Woody Taylor normally occupied desk space as supervisor. Cecil had attended the monthly supervisor's meeting with the director in Woody's stead, and this meeting was to keep us abreast of what had gone on at that meeting. Cecil told us that Woody should be back in two more weeks, depending upon the outcome of a workers' compensation hearing scheduled for Friday. The biggest plus in Woody's return was that it would free up Cecil to handle more cases himself, thereby easing the pinch our unit felt when Barb Komosinski left us to take a job with probation four months ago. Still no word on her replacement as yet.

The rest of the stuff was garbage, a waste of time. I always found it counterproductive to spend hours debating which form should go where, or who was retiring next month and would be given a luncheon, or why we needed administrative approval to interview children in school when the school made the report, when there was so much else that required our attention.

By the time we broke up to return to normal duties, it was after eleven o'clock. Before anything else could deter me, I called the police to file a missing persons report on Jenny and was told the covering officer would get back to me. Two more messages had mysteriously appeared on my desk during the meeting, along with a cover sheet that showed that Sex Crimes had tried to fax me the copies of the Riordan statements just before the machine had broken down. Reese had also left a message indicating that although he still hoped to be able to arrest Mr. Riordan by tonight, there might be a problem with that. I wondered how the Riordan family had made out with their long weekend of charade-playing in the meantime.

I began filling out the survey questionnaire while I returned phone calls. By the time I was ready to see a few cases in the afternoon, I already felt like I'd put in a full day's work, a duality I'd felt many times before. As it turned out, I had a long afternoon still ahead of me, which would not include seeing cases.

I was finishing up my last returned phone call when I noticed someone standing patiently by my desk, waiting for me to be done. It was Bill Kahn, an elderly senior worker from an undercare unit. (CPS undercare units get the long-term, ongoing, or court-supervised cases when we're finished with them.) Like Cecil, Bill was covering a unit whose supervisor was away, fielding whatever problems the supervisor would normally handle, while writing all the court petitions for every case in the unit, coordinating workers' testimonies and court appearances, as well as trying to keep up with his own caseload.

Another call came through for me from a Detective McKenna, who was handling the missing persons report on

MacAvoy. He wanted some background information, which I gave; Bill scribbled a hasty, impatient note and huffed off. I glanced at it while McKenna was checking something: NEED YOU IN COURT, JUDGE O'CONNOR, 2:00, ON NUÑEZ. I rolled my eyes heavenward. Kahn had mentioned this to me last week, that I might be on call for court today, to testify to my involvement in the Nuñez case. They'd even subpoenaed me to insure my presence; it had simply slipped my mind. Normally, I'd immediately write such an important "hafta-be-at" in my appointment book, but something else must have diverted my attention away before I'd gotten the chance.

The case involved a nine-year-old boy who hadn't gone to school for three months, caught between parents who had fought constantly, physically, and in front of the child, had a long history of separation and reconciliation, and had bounced him around between "friends," grandparents, and the parents' home. Currently separated again, each parent was fighting the other for custody, and CPS was recommending custody be granted to his paternal grandparents, who'd provided the only stable environment he'd ever known.

Kahn's notification had been just one more item I'd had to try to keep in mind during a particularly hectic day in a hectic week, and as it turned out, I'd had no chance to prepare for delivering my testimony. So now I had to quickly scan my notes and try to memorize certain key events and the dates they'd occurred so I'd be ready for whatever questions they threw my way in court. I also had to try to borrow a tie someplace so I could look, as well as act, the part of the confident, well-prepared professional. (Normally, I would wear a suit for a court appearance.) It was 12:45, giving me just over an hour to accomplish this, switch my appointments around to accommodate, and try to grab a bite to eat somewhere along the way.

I hastily packed up my briefcase with the stuff I anticipated needing, including my appointment book and Nuñez notes, trying to get away before something else came up or the phone rang.

My instincts were correct, but luck ignored me. As I snapped the clasps closed on my briefcase and wrestled into my jacket, Lynne announced a phone call for me. It was Mrs. Riordan, and rather than play the tell-her-I'm-not-here game, I took the call.

"This is Mr. Richards."

"Oh I'm so glad I got a hold of you, Mr. Richards. I'm really sorry to bother you, but I was wondering if you'd heard anything from Sex Crimes. Jack called again last night, twice, and it's hard to have to hide what's going on from him. He wants to come over, he wants to see the kids, and he makes me feel like the nasty old witch who's keeping him from his children."

"But you're not the perpetrator in this case, Mrs. Riordan," I said, "and to be honest, I thought you kept your broomstick hidden pretty well."

She snorted dubiously. "Thank you, you're very kind. I just don't know what to do, what to say, to keep him away. I don't want to see him, and neither does Cindy, but Jody keeps pestering me about his father, so I'm getting it on both ends. I'm afraid I'm going to slip up and say something to tip him off. I don't know how much longer I can keep this up."

"Sex Crimes told me this morning that they expect to pick him up tonight, but in the meantime, the best thing I can tell you is to make like you're too busy to talk, like you're on your way to a doctor's appointment or something. Tell him you can't talk to him. Tell him you're going out."

"Then he'll want to know where, and he might come over here."

"You have that order of protection. If he gets troublesome, you can still call the police for violating that."

"Yes," she said, "but that'll tip him off that I've been to court, talked to outsiders about this situation, and he'll know something's up. I don't want to mess up the detective's case, but I hope they resolve this tonight."

"I know, ma'am, it's holding up my case, too." I checked my watch. 1:05. "Look, I hate to have to cut you short, but I have to get to court myself, or they'll hold me in contempt. If there are any problems, or if for some reason they don't arrest Jack tonight, I'll be back in the office tomorrow morning." I hated sounding this callous. She needed more than the typical cold shoulder the system gives to victims, and it suddenly became important that she know that somebody cared. "If you'd like, maybe you can call me tomorrow and let me know how things went? We can talk more then, okay?"

"Okay. Thank you for your time." She hung up.

I grabbed my jacket and suitcase and scooted out the door. I had about three-quarters of an hour to prepare for my role as an intelligent, caring professional who would remain unflappable on the stand.

CHAPTER FIFTEEN

The Pelham County Family Court Building is located across town from our offices in a separate complex from where both criminal and district court are housed. The probation department and child support both have offices in the building, as do the various county attorneys and juvenile legal advocates (JLAs). Yet, despite all these offices and a large main lobby, space is always a problem.

In order to gain entry to the building, you must pass through a metal detector, the same type set up in airports, jails, and police stations all over the world. After you've replaced your watch, keys, and loose change, you are greeted by a large precinct-type desk with a sign over it exhorting you to check in with the clerk, who keeps a copy of each court's calendar for that day. This bit of business accomplished, you are then almost always invited to "have a seat in the lobby."

Anyone who has ever been there will tell you, bring a book. Even when you're "on call," and going about other duties in your office, even when you get the call and are told your presence in court will be required at 2:00 P.M. sharp, even if you bring paperwork to catch up on while you're waiting, bring a book. You'll often wind up with enough time on your hands to polish off a couple chapters; sometimes the hard part is remembering what you're there to testify about in the first place.

The halls resemble a darkly-lit elementary school, and the few benches offered are the wooden kind you might encounter in a principal's or nurse's office. The doors lead to courtrooms, not classrooms, however, and the lessons taught and learned in them are triggered by lawbooks (and pocketbooks), not textbooks. They've sworn for years that the place is air-conditioned, but on a hot, busy day, it looks, feels, and smells like the inside of a cattle car.

There's almost no room for chairs, so people either stand around, pace nervously, or walk along slowly while consulting, adding to the general clog. To remedy this, court officers are stationed at desks throughout the halls, checking IDs and directing traffic, lending even more confusion to the whole melee. The trick is to get past them in the first place, a feat not as difficult as it sounds.

These hallowed halls are also one of the few places on earth other than Roxanne's office that smells like the inside of a chimney. Though there are No Smoking signs posted in the lobby/waiting room, and no one would dare defy such a rule in a room with so many uniformed police and court officers about, there aren't any signs in the crowded hallways. This is where interested parties in about-to-be-heard, recessed, or just-heard cases can grab a quick smoke while consulting in quick-cram preparation, figuring case strategies, or discussing the judges' orders and what impact they may have. On rainy days nobody goes outside, making things still more cramped.

My involvement with the Nuñez family had consisted of three contacts. I had secured attendance records from the school (which proved how many days Stephen had missed and had resulted in both parents being indicated for ed. neglect); I had interviewed the mother on one day when she and the boy were staying at a friend's house because the father and mother had had another of their violent, physical fights, which Stephen had admitted he'd witnessed; and I'd held an interview with Stephen at the Juaristi home, his paternal grandparents', during which he related a history of often being dumped without warning at their home when Mom and Dad wanted to party with friends and couldn't be bothered with his care.

One of the basic differences between the parents was the substance each chose to abuse; Dad was heavily into cocaine and, according to Mom, had started smoking crack; Mom would swear she never touched the stuff—she only hung out and swilled cans of beer with her leather-jacketed, motorcycle-gang cronies. Stephen told me that his mother sometimes worked part-time off the books at a motorcycle repair shop, and was so good at repairing engines that her friends had nick-named her "The Wrench."

The Juaristis had told me that Dad was the meeker-looking of the two, though he had thin, wiry strength; by the looks of the mother, he had to be strong, maniacal when pro-voked, and violent beyond belief to drive her out of the house. When I mentioned that I'd never met him, nor had anyone from the school, they told me I wasn't likely to, because all he cared about was his next high, and when it came to his son, he quite frankly couldn't give a damn.

The grandparents sometimes would receive a phone call from the boy and would go and pick him up to remove him from the parents' playground/battleground. Mom got in the habit of showing up on her in-laws' doorstep at three in the morning to demand his return, sometimes with the police, of-ten on the morning before she wanted him to accompany her on a Public Assistance recertification appointment, or other-wise needed him to further her image of a poor victimized woman with a hungry child to feed and clothe. After several years of this, and at my suggestion, the Juaristis decided they would file for custody since they were the boy's primary care-takers anyway.

On this particular day, Mom had really put on the dog for court: tight blue designer jeans; a brown crushed-leather fringed vest, which partially covered the Harley-Davidson in-signia silk-screened across the chest of her black t-shirt; and brown hand-tooled leather boots, which must have been fairly new because they looked like they'd actually seen polish with-in the last month or two. A silver razor-blade hung from a thin chain around her neck. She also wore matching dangle-earrings in the shape of a screwdriver from her left earlobe, and an open-end wrench from her right, affirming her nickname.

I was filled with anticipation that something would be ac-complished today; we'd had numerous adjournments because neither she nor Stephen's father had bothered to show up, and

Judge O'Connor had finally ordered a hearing be held today, with or without them. Bill Kahn had tried unsuccessfully in the past to petition the court for custody of Stephen, only to have the judge order the child to remain with his mother at a new address she had established apart from the father. Now, we were two-and-a-half years older and wiser, Mom had moved back with Dad (and out again, and back again, and out and back and now out), and the only schooling Stephen had received was through the efforts of the Juaristis. Bill, who'd been the ongoing worker after my involvement, was now petitioning for custody to be granted to them, with CPS's approval. It was also where the child had repeatedly stated he wanted to live.

I was sitting on the hardwood bench outside the courtroom. A small engraved plaque on the door read, "The Hon. Cyrus M. O'Connor" and under his name read, "Part VII." This referred to a particular judge's seat. The actual hearings might take place in different courtrooms depending on scheduling conflicts, but during a given term (family court judges are elected to their seats), a particular judge will stay with his Part. Another sign, white letters engraved into a red background, read, "Absolutely no persons may enter the courtroom without clearance from the court officer." Meaning this bench was as far as you got until your name was called.

I glanced at my watch, and gave the results to someone on the bench opposite me who'd noticed and asked. 2:37. With luck, I'd be done within an hour. It was also possible that I wouldn't get to testify today at all, which is another sad fact of life you just have to grin and bear. You could be forced to waste whole mornings, afternoons, or even several days, just waiting to give twenty minutes worth of testimony.

Not only was there no guarantee you'd be called, there was nothing to insure you'd be allowed to testify if you were called. One such custody hearing saw me sitting on a similar bench, under subpoena, for two-and-a-half hours; finally getting called and being sworn in; answering a total of three questions, and nothing more. The fourth question asked of me was objected to by the father's obnoxious attorney, the judge sustained, and almost every other word out of the mother's attorney's mouth was likewise objected to and sustained. The father's attorney did not even bother to sit down after each attempt to paraphrase the question; he just stood there with his back to the mother's attorney, finally explaining that he intended to object to every word out of the other man's mouth, and while the judge reminded him proper protocol was for him to sit down and then re-stand at each objection ("but this will save time in the long run, Your Honor"), the judge pointed out that he would sustain each succeeding objection because what I was testifying to was essentially outdated. I was dismissed, having waited the entire afternoon to tell them who I was and how long I'd worked for Child Protective Services.

They were interested in what I had to say on the Nuñez case, though. It had already dragged on for so long, even the judge seemed genuinely glad to be making progress at last. Rosalinda Nuñez sat there, heavy-lidded eyes boring right through me in an attempt to intimidate. I stared right back, with the same indifference I had frozen on my face the day she claimed that she would make it with just about anybody if the price were right, including me. I wondered if that offer would still hold after my testimony.

I testified to my involvement, my contacts, and the results of those contacts. I also stated the reasons why we had indicated the parents, and especially the mother, and why we felt the paternal grandparents were the most appropriate caretakers for the child. The mother's attorney tried the usual tactics to discredit me, which included attempts to confuse me as to what actions were taken on which dates and who said what to whom; implications that I was burned out and couldn't remember anything properly; implications that I had a vested interest in seeing the child placed with the Juaristis; and forcing me to acknowledge that there was a chance, however slight, that my case decisions could be wrong and thus it was at least possible that I was in error on this case. I followed all the rules of testimony I had set forth for myself over the years: always pause before answering, to give the impression that you're being thoughtful and to give your attorney a chance to object (it also helps keep the cross-examining attorney from working up a momentum that might cause you to blurt out an answer you don't mean to give); don't become flustered, and keep a professional demeanor no matter how much your competence or professionalism may be questioned; remember that you are the professional by virtue of whom you represent and the only way you can be discredited is if opposing counsel can get you to do it yourself; and finally, in the words of a popular commercial, "Never let 'em see you sweat."

I'd testified enough times to know when I had done well, and this was one of those times. The mother's attorney confirmed this for me when his last-ditch effort was to ask the question: "Do you have any children of your own, Mr. Richards?"

It's a question that most clients ask me at one time or another, and it's something of a catch-22. If I admit that I do, the parents expect that I'll be more sympathetic towards them since we're all part of the Brotherhood of Parenthood; if I state that I don't, then it implies that I'm not competent to do my job effectively since I can't possibly know what parents must go through in raising children if I haven't gone through it myself. In this case, I suspected that they were hoping I'd answer in the negative, so they could take a parting shot at tainting both my image and my testimony.

I answered with my standard reply. "I had parents. And I know what it's like to be a child raised with love, warmth, and fairness, to be encouraged to feel good about myself. I've also been doing this job long enough to see the pain, anxiety, and depression felt by children whose parents don't raise them that way." At this point I usually ask my clients whether they've talked to their children recently about what they're feeling, and by then, regardless of the answer, the interview's focus has shifted back to the clients' parenting, where it belongs.

This attorney was sharp, curt, and downright obnoxious, and came back at me by demanding a yes or no answer. I was going to give in and oblige him, but a glance at Mrs. Nuñez's expression made me realize that I didn't particularly want her knowing. So instead, I answered that being a parent was not a prerequisite for my job. He asked once more, and when I hedged, he said, "May I remind you that you're still under oath?"

I paused, glaring at the county attorney, who finally caught on, stood up, and objected. "Mr. Richards's parenting, or lack thereof, is not the matter under consideration here, Your Honor."

"Objection sustained."

"No further questions," said the mother's attorney, and I was dismissed.

"Court will recess for ten minutes," announced Judge O'Connor, and we returned to the cancerous corridors outside Part VII.

■   ■   ■

"You were great!" said Bill Kahn, lighting a cigarette as we stood talking with the county attorney, the juvenile legal advocate, and Mrs. Juaristi, the child's paternal grandmother. "I wish you could testify on the other nine cases I'm petitioning." On this particular case, Bill was trying to win a judge's approval for removal *before* protective custody was actually taken, but many was the night he'd be working the overtime trail to get an after-the-fact petition written in time to present the next day. He was one of the better court workers, who knew his stuff and did his job without arrogance or pomposity. He was looking tired, though, and I supposed he was another one of us who really could have used a vacation.

"Just so the judge rules in Stephen's favor," I said. "None of it means anything if he's forced to stay with either parent."

"I agree," said Mustafa Wadir, the juvenile legal advocate, "and if our office holds any sway at all with the judge, your grandson will be with you this very night," he told Mrs. Juaristi.

A court officer approached us, informing Kahn he had a phone call in the small office assigned for DSS workers' use. "Probably Mother, checking up on me again," he explained, referring to his supervisor, who mercilessly kept him under her thumb because he knew the job better than she did, and thus she needed to continually remind them both who the supervisor was (something akin to the Richards/D'Angelis relationship). Kahn managed to take it in stride, but he'd often said that it made the job about ten times tougher than it was already.

Across the hall, on an opposite bench, sat Mrs. Nuñez. Her attorney was speaking to her, but she wasn't really listening; she'd been glaring at Bill, and I could almost see little knives lining the air between her eyes and his chest, as in a comic strip. When Kahn passed her to take his phone call, she whispered something vehement to him. This was a typical hallway intimidation game people often played with success, though I knew Kahn had been around too long to fall victim to such maneuvers. Still, the right to face one's accuser seemed, at times, to be more like the right to try to scare your accuser into dropping the whole thing.

Though this has never been my favorite way to spend an afternoon, at least I'm being paid for it. What breaks your heart is to see the turmoil in the eyes of children who must face an abusing parent from the stand, caught between admonitions "never to tell" from someone to whom they still may feel loyalty and whom they have no desire to betray, and encouragements from the lawyers and judges who made them swear an oath in front of a whole roomful of people to tell the whole truth and nothing but the truth.

Another officer announced Judge O'Connor's court was reconvening, though Kahn was still on the phone. After a moment or two, the officer came back out, and seeing me still in the hallway, asked about Bill. Since I knew where he'd taken the call, I offered to find him and tell him that Judge O'Connor was reconvening.

"Bill?" I poked my head in the small, cramped DSS office. It was empty. "Bill?" I noticed the phone was off the hook, and thought it odd. Maybe he had someone holding, and was checking on something. Whoever was on the other end of the line would know, but I didn't see the receiver. I grabbed the phone cord from the base of the phone, and traced the cord to the receiver's end, and that was when I found Bill.

Lying on the floor behind the desk.

"Hey, man, are you okay? They're reconven—"

He was on his back, mouth agape in a silent scream, eyes glassy and unmoving, not seeing the spot on the ceiling at which they were staring. I bent over him, shook him gently, and felt for a pulse.

Found none.

I raced back into the hall, grabbed the first officer I saw, appointed him to call an ambulance. Then, yelling for help, I returned to Bill, and tried to begin what I remembered of an in-service CPR training course the county had bestowed upon select employees about three years before.

I repeated the CPR cycle several times, praying that I could revive him, cursing him when I couldn't. Trying to keep the rhythm steady, I was aware of the blood pounding in my own ears, but unaware that anyone else had entered the room, until they pulled me off him and took over the CPR routine.

"I just walked in and found him like that," I said, a phrase I would repeat many times over the course of the next few days.

Whatever Judge O'Connor had in mind for Stephen Nuñez, Bill would never know. He would not be working overtime tonight, nor would his easy smile grace the halls of family court again. The demands of the job would torment him no more; Bill Kahn had written his last petition.

Ironically, the judge did ultimately rule in favor of the Juaristis, granting them full legal custody of Stephen. Ms. Nuñez disappeared from the boy's life shortly thereafter. But what I remember most of that day in court was the look of triumph on Roz Nuñez's face as they carried Bill's stretcher past her in the hallway. Maybe she'd lost her son at long last, but she'd somehow managed to exact her pound of flesh from the man she blamed; not her snotty lawyer, or her dirtbag husband, or any of the motorcycle grease-monkeys she hung around and slept with, but the dedicated social worker who only wanted what was best for Stephen.

And they wonder why our staff turnover rate is so high.

CHAPTER SIXTEEN

Whenever civil service test results are published, new job assignments or promotions are announced, or some tragedy befalls a staff member, almost no work gets done that day or the next. People mostly gather in clusters to talk about what they knew, what they'd seen, what they'd heard, and Bill Kahn's name was on everyone's lips the next morning. Since I'd found him first, my account was much sought after, but once I'd gotten the first two or three retellings out of my system, I just wanted to roll up my sleeves and lose myself in the job. As with time and tide, life marches on, and no one ever takes a vacation from child abuse.

The coroner's report said Kahn died of a massive stroke induced by stress and compounded by his smoking. I would have loved to have overheard the last comment Roz Nuñez made to him, but I'm sure it was just one more stressor heaped upon a man who'd already suffered more than his fair share. I stopped into church on my way to work that morning and prayed for his soul. I also prayed for Stephen Nuñez's future, that Kahn's efforts on his last case would not have been in vain. I prayed for the safe return of Jenny MacAvoy, the adjustment and healing of Meg Riordan's new family of three, and the well-being of the Zifarellis and the Brownes. I prayed for all Child Protective Services workers everywhere, and asked that "God help us, every one," for if He did not look out for us, nobody else would.

Another poignant bit of news made the rounds that morning. My supervisor, Woody Taylor, who had been out the past month, had decided to try to extend his workers' comp. benefits, and would remain out indefinitely. Inside information had it that Woody was not in such bad shape, but was playing the system for all it was worth, and if he won his case, he would take his compensation and his pension and call it a career. Compared with the Kahn alternative of breaking your back until the job ultimately chewed you up and spat you out, sentiment was running high in favor of Woody's attempt to sweeten his retirement kitty.

The phone jangled, and I answered on the first ring, glad to immerse myself in something as mundane (when compared to death and mortality) as a routine phone call. It was Meg Riordan, and she sounded anxious, tentative.

She'd managed to avoid her husband's call last night by taking the kids to the movies, hoping he'd be in jail by the time they returned home. But he'd called again this morning while they were readying themselves for school, and he'd started pressuring them to see him, to ask their mother to let him visit. They hadn't known what to say, other than he'd have to talk to Mom about it and she couldn't talk right now. He'd ended the call by stating he would come over right after work this evening, and now she was scared. She could go to another movie, but that wasn't facing the problem; still, she doubted if any of them had the strength for a confrontation just yet. Besides, she said, despite being married to the man for almost ten years, the thought of touching him, let alone trusting him again, was totally repugnant to her. And what, she wanted to know, had Sex Crimes been doing last night?

She knew there probably wasn't much I could do, since we'd been waiting for Mr. Riordan's arrest to fit into Reese's shift schedule, but—well, she said she had to tell someone, and mine was the most sympathetic ear she'd spoken to these past few days. I told her I'd do what I could, knowing she was probably right about our ability to help.

I packed my briefcase, and was slipping into my jacket when the phone rang again. It was Detective McKenna, following up on Jenny MacAvoy, and he had some questions which, surprisingly, I was able to answer off the top of my head. I also ran the Riordan situation by him one time, and he said it sounded to him like a matter of convenience for Walt Reese. He didn't put it quite that way, but that was how I read it.

I called the number for Sex Crimes. We'd gotten the word yesterday that Mark Vlasic, a senior caseworker from another team, would be helping us out on our own court petitions, and he would need copies of the Riordan statements, which between our finicky fax machine and Detective Reese's busy schedule, we were still waiting for. Thus, I was justified in calling for those copies, and while I was at it, I was going to run the situation by Walt Reese's superior, since I was certain Reese would not be there.

I spoke to Detective Sergeant Nessa Wallace, who functioned as a sort of coordinator of assignments for Sex Crimes. I'd dealt with her once or twice before on the phone, and found her to be competent and knowledgeable without sacrificing compassion. Like all cops, she could be a little rough around the edges, but for a black woman to rise to a semi-supervisory position in any section of the police department took brains and guts, and Detective Wallace continually had to prove she could do the job. And she did.

Reese had earned a few days off, Wallace said, and had been slated to start the night shift last night. Thus, he was probably figuring to pick up Mr. Riordan tonight, she said. I ran the family situation past her, knowing I was risking seventeen kinds of flak from Reese should I ever have to work with him in the future, as well as scorn from Wallace, who was still a cop. Though cops may recognize snitches as a necessary evil, they don't think very highly of them. However, if there was derision in her voice, I couldn't detect it; all she told me was that she'd look into it.

I finally was able to escape the office to the field, although on some days it was like tunneling out of Treblinka and right into Auschwitz. Today wasn't too bad, though. I visited three cases that afternoon, and when I called in for messages at about quarter of four, Lynne told me I had only one—Detective Sergeant Wallace had called back to say that Mr. Riordan had been picked up at three o'clock from his job, and arraignment was scheduled for first thing tomorrow morning. This meant he'd spend at least tonight in jail, regardless of the amount of bail ultimately set and whether or not he could raise it. Lynne also told me that she'd put the faxed copies of the Riordan statements on my desk.

This, of course, was terrific news, and I resolved to call Wallace in the morning to thank her for her help. Since I was in the next town over, I decided to deliver this news to Mrs. Riordan personally, and explain to the children what it all meant.

She opened the door tentatively, looking very anxious until she recognized me. Then, she broke out in a relieved smile, and invited me in.

"I'm glad it's you," she said. "Jack told me this morning he was coming over later, and I thought you might be him."

"Well, the reason I'm here is to tell you those plans have been changed. Mr. Riordan is going to be the county's guest tonight, and I doubt he'll spend his one phone call bothering you."

It took a moment to sink in, then a Christmas morning smile of sheer delight crossed her face. "He's been arrested? The police picked him up?"

"About three this afternoon. His arraignment's tomorrow."

She clapped her hands, as though her prayers had been answered, and hugged me in gratitude before either of us realized it. "Thank you so much," she said, "this is great news. The children can sleep in peace tonight."

"Speaking of which, are they home from school yet? I can explain to them about what happens next, if you'd like."

"That would be terrific, thank you, but they're not here. I sent them to my mother's for the night, so they wouldn't be here if Jack showed up."

I shook my head in amazement and admiration. "Once again, you've managed to stay one step ahead. You're incredible."

"I'm not so incredible as you think. I feel like I'm falling apart."

"But you haven't. The worst is over now. You can go about getting on with your lives."

"But I feel so stupid," she said. "I had no inkling of what was going on. I mean, it had been some time since we'd slept together, but how could I know that meant he was—" she spat the word out as though it were full of maggots, "*molesting* his kids? And yet, somehow, I should have known what was going on."

"You know, Mrs. Riordan, it's one thing to read about it in the paper, or see it on television. It's another matter entirely when it happens in your own home, to your own family."

"But I should have seen *something*. How can a man be raping your daughter—right under your own roof, and you don't have any idea?"

"It's not your fault."

"In some ways I feel like a boat adrift in a monsoon. I mean, my kids come first, but . . . I've got no man, no income, and even though Jack's away for now—thanks to you—God only knows what he might try when he gets out. I feel like the world's biggest jerk. I don't even have him to lean on to get me through this. And who's going to show any interest in somebody who—"

She'd been worrying out loud, and suddenly became self-conscious about it. She stopped, a curious look seeping into her face. "I'm sorry," she said, "I'm heaping all this on you, and you've been nothing but kind and helpful. I . . . know this may sound corny, but I wish there was some way I could show my appreciation . . ."

"If we take good care of you, then you'll take good care of your children. The old Care for the Caretaker theory."

She'd been sidling closer as we spoke, and now was a mere foot away. "Take good care of me," she said, and suddenly was in my arms, burying her face in my chest. Her smell came to me, a pleasant, musky fragrance which bespoke no special preparation other than good hygiene. Her shoulders started heaving while she literally cried on my shoulder. When she pulled her head away to grab a tissue, my shirt had dark tear-stains above the breast pocket. Dabbing her eyes, she returned to my shoulder.

We stayed like that even after she'd stopped crying, and we both started breathing heavier as we realized it. After another moment, she reached up, tilted her face to meet mine, and without speaking, pulled my head down to kiss me.

She's still your client, a voice inside me protested, as I moved my lips away from hers. *This isn't consolation any more.*

"No. I'm sorry," I gasped, both fighting and wanting to give in to the urge. I gently pulled her hand away. "You're my client, and besides, I'm a married man."

"Please," she whispered, "don't make excuses, make love to me. I . . . need you to." Checking to be certain the front curtains were drawn, she then began to slowly unbutton her blouse.

"Do you think I have a nice body?" she asked. I thought I understood her reasons for doing this, and I *did* want to feed her self-confidence, renew her belief in her own sexuality and desirability. I knew it was what she needed to hear, but all I could offer her were words.

"Meg—Mrs. Riordan, I think you are an incredibly attractive, sexy woman, and I'm sure there's another loving, caring, virile man in your future," I said, taking her hands away from her blouse. "But it's not me. I can't. It would be the biggest mistake we could make."

"But I need you. If you won't make love to me, I don't know what I'm going to do." She collapsed on the couch and began to cry again.

"You'll go on with your life. You'll keep doing all the wonderful things for your children that have made you such a great mother. In time, you'll realize we did the right thing."

"What's wrong with me?" she kept sobbing. Again I felt like touching her, rubbing her shoulder to reassure her, but that could have been what gave her the wrong idea in the first place, and I restrained myself now.

"Nothing's wrong with you, Meg. It's the situation that's wrong, that's all. You don't really need sex with me, you need reassurance that you're still attractive, still desirable—and you are."

She dabbed her eyes with a tissue, sniffled, blew her nose, and made a visible effort to pull herself together. "I apologize, Mr. Richards," she said, buttoning her blouse up hurriedly,

"I've made a terrible fool of myself, and put you in an awkward position. I just hope you don't think this is how I spend all my free time."

"I know better." I gathered up my clipboard, took my keys from my pocket. "I guess it'd be best if I go now." She just nodded.

I let myself out, feeling like I was covered with slime, knowing what I'd just done was proper, but sorry I'd had to hurt her in the process.

CHAPTER SEVENTEEN

The next day saw me back in the field, out on another sex abuse case, albeit one of those "fairly easy" ones where everybody is cooperative; still, the case was full of irony and paradox, and the whole thing was one big emotional drain. The victim was twelve-year-old Susan Ashburn, who had been molested by her father. He'd fondled her around Christmas last year, but as she explained to me, Sex Crimes, and the school nurse, "it was only once, and I didn't want to ruin everybody's holidays, so I shut up about it. Then he stopped, and we just never mentioned it again."

Mom and Dad Ashburn had had their share of screaming arguments, and though their relationship did not improve, peace was somewhat restored when Mom began working the night shift and both parents were seldom home at the same time. One night last weekend, however, while Mom was working, Dad had gotten drunk again and had gone into his daughter's bedroom. Her two younger sisters were asleep in another room they shared. Dad thought that twelve-year-old Susan was asleep, lifted her nightgown, stared at her naked behind and privates for awhile while rubbing himself, and started to rub her legs, her thighs, and finally, her vagina. She pretended to be asleep, but rolled over, and the father stopped, leaving the room. This not being a holiday, the girl told her mother the next day, and another terrible verbal argument ensued, with all the girls crying and pleading when Dad threatened to leave them all.

On the plus side, it was "just" a fondling case. Without minimizing what he did, at least he didn't rape or sodomize the child, impregnate her, or beat her up; the family realized they needed help, and immediately sought counseling. But in one of the true paradoxes of the CPS reporting system, those the family turned to for help had to be the ones to turn them in. Mandated by law to make a report, the counseling agency had called the hotline with what vague information they had, so we could get involved and investigate.

In most cases, seeking help on their own is a most difficult step for a family to take. Most decent therapists tell the family what they, by law, are going to have to do; however, once the report is made, the clients often feel as though they can no longer trust that therapist, cannot continue in counseling, and can never trust anybody again. They feel their confidence has been betrayed. Many won't cooperate with us either, thereby cutting themselves off from the help, therapy, and support they were originally seeking.

Fortunately, this particular family was very understanding about all that. But the situation placed mother, father, and victim in their own singular niche between the proverbial rock and hard place. All were worried about the father being arrested, and the family name being splattered with sensationalistic mud all over the newspapers.

Susan had to deal with the guilt of disclosure, worry over upsetting her mother, feeling that she was the one breaking the family apart, and all the inner confusion and turmoil such a victim encounters. Mrs. Ashburn, a nursing aide who worked the night shift to earn a little extra money, felt guilt over not being there; anger and betrayal with her husband for violating such a trust regardless of whatever marital problems they had; concern over her daughter and the changes and havoc this situation would now wreak on their lives; and the same what's-wrong-with-me feelings Meg Riordan had had to deal with.

In yet another case paradox, I even found myself empathizing somewhat with Mr. Ashburn, despite his being the cause of it all. He'd made a bad mistake, and deserved whatever he had coming, but to see him sitting on his own couch, crying and sobbing like a nine-year-old caught stealing, was absolutely pitiful. Stewing in his own juices as he had to face both myself and the Sex Crimes detective was part of his punishment, but at least he admitted and felt remorse over what he'd done. (We get an awful lot of perpetrators who blame the child or the wife, or otherwise will deny with their dying breath that anything ever happened.) Maybe he deserved triple this much misery, but there was no pleasure for me in witnessing it.

Even the two youngest girls, too small to understand what was going on, knew that everybody was upset, Daddy had to leave the home, and they had to be dragged all over town to the offices of strangers. Everybody loses in a situation like this, and I felt sorry for all of them.

I returned to the office about two o'clock already pretty drained. Lynne gave me two messages that were waiting, however; the first was that a school nurse had called on the Ramirez case, and the other was that Roxanne had said for me to report to Brandon Ericsson's office at 2:15. Since that left me with a couple of minutes yet, I turned to my file cabinet to pull the Ramirez record so I could return the call, but found I had another problem.

The cabinet was locked.

"I-didn't-do-this," I sang out, an uneasy feeling sliding its way into the pit of my stomach. "What's-going-o-on ?"

"Oh, Roxanne took all your records off your desk, put them in the cabinet, and locked it," Lynne reported, her hand over the mouthpiece of a call she was taking, "then she gave me the message I just gave you. That's it." She returned to her phone conversation.

I didn't like it. I ducked into the men's room to freshen up and regain some measure of calm before my command appointment with my center director, but I had trouble combing my hair. The comb kept jumping around, I dropped it twice, and finally, I gave up.

A call into Brandon's office was not necessarily catastrophic. It was the locking up of my case records that unnerved me. They only did that when a worker was going to be away on vacation or extended sick leave or something. Only the director and the team supervisor had keys; Roxanne had already taken her own protective custody of Woody's copy—and, apparently, my case records as well. I wondered if she'd been humming as she'd locked the cabinet. The only thing I knew for certain was that it would be a while before that school nurse and I discussed the Ramirez case.

Bolstered by the splash of cold water on my face and a couple of deep breaths, I dried my hands, popped a mint into my mouth, and marched into Brandon's office.

As my feet sunk into the plush carpeting, I should have felt more comfortable, but in fact, it only added to my uneasiness.

"Have a seat."

Brandon sat at his desk in his swiveling brown-leather chair. A long hardwood conference table ran perpendicularly into the room from his desk, and both Roxanne and Cecil Perry, our senior worker, were already seated on one side. The only other empty chair was situated on the opposite side and I took it as instructed. Aware as I must be of how the physical set-up of tables and chairs in an office can reduce children's uneasiness when I interview them, I was keenly aware of how this set-up was adding to mine. I was already beginning to feel like some mutant paramecium being examined under a microscope.

Pulling the armchair under me, I noticed the droplets of moisture my hands had left on the armrests, and the fact that my nervousness was showing made me even more nervous. Smoke from Roxanne's latest lung-leveler caught in my already dry throat, and between coughs, I waved the smoke away and gasped at her to do something about it. She appealed to Brandon in a do-I-really-have-to look, and he closed his eyes and gave a subtle, let's-go-along-with-it nod. She snubbed the butt out as though she were trying to stab right through the ashtray.

"Keith, tell us of your involvement with the Hart case," Brandon said.

"Monica Hart? Name rings a bell. Where do they live?"

He recited a Brentwood address, and the case clicked. It may sound awful, but names don't usually help me recall a case situation; only addresses do. I must be able to see in my mind the setting where I dealt with the clients; that usually is what I remember to differentiate the hundreds, probably thousands of cases I've seen. "I think we just closed that case 'indicated' this past spring."

"Yes, we did."

I tried to remember. "As I recall, the stepfather was a teacher who was playing head games on the child. Scapegoating, falsely blaming, inappropriately punishing, that sort of thing. Six-year-old girl, maybe seven. Mother just let it pass. We didn't feel we had a strong enough case to go to court on emotional maltreatment, so we indicated the case—both parents, I think for Inadequate Guardianship—and closed it out "

"You have a good memory."

"Thanks." I smiled briefly, still not daring to relax.

"Tell us about your interview with the child, can you remember?"

"I spoke to her in her room."

"Alone?"

"Of course. Otherwise there's no point in speaking to her in her room."

"Did Mrs. Hart give you permission?"

"Most likely. I mean, I always ask, and if the parent has objections, I don't press it. I can always speak to the child in school, if it's really important."

"But did she specifically state that it was all right with her?"

"I don't specifically recall, but she must have. Why?"

"Did anything happen while you were talking to this child?"

I shrugged my shoulders. "No, not that I remember. Just your average child interview. 'How do Mommy and Daddy punish you when you're bad? What do they say? Do they ever use a belt or something in their hand? Do they ever call you names, or use bad words?' that sort of thing. She gave her answers, I wrote 'em down, I thanked her and left. No big deal. So why the third degree? What's going on?"

For the first time, I sensed their uneasiness: Cecil used his pen as a bell-clapper between thumb and pinky, Roxanne fiddled with her cigarette case, Brandon scratched his temple and looked to a far corner of the ceiling. I felt the need to break what was becoming an awkward, unwarranted silence. "I mean, I conduct a lot of investigations this way. What's so special about this one?"

Brandon drew a ponderous sigh and asked, "Did you at any time physically touch this child?"

"I don't know, I might have . . ." His implication finally hit me, due as much to their reactions as to the questions themselves, and I leaned forward on my chair, muscles tensing, beads of moisture popping out on my forehead. "*Why?*"

"In what manner did you touch the child?"

Suddenly I realized why I'd felt ganged-up upon, all alone, three against one. "Wait a minute!" I said, making a time-out sign with my hands. "I don't like where this is heading. I'm not answering any more questions until I'm told what this is all about."

"It would be in your best interests to cooperate, Keith," said Roxanne, in one of the most hard-nosed, unfeeling, off-putting tones I have ever heard uttered by someone purporting to be a social worker.

"Cooperate? With what? Is this some kind of formal investigation? Has some kind of report been made against me?" I leaned forward even more, gazed directly into Brandon's eyes, and spoke as though there were no one else in the room. "For God's sake, at least have the guts to tell me straight up what's going on! We give even our clients that much!"

Brandon placed his hands on the table in front of him; for a moment I thought he was going to start twiddling his thumbs. He looked directly at his hands as he said, "We have received a report that Mrs. Hart's daughter was sexually abused by her caseworker, naming you as the alleged perpetrator."

"*What?* Is this somebody's idea of a joke?"

"No joke."

"But I never even touched her!"

Roxanne jumped in, obviously enjoying this. "You just finished saying that you might have, you weren't sure."

"Physically touched her, maybe. An encouraging pat on the back, a . . . a smoothing down of her hair, maybe a reassuring squeeze on her arm—but sexually, never!!"

I glanced at each person in the room. "You folks don't really believe there could be any truth—"

They didn't know for sure, but their expressions weren't encouraging.

"I'm sorry to have to hit you with this, Keith," said Brandon. "This meeting is preliminary only. The family is still deciding whether or not to press formal charges. I have every confidence this will all work out."

"Yeah, but in whose best interests? The child's? My own? I mean, my professional integrity is being challenged here, my reputation is at stake!"

"You finally appreciate the gravity of your situation," Roxanne put in. Maybe her face was impartial, but there was gloating in her voice. Brandon glared her into silence but let the remark pass.

"Keith, can you be more specific about the manner in which the child was touched?"

"I thought I already expl—" I stopped myself, set my jaw firmly. Somehow, the fact that this meeting had been labeled a "preliminary hearing" didn't ease my suspicions. "I don't think I want to say anything more unless I have a lawyer present."

"As you wish." Brandon sighed in a tired, bothered way. He seemed to want to believe me, but just wasn't quite sure enough. "I could suspend you for a week or two pending completion of our investigation, but we need our experienced staff in the field. Besides, we've received a subpoena for you to testify on another case in two days."

He sighed again, as though he was sticking his neck out and handing me an axe. "I'm going to allow you to continue at your duties, but especially now that you're aware of what's happening, I remind you to watch your step. If formal charges are pressed, I'll have no choice but to effect your suspension pending investigation."

I ignored Cecil, who was smart enough to know he was merely here as a formality, and thus said nothing, and stood over Roxanne, gaining little satisfaction from the disappointment I saw in her face. "How long will it take you to spread this around the office?"

"Everybody already knows."

"You mean now that you've told *me*, everybody knows." I turned back to the director. "I appreciate your vote of confidence, Brandon, but I wish you had spoken to me first. Alone. I feel like *my* confidentiality has been violated." I shook my head. "Even the clients get better treatment than this."

"That's enough," he said, reaffirming his authority. "You still have a job to do, I suggest you get back to it. Roxanne, you see to it he gets his copy of the subpoena this afternoon."

"Would you be kind enough to unlock my file cabinet again, please?" I added, as sugary-sweet as I could. Roxanne held the key out to me, almost too fast. "Just make sure I get these keys back," she snapped, trying to save some face. She'd acted prematurely, and she knew it.

"Answer me one question," I said. I looked each of them in the eye, and each avoided my gaze. "If it comes down to this child's word against mine, who are you going to believe?"

No one answered. No one could expect them to.

Staff integrity is often questioned around here, and seldom is it blindly assumed. Until these people had learned all the facts, silence was the only answer they were going to give.

■ ■ ■

That afternoon, back at my desk, I had a hard time keeping my mind off my "preliminary hearing." I'd heard about workers having charges made against them by clients in the past, usually as retaliation or as an attempt to manipulate the system.

However, I had no idea why Monica Hart should have an axe to grind with me. Perhaps the girl actually *had* been abused by someone, and the mother decided to blame me, rather than confront the real perp; perhaps there was no conclusive evidence, so the family decided to take a shot at blaming the caseworker. Perhaps the child was making the whole thing up.

I already had enough stresses in my life right now, and I resolved to try not to worry about this one now. I knew I was innocent; if the department had anything specific, any evidence that might hold water, I would not have been asked to sit in on a "preliminary hearing"; they would have already "thrown the book at me." I most certainly would not have been allowed to continue my normal duties. If they felt they had enough evidence to proceed with formal charges, they would do so, and there would be plenty of time for panic then.

Still, the lack of support by the administration concerned me greatly. My innocence or guilt was not the real issue here; the real issue was which course of action would hurt the agency's image least. Would Pelham County's interests best be served by appearing to quickly get rid of one bad apple, or by ignoring such idle accusations? I could feel myself getting angry, but I knew that such feelings were premature and useless at this point, so I decided to forget about the charges for the time being and concentrate on getting some paperwork done.

As there were no new cases in my bin for a change, I gathered up six cases I really needed to update or transfer and found a small interview room that was unoccupied. We only had three interview rooms in the building, and there was a sign-up sheet outside each one; nobody had scheduled anything for this room for this time slot. So, I wrote my name, entered, closed the door, and spent three hours, away from phones and clients, catching up on the cases.

About a quarter to five, there was a knock on the door, and Rick Beconsall poked his head in.

"I saw the light on in here," he explained, "and I didn't know if anyone was still around. How's it going?"

"Good. I'm just wading through some backlog here."

"What a dedicated guy! Listen, we're starting a special CPWA night meeting in about fifteen minutes in the conference room. Want to join us?

"Well, maybe for a little while."

■   ■   ■

Gloria is very understanding about my occasional need to exorcise the job demons from my system with people from work. After phoning home, I was introduced to the group, which included first-timer Glenn Goddard, a young bachelor from Rick's investigative team who had only been hired two months ago. He made the usual observation about my name, and I earned a few giggles and derisive comments when I replied that the rock star was the exceptionally wealthy Keith Richards whereas I was the exceptionally good-looking one.

I learned about some personnel changes that would impact us in about two weeks. There were comments about Bill Kahn's death and the manner in which Woody was able to milk his compensation claim for all it was worth to try and avoid the same fate. "So, Glenn," asked Deanna Randall, a caseworker aide, "have you been up to Ithaca for your training yet?"

"Next month is what they're telling me," he answered, rolling his eyes to the heavens. "Is it any good?"

"I think it's generally helpful," said a woman I didn't know, "especially if you get up there with a good group. They never sent me until I was here almost a year, and by that time, I'd learned a lot of stuff by myself, the hard way. Nobody should be on the job more than about a month before they're trained. It can save a lot of grief in the field."

"It'll also help you get over that feeling of not knowing what you're doing, though it'll take about a year to really learn the job," said Rick.

"Is the training actually given on the Cornell campus?" Glenn asked.

"No," answered Marsha McKay, whom I was surprised to see. "They usually hold it in the meeting rooms of some hotel, though the instructors are all affiliated with Cornell's College of Human Ecology/Family Life Development Center, or something like that. The legal stuff helped me not be so afraid of doing something they'd crucify me for in court. That's one of the biggest pressures we face in this damned job."

"What's that?"

"That no matter what you do, you feel your head's going to roll for it. Everybody's looking to you to make the decisions, to take the responsibility no one wants. If a child needs to be taken from his parents, you're the storm-trooping fascist who makes that decision, initiates the action, and who has to convince a judge you made the right choice; yet if you allow an abused child to remain in the home and he or she is further abused—"

"Or, God forbid, killed," put in the woman I didn't know.

"—or, God forbid, killed," Marsha continued, "everybody still looks to you for answers. 'What happened?' 'Why wasn't the child removed?' Either way, you're in the hot seat."

"I get tired of always having to defend my actions, especially to people who don't have the slightest idea of what we do or how we have to do it," said a senior worker named Shaniqua Mosely.

"I get tired of all the upper-level administrative bullshit from people who make the decisions that affect us but never set foot in the field," said Buddy Hollister. "If they really want to know what's going on, they should ask us, not the little toadies hired to yes the commish to death."

"I'm tired of the paperwork," added Mark Vlasic.

"But don't get us wrong, Glenn," said Rick, grinning, "it's a great job!"

"My question was," said Glenn, "if this is such a great job, then how come all I ever hear is everybody bitching about it?"

"Because we all gotta blow ballast sometimes," Buddy said, "and nobody can know how tough a job it is unless they do it. You can bitch to your wife or girlfriend, to school people, to the police, even to your congressman, but only those of us who do it can understand."

"That's why these little bull sessions are so important," said Rick. "Otherwise you wind up like Bill Kahn."

"Not to scare you off or anything, Glenn," said Marge Sternberg, "but odds are you won't be doing this job longer than two or three years. The turnover rate is incredible, and if you stay too long, you get burned out, like all of us here."

"Speak for yourself, Margie," said Shaniqua.

"Seriously, though," said Rick, "it is one bitch of a job, and you have to look to the other CPS workers for support. Nobody else wants to hear it."

Other issues were discussed, including how we might implement a mandated caseload size, how we might upgrade all the casework positions in CPS to senior worker positions, and how we might approach the union to put pressure on administration to rectify some of the plumbing and heating problems we'd been suffering in the building.

We adjourned at six o'clock. Although I'd let the opportunity pass to gripe about my administrative roasting, I'd agreed with Rick's statement about worker support the moment he'd said it. Someone asked me if I would prefer another meeting at night, and I told them night meetings were just fine—provided I wasn't forced to work overtime.

■   ■   ■

As I was leaving the building, Cathy walked up beside me and took my arm. "I wonder if we could talk privately."

"Sure," I replied, "but how come you're still here? Earning brownie points with your boss?"

"No, actually, I . . . something happened to me today and I need someone I can confide in. Maybe we could grab a cup of coffee?"

Realizing I hadn't spoken with Cathy since she'd warned me about Roxanne and the Hart case, I readily agreed.

We settled into a booth at the local diner and ordered.

"I was questioned about the Hart case today, though it felt more like an interrogation," I opened, adding, "Thanks for the warning. And how are things with you?"

"Same shit, different day," she answered. "Did they formally charge you?"

"No. With the hiring freeze imposed by the county legislature, I suppose they have to make use of every warm body they possibly can. Still, between Bill Kahn's death, my Browne fatality, and Joe Picante's bathwater baby-dropper, administration's pretty jittery about everything."

There was silence for a moment, but then she blurted, "Have you ever had a client come on to you?" and the water I'd been sipping dribbled down my chin.

"I suppose it's happened to all of us at one time or another," I answered, as noncommittally as I could. "Why do you ask?"

"I . . . I found myself in a bit of a situation this afternoon."

I said nothing. My first thought was that she'd somehow found out about Meg Riordan, and if she knew about it, other people did, too. But assuming my secret had gone no farther than Meg's living room, I most definitely wanted to hear what Cathy wanted to share.

"I was interviewing this newly-licensed foster mother, you know, just to meet her, find out her preferences, and see about a possible placement. Nice, clean home, somewhat affluent. Her husband was at work, but while I was there, her son Bart walks in. Bart Fontaine. Twenty-four, single, a manager at a fast-food restaurant enjoying his day off. He just finished jogging, and he's wearing sweatpants, sneakers, and nothing from the waist up. The guy was utterly gorgeous. When he saw me, he immediately put on a t-shirt, and it was cute the way he seemed embarrassed, but Keith, I'm telling you, when I saw him, I just . . . I don't know, I lost track. He seemed like a real nice guy, but I felt like . . . like an insecure teenager again, you know?"

"Well, we started talking over tea with his mother, and the next thing I know, he'd showered, dressed, and was taking me out to lunch. We had a real nice time. He's witty and charming, and I couldn't believe nobody had reeled him in yet."

"A lot like what people say about you," I observed.

She slapped my arm. "Let me finish. I've got maybe fifteen minutes left before I have to be back at the office, so he drives up to the Overlook, by Bald Hill? We started necking, like a couple of teenagers, and things got pretty hot and heavy—he's a good kisser, too. I haven't felt this way about anybody since Rob, and I just kind of allowed myself to be swept away."

Rob had been Cathy's deepest relationship since her divorce, and they had actually been engaged, before she caught him stepping out with somebody else. Cathy had effectively ended their wedding plans by pouring a pina colada over Rob and his "friend" while they were smooching it up at a local dance club. ("Like pouring cold water on mating dogs," Cathy later explained.)

She continued. "It was like I was in some sort of trance, and all of a sudden I woke up to find myself smooching with this Adonis-like client in the front seat of his car, and he's got me half undressed! I mean, he's not actually my client, but his mother is certified as a provider for the agency, yet at that moment, I just didn't care. I'm sitting there letting him do these things I don't let anyone do, at least not right away—" she grinned, averted her eyes, and began to blush. It was like I was out of control. I mean, you know me pretty well, Keith, and that's just not me."

I nodded. "So how'd it end up?"

"Well, as I put myself back together, I explained to him that I liked him very much, and I talked about my job, and our professional relationship, and all that jazz, and he took it really well. He didn't get mad, or all hurt, or anything. He drove me back to my car, but just before I got out, he asked me out for Friday night! And after the whole routine I'd just finished running by him, about responsibility, and the wrongness of it, and how unlike me this really was, I said yes! The rest of the day, I've felt torn between liking this guy, wanting to give him a chance, and fear of losing my job. I don't know what to do."

"Are you asking me for my opinion?"

She looked at me for a moment, waited for the waitress to serve us. Then she reached across the table and gave my hand a squeeze. "If I can't trust my best friend, who can I trust?" She smiled that warm Cathy smile, sunshine at eleven o'clock at night. "What do you think?"

I sighed, resigning myself to return her trust. I needed to tell my tale, too, and for all the secrets I don't hesitate to share with Gloria, this was one I felt it might be better not to mention. "I think I may not be the best person to advise you. We're sort of in the same boat."

"You're going out with Bart, too?"

Now it was my turn to slap her arm. "No, but I started getting involved with somebody, myself. The only problem is, I'm already married, and she *is* my client. Though we didn't get quite as far as you and Bart, for a while it seemed like we were going to, so I know what you mean about being in some kind of trance, and also about being scared, Cathy.

"It wasn't fear of job repercussions that ultimately made me put on the brakes, though. It was Gloria. I just realized that she's put up with so much of the shit that splatters onto her from this job, she didn't deserve an unfaithful husband on top of it."

"Is there a full moon, or something?" she asked. "This is incredible. So what did you tell her?"

"Oh, you know, all the stuff about job responsibilities, and guilt, and it being wrong, the same stuff you told this Bart, I'm sure. I tried my best to let her know how tempted I was, but just couldn't, you know, so she didn't feel there was anything wrong with her, but it all sounded so hollow, like just a bunch of empty words. I didn't want to hurt her, although I probably did anyway. You see, her daughter had been sexually abused by her husband, and I'm sure that part of why she was coming on to me was her need to reaffirm her own sexuality. Rejection was the last thing she needed."

"But you did end it?"

"Yeah, though it was more like not letting it get started. I suppose once you start kissing, you've already crossed that line of demarcation, like the first crack in the dam. The wall of self-control crumbles pretty quickly after that, and it gets awfully tough to hold the waters back."

She was thoughtful. "Good analogy! It's just that Bart seems so nice! And it has been such a long time for me."

I nodded sympathetically. "You're just going to have to decide whether or not it's worth the risks you'll be taking. I mean, your secret's safe with me, kid, but for openers, I can't believe you're going to be able to go out with him, or carry on a relationship, without his mother knowing. And it's all downhill from there."

"I know," she agreed, "but I don't want to hurt him, either."

"You may have to."

CHAPTER EIGHTEEN

I was spending the morning in the field, catching up on cases that needed seeing. The first involved an inadequate guardianship on a drug-abusing mother who had left two children with Grandma (who began to panic when mother didn't return, and wanted help gaining custody of her "grandkids"), and the second involved a nine-year-old boy with a horrendous school attendance record (ed. neglect). Both visits were negative, meaning Grandma was probably either at the Department of Social Services offices applying for benefits or at the store, and wherever the nine-year-old was, he wasn't in school, or home sick, either.

I was making my third negative visit of the morning, standing inside the front porch writing out my third note requesting contact, when I heard a car engine starting up. I left the note on the door, then began to walk around the back of the house toward the noise. The neighborhood was cramped, the houses built practically on top of one another, so I wasn't sure at first if the driveway I was entering belonged to my client or the person next door.

The engine revved, and I saw the flash of chrome and metal rolling toward me. Being in the driveway, the car wasn't moving that fast, so I was able to push off the fender and roll away from the car, which kept right on going. I noticed the color was brown with red primer paint; I noticed that the tan vinyl roof was dirty, torn, and peeled; I even got a glimpse of the person driving, though it was impossible to determine whether the driver was male or female. I didn't get a look at the license plate.

I was annoyed with myself. Eight years as an investigator with Child Protective Services, yet I hadn't noted the plate number, something that was almost automatic with me since the Pressman case.

■   ■   ■

Pressman had been my first removal, the first time I'd had to take protective custody of a child. I'd been summoned to a day care center to observe bruises on the backside of four-year-old Stephanie, who had complained in the past about being paddled by her mother's boyfriend and was afraid to go home. (We suspected Mom and Carlos, the boyfriend, were running drugs, based on the fact that the children were left with different families to babysit for weeks at a time, and just about once per month, while Mom and Carlos went to Florida. When the parents returned, the children would be paying for their lunches with crisp $20 bills.)

I'd taken the 35-mm camera to get the best color shots possible. The child's buttocks were dark purple and puffy, and she had refused to sit down, which is what alerted the center staff to check her out in the first place. She was limping, and more bruising was noted down the back of her legs; an angry red semi-circular bruise marked the spot where the paddle's edge had bit into her buttock; but what concerned me most were bruises and scrapes extending about a third of the way up her spine that looked like the paddle had struck her directly on the vertebrae. I'd wanted X-rays, and we hadn't been able to reach the mother at work. The child's father lived out of state and hadn't contacted the family in years.

A series of phone contacts, to my office and then to family court, resulted in verbal permission to take protective custody in order to get Stephanie to a hospital. This I did, although she had to lie on her stomach across the back seat of my car because she was literally too sore to sit or to be seat belted properly. I'd left word at the day care center as to which hospital we'd be at, in case the mother showed up.

What happened next took only a minute or so, yet in replaying it over in my mind, it seemed like I'd had hours to do all the things I should have, but didn't.

Ms. Pressman, of course, showed up at the day care center right after we'd left. She followed us to the hospital emergency room. Stephanie was putting her coat on a chair near the door while I was at the receptionist's window making arrangements. The mother flew in like a hurricane, cursed me out, grabbed the child by one arm, and flung her over her shoulder like a bag of dog food. Then she spun around and stormed out.

I followed her into the parking lot, informing her that the judge had granted us custody and that she was about to commit custodial interference. In effect, she was kidnapping her own daughter. The mother opened the driver's door of her brand new, two-toned Cadillac, her gold jewelry flashing in the pale November sunshine, her fur coat flapping in the icy breeze. She literally threw the coatless child across the front seat. When I begged her not to do this, she said she didn't give a shit about CPS, or judges, or anything, and she was "taking my fucking kid back." She then suggested an anatomical impossibility, flashed her middle finger in the air at me, jumped in the car, and sped off.

I'd noticed that she hadn't bothered to grab the child's coat; I'd noticed that she hadn't buckled the girl into a seat belt; I'd noticed all the material luxuries we were supposed to believe Ms. Pressman earned on a factory assembler's salary; I hadn't noticed the license plate number, which the police would have found most helpful. Ms. Pressman and Carlos were never seen again, and I like to think that they got what they deserved in some drug deal gone sour. Still, like a pair of boots left behind after an oncoming train has just horribly jacked their occupant right out of them, the image of Stephanie's coat lying across the chair where she'd just put it haunted me all through that winter.

She was discovered on that same hospital doorstep three months later, crying but alive, thank God. Unfortunately, she was suffering from a concussion, pneumonia, multiple bruises all over her body, and two broken fingers, all of which I felt responsible for. If we could have found her sooner, perhaps we could have saved her those additional injuries. I swore never

again to forget to note a license plate number, and never had—
until today.

■ ■ ■

As I got back in my car, I couldn't be sure the driver had inten-
tionally been trying to run me down; I just figured he or she either didn't know I was there (in this neighborhood, being
drunk at eleven in the morning and then taking the car out for
a spin was no particular rarity) or didn't care. It was also possible that with my clipboard, my straight-laced, clean-cut image,
and my official bearing, the person thought he or she knew
who I was and just wanted to get away (people often tell me, after I've identified myself, that "we thought you was police, or
probation, or sumthin'").

With the three negative contacts, I had a little extra time
on my hands, and while I was trying to decide what to do with
it, I noticed that my car seemed to be driving me over to the
neighborhood in which the MacAvoys lived.

What was I doing here? I asked myself as I walked up the
rutted dirt driveway. What was I going to say to them, especially after my last phone conversation with Mr. MacAvoy? I decided to confront them with the fact that Jenny didn't appear to
be at either place her parents had indicated she'd be, and to
make sure they understood that if Jenny could not be located
within forty-eight hours, they'd be expected to file a missing
persons report on her; and if they didn't, I would. I suppose it
sounded weak and contrived, but it was the best excuse I could
come up with on short notice.

As on the last occasion, Mrs. MacAvoy was in the yard,
and when I pulled up to the curb and got out of the car, she saw
me, fear creeping into her face. She turned and started walking
toward the house. At that moment, a man I took to be Mr.
MacAvoy came outside and demanded, "What's the problem
here?"

"This is CPS again," she said, sublimating some of her fear
into anger. "I'm calling Lenny. He told us there'd be no more
harassment."

Mr. MacAvoy, a tall, wiry, unshaven man with crewcut
short brown hair, blocked her path. The tattoos on his arms

and his general scruffy appearance pretty much fit the picture of what I'd expected Amanda's husband would look like. "Lemme handle this," he told her, and turned to me, his face getting ugly. "What the fuck do you want? I already told you we're done with this bullshit, so I want you outta here. Now!"

I tried to tell him he was named in a report and had the right to speak to me about the allegations, but this didn't achieve its usual calming effect. "The only right I want is the right to kick your ass offa my goddamn property! You got any more questions, I'll see ya in court. Right now, you take a fuckin' hike!"

"Mr. MacAvoy," I said in an imploring tone, "it doesn't look like Jenny is anywhere upstate or in North Carolina. If she's disappeared, we can help you find her, but you'll have to file a missing persons report with the police."

"Were you born deaf? Or just plain retarded?" he said, moving toward me angrily, not a trace of question in his voice. *"Get off my property!"*

"Jud, don't do nothin' stupid!" his wife implored.

Though I'm already taking out my keys, zipping up my jacket, or slowly backing away as I do it, I usually try to reason with the people after the first order to leave, and often they've merely overreacted, or misunderstood, and can be reasoned with; once the demand is repeated, though, I do leave. At that point, you no longer have a right to be there without a warrant, unless a child is in imminent danger at that moment, and at that moment, there was no child to be seen, and no reason to suspect there were any children on the premises who were in imminent danger.

As I was getting into my car, Mrs. MacAvoy asked him what would happen if I came back while he was away, and he'd told her not to worry about it, I wouldn't come back.

"Well, that went over really well," I told myself in the rearview mirror as I turned the corner. Still, I couldn't shake the feeling that if I could get Mrs. MacAvoy alone, she would respond to reason.

I was reminded of a summer in my childhood, when we'd visited a great-aunt in Virginia. She lived at the edge of the Great Dismal Swamp, on what was left of an old, ramshackle farm, which hadn't been worked properly since her husband had died years before. Television reception was usually pretty terrible, so on most nights we'd talk, read, or play cards. Sometimes we'd do jigsaw puzzles.

I remember one such puzzle, which contained about a zillion pieces, and was really two puzzles in one. On one side was a late spring landscape of a shimmering lake with an old-fashioned covered bridge spanning it; on the other, the pieces would fit together to form the majestic beauty of a redwood forest in autumn. Part of the puzzle was to figure out which side of each piece belonged to which scene, the bridge or the forest, and after each match was made, we applauded and congratulated ourselves on at least being one step closer to finishing what Aunt Sarah called, "that infernal conundrum." It had taken us the whole summer to put it together, and we ceremoniously tapped the last piece into place on the night before we were to return home. Aunt Sarah told us she was going to have the puzzle mounted and laminated, and send it to us, but she died that winter and I never saw it again.

This whole MacAvoy case was beginning to feel like that puzzle; each new question was another piece. Where was Jenny, really? Was she bouncing from relative to relative? Was she still with the MacAvoys, hidden away to keep her from being seen by any more nosy CPS workers? Why had she never been in the Public Assistance grant? Most people would have tried to continue collecting money for her long after she was gone! Why had she gone to live with Jud and Amanda in the first place? Which piece went where? The bridge or the forest?

If I was ever going to solve this puzzle, I needed more pieces, and I was convinced Amanda MacAvoy still held a few. Unfortunately, today's little excursion had pretty well ended any chance of getting any more information from her, and at the moment, I was out of ideas. I still had ninety days to complete a report, so I'd keep the case open to see if perhaps Jenny reappeared somehow. A slim chance, certainly, but nothing would be lost by doing so.

In the meantime, I still had other clients to see.

CHAPTER NINETEEN

O ne of the reasons given by people who decline to work in Child Protective Services is the fact that your schedule is subject to constant change, on short notice. It doesn't happen every day, but it happens periodically, and when it does, you must drop everything and attend to the presenting crisis. The remainder of this day turned into just such an afternoon.

I returned to the office around twelve-thirty, planning to use the bathroom, check for messages, and grab my notes on two or three other cases I would follow up on after lunch.

I never got the chance. I never even got lunch. The minute I walked through the door, and O.J. said, "Here he is, the man of the hour," I knew something was up. Cecil briefed me as I took my jacket off and made a trip to the men's room.

"This one looks nasty, Keith, but it might be resolved by a phone call. I had assigned you a case called in this morning about a three-year-old girl who was riding with her parents when they were involved in a head-on collision. No seat belt, no car seat, nothing. Girl went right through the windshield. She and her mother were admitted to Bay Haven Hospital, father was released with a few bumps and bruises. That part's indicatable right there.

"But the child's condition has worsened, and she had to be taken by helicopter to Rocky Glen Hospital for emergency surgery. They need to relieve pressure in the child's skull, but she's also lost a lot of blood. They want to give her a transfusion to stabilize her for surgery, but her father, who's at Rocky Glen now, won't give consent. The doctors feel that even with the transfusion, if they don't alleviate the pressure on her brain, she could die. When you walked in, I was just going to call Bay Haven, to see if perhaps the mother will give the OK. Hopefully, this can be resolved by a phone call. I hope so, because this girl doesn't have a lot of time."

"So the mother's still at Bay Haven Hospital? Was she admitted?"

"She was still in emergency when I called back the reporting party. A social worker from Bay Haven," he added, before I could get the question out. "Life-and-death situation, Keith." I finished drying my hands, and we returned to the unit.

"Did the father give a reason for his refusal? Are the parents Jehovah's Witnesses or something?"

"He didn't say exactly. Don't forget, I'm getting this info from the hospital staff."

"Okay. Let's see if maybe the mother will give consent right now. I don't know if she'll go against the father, but it's worth a shot. In the meantime, Cecil, can you call the doctor who's recommending the surgery? We should have something in writing for the record no matter what, and if we do have to go to court, the judge will demand it."

"Speaking of which"—Cecil turned to Marsha McKay—"would you see if Mark Vlasic's available, in case we need petitions drawn up?" he asked, and she scurried out of the room as we both started dialing phones.

As it turned out, getting through to the mother in the emergency room was the easiest part.

"Mrs. Calvin? Mr. Richards, CPS. Look, I know you must be in pain right now, but I have to tell you that your daughter, Dianne, is in pretty bad shape, too. She's going to need a blood transfusion in order to stabilize her for surgery, and then she'll need a procedure done by a neurosurgeon to relieve pressure on her brain. If she doesn't have these things as soon as possible, there's a good chance we'll lose her."

"My husband is at the hospital with her right now, Mr. Richards. What does he say?"

"He would not give his consent. We were hoping you would. Dianne doesn't have a whole lot of time left before there'll be nothing anyone can do to save her."

"I'm sorry, sir, this whole thing is jus' a terrible tragedy, but it's the Lord's way, and His will be done."

"His will is not to let people die when doctors have the knowledge and the means to save them."

"His will is somethin' that mortal men should not be tamperin' with."

It was time to switch approaches. "Mrs. Calvin, I'm obligated under state law to do what's necessary to save your child's life. If you and your husband refuse to give your consent, we will go to family court immediately and seek an order granting the transfusion and surgery be done. But by the time we go through all that, it may be too late, and I'm asking you to give your permission so we don't lose precious time."

"I'm sorry, sir, but you're askin' me to do something I cannot."

"Would you consent to voluntarily granting the Department of Social Services temporary custody of Dianne so that we might authorize the treatment?"

"No, sir, I would not. She's still my daughter."

My awareness of my increasing frustration level was almost as acute as my awareness of the seconds inexorably slipping away. Keep calm, I told myself, getting frantic isn't going to help anybody. At the other desk, Cecil was speaking with the doctor, and I caught his eye, pointed to my phone, and grimly shook my head no. "Are you refusing on religious grounds, Mrs. Calvin? The judge is going to want to know. Are you Jehovah's Witnesses?"

"Something like that."

I gave a short sigh. "All right, ma'am, someone will be in touch with you to inform you of where and when the court hearing will take place."

"Mr. Richards?"

"Yes, ma'am?"

"I'm really sorry, sir, I know you're just tryin' to help. You go and do what you have to do, and may God bless you."

I knew immediately what I said next probably wasn't the best thing to say, but it was out before I could stop it.

"May God forgive you if she dies, Mrs. Calvin."

■　　■　　■

What happened next occurred very quickly, but at the time, it seemed as though we were moving underwater. The doctor faxed us a copy of his diagnosis and prescribed treatment. We notified both the county attorney's office and the Juvenile Legal Advocates. We got on the court calendar for 2:00. Mark wrote up a quick summary on a form that would promise the court a formal petition within seventy-two hours. The parents were notified of the hearing, though both declined to attend. I borrowed a tie from somebody so I'd look semi-presentable in court.

Mark and I grabbed a quick burger from a local drive-thru, and ate on our way to the hearing. We got there at 1:55, but there was another obstacle we had to hurdle.

The judge for the day was Judge Austin, who normally covered a different geographic area, but on this particular day was hearing cases in Hauppauge. I'd dealt with him before. Generally, he was a pretty savvy, fair-minded magistrate, but every once in a while he got his dander up, and his pique could be as intense as most people's rage.

Today he was not only backed up with cases to be heard, but in a sour mood, and those around him were giving him a wide berth; no one, therefore, had informed him of the seriousness of this case. After having reluctantly approached His Honor while we waited outside the courtroom, the court bailiff returned with a verdict, "Judge says you'll have to wait, he's gotta clean up his backlog. Why don't you have a seat in the lobby?"

"Didn't you tell him we don't have time to wait?"

The officer adopted an I've-heard-it-all-before expression. "Yeah, yeah, everybody's in a hurry. Judge knows what he's doing, and I'm not gonna piss him off any worse than he already is."

"But this is a life-and-d—"

"Judge says wait, you wait." He stood there, glaring, with his arms crossed over his chest, and nodded toward the lobby, "Now please have a seat outside. We have to keep these hallways clear."

As I moved away, complying grudgingly while I mulled over the best way to handle this, the answer presented itself to me in the form of a face poking out the door to the courtroom. "Eddie? Judge is ready to proceed." Out of the corner of my eye, I saw the bailiff abandon his post and head inside; I grabbed Mark's arm and tugged, following through the door and into the courtroom on the unsuspecting officer's heels.

"Your Honor, please, a young girl is dying and I need your help!" I yelled out, earning wrathful stares from bailiffs and judge alike.

"What the hell's going on?" growled the judge, as the court officers grabbed me to escort me out.

"Please, Your Honor, hear me out. Her death will be on your head if you don't!"

They had me turned around and almost out the door when the judge called, "Bailiff, bring him up here!" As they fairly carried me toward the bench, he added, "Who the hell do you think you are, bursting into my court like this? You've got a hard lesson to learn about protocol, young man, and I'm in just the mood to begin your education!"

"Please, Your Honor, I meant no disrespect. Please hear what I have to say before you punish me."

"This had better be damned good, or you're looking at a couple of days in jail for contempt."

"Thank you, Your Honor. I'm Keith Richards, and I'm a caseworker for Child Protective Services. We have a young girl in critical condition. . . ."

I explained the situation, and Mark presented our temporary request for permission. The judge asked a few questions (some of which I'd also asked when I was first learning the details of the case), and I answered as honestly and respectfully as

I could. When I'd finished, the judge ordered the officers to un-hand me, then glared at the bailiff. "I wasn't informed as to the urgency of your request, son. It took a lot of moxie to take the risk you did, but I see now you had no choice. I'm going to grant your request. Still, I hope you understand that this was an exceptional situation, and under normal circumstances, protocol must be adhered to."

"Your Honor, I assure you that if time wasn't so critical, I never would have done anything this drastic or disruptive."

"The court clerk will enter an order granting temporary permission for emergency medical treatment. I want to be kept abreast of this situation, Mr. Richards, and I expect a formal petition before this court on Monday morning."

I nodded my compliance, but before I could even say "thank you," he banged his gavel and ordered, "Next case."

We informed the hospital by phone the moment we left the courtroom and faxed copies of the order to both the DA's office and the hospital once it was typed up. It was after three-thirty by then, and by the time they had given the child her blood transfusion, assembled the surgical team, prepped her, and wheeled her into the operating room, it was after five o'clock. I'd have to wait until tomorrow to find out Dianne Calvin's fate.

My work day was over, but I still had Bill Kahn's wake to attend at 7:00. Just enough time to rush home, grab some dinner, spend twenty minutes with my family, throw on my own jacket and tie, and get over to the funeral home.

There were so many CPS people at the wake Brandon Ericsson could have held a bureau meeting. It seemed to me that Bill's family took particular comfort in all these people turning out after a full day's work to pay respects to a man who had given the job all he'd had. What the family wouldn't know, and what agency people wouldn't let on to them, was that Bill had already become a symbol of what the job could do to you if you let it.

Sure, it's possible that Bill would have met the same fate no matter what job he worked at. It could be that even had he retired a year ago, he would've collapsed wherever last Monday would have found him. But no one in CPS believed it.

I overheard the hushed tones of voices kept low, remarking how this would motivate them to retire, transfer, or quit, as in "I've been thinking about retiring for a while, and maybe now's the time to do it," or "If that probation job doesn't come through, I'm going to pack it in before something like this happens to me." The rejoinder, which would be heard even more in days to come, was, "After all, you don't want to end up like Bill Kahn."

I left the funeral home tired, drained, wanting only the comfort of my wife's arms around me and the restful oblivion of sleep. There would be plenty to do in the morning. I would have to try and see the Calvins sometime tomorrow; I would have to help Mark Vlaoic draw up the petition; but the first thing I would do would be to call the hospital and find out the little girl's status.

I never made that call.

For all the resolutions you form about not taking the job home with you, sometimes it invites itself, and isn't always the most gracious of guests.

I was getting ready for work the next day, rushing around in the usual early-morning craziness of getting two children off to school and two adults off to work. Gloria had already left when the news came over the radio that a young girl had died last night at Rocky Glen Hospital, despite efforts of doctors to save her, because her parents had refused permission for treatment and court approval for surgery had apparently come too late.

I wonder if years from now, my children will remember the day they came to the dining-room table, expecting to find their breakfast set out, but finding instead their father, with his head cradled in his arms, weeping. Should the memory ever visit them, then they certainly will recall the ferocity with which he clung to them when they went to console him.

CHAPTER TWENTY

The only consolation brought by the next morning was that everyone in the working world was winding down the week, gasping, "TGIF!" Only one new case was in my IN bin, the type that always makes me wonder about misuse of my time and taxpayer dollars. This was called in by a public health nurse who had tried to visit a client at the Island Lodge, a run-down motel complex where the Department of Social Services placed homeless families. The nurse had found a four-year-old child and a five-month-old baby, both asleep, alone in the room. Mother's whereabouts were unknown. The nurse's knock had awakened the four-year-old, who didn't know where her mother was or when to expect her return; before the nurse could finish questioning the child, the mother returned, apparently having stepped out to a local convenience store for a cup of coffee and to call her housing worker. The children were alone for between ten and twenty minutes and were unharmed.

Sure, the mother left them alone unsupervised. Sure, this could be indicative of an ongoing pattern of neglect and poor supervision. Sure, any one of a number of things could have happened in the mother's absence.

But they didn't.

The children were unharmed, and the mother came right back. So what was I investigating? The crux of the whole report was the potential for harm ("child placed at risk" is the popular

165

phrase), and while the nurse was charged by state mandate to call it in, she was also protecting her posterior. Our involvement would be to slap Mom on the wrist and teach her about making better choices to minimize this dread "potential." Thus, high-level administration would be able to boast that we left no stone unturned in our never-ending crusade to insure protection of children, but what actually happens in cases of this type is that we are placed in an (officially unrecognized) teaching role rather than an investigative or protective one.

This was just one more example of how people try to manipulate the CPS referral system to their own ends; in this case, it's the wrong thing being done for the right reasons. If people want parents taught, they should set up parenting curricula in schools. If they're worried about the agency's image, they should refer it to our public relations people. With all of the chronic abuse that really is occurring out there, with all the gross neglect, I don't believe a case like this should be accepted by the State Central Registry. Even if we indicate the mother, there's nothing we can do about it other than to give her an official scolding.

There are those who will tell you that it's good to have a record of this, to see if it reflects an ongoing pattern, and their argument is well taken as far as the theory goes, but there comes a point where finer aspects of theory must be sacrificed for the sake of practicality, not to mention economics. That'll be the day when you see a police officer spending like amounts of taxpayer dollars to lecture people about jaywalking, double-parking, or spitting on the sidewalk, or keeping volumes of paperwork to see if it reflects a pattern!

But, once again, I could not allow my own personal feelings to interfere, and would have to place them on a back burner in order to get the job done. I'd make the contact sometime today.

I noticed, as I began to pack up my briefcase and put on my jacket, a clerk from our local register unit dropping three more cases in Lynne's basket. One of them was for me, a subsequent report on MacAvoy, which had been called in by Amanda's mother, Carla Simmons. This report alleged domestic violence by Jud against Amanda (in presence of the children), mentioned how "the family lives in filth," and accused Jud of spending all their PA money on crack. While it didn't list Jenny in the family composition, it alleged maltreatment against the baby Carlotta, and hoping that maybe the maternal grandmother could give me some updated information, I called her back right away.

Other than confirming the allegations and giving me an updated address in Bellport for her daughter Charlene "Charlie" Simmons (Jenny's real mother), she wasn't able to help much. When I'd asked her why she had decided to call the report in at this particular time, she replied that she "just knew something was goin' on over there with that poor li'l baby, and I want you CPS people to check it out. If you ain't too busy!" she added, answering my unasked question as to whether or not she remembered our phone conversation the day Mrs. Zifarelli overdosed. "But listen, Mr. Richardson, you ain't gonna tell them I called it in, are you? That Jud MacAvoy is one mean sonofabitch, excuse my French, and I don't want no troubles."

"You could call the police if he comes to your home and starts trouble."

"And I will, too, don't you worry 'bout that, but I'm a-scared he'll only take it out later on poor Mandy."

"Don't worry, ma'am, reporting parties are strictly confidential." I didn't tell her that it often isn't difficult to figure out who phoned in a report just from having heard the allegations, which the perps (alleged perpetrators) are entitled to hear. "You wouldn't happen to know anything more about Jenny's whereabouts, would you?"

"Only what I told you before. Mr. Richardson, one more thing. You will remember that if you take that baby, you place her here with family, not with some strangers, right?"

"I'll remember your offer, ma'am."

No sooner had I hung up than the phone rang again. It was Meg Riordan, who'd called to tell me that she and Cindy had had their first counseling session last night, and they both liked the counselor. She also wanted to thank me again for all I'd done for them.

Then she got down to the real reason she'd phoned.

"I was wondering if maybe we could get together, Keith. I...I really need to talk."

"If you like your counselor, can't you talk to him?"

"Her. It's not that easy for me to open up to the counselor. I trust you, you know the case already, and—" she paused, and I heard her sigh as an internal battle was decided, "I just like you better, that's all."

"I'm sorry, Meg, but I don't think so."

"Please, Keith, I really need your shoulder to cry on."

"I'm sorry, Mrs. Riordan, but I can't do that."

I could hear her starting to sob on the other end.

"I thought you were different. I thought you really cared about me. I trusted you, and you turned out to be as heartless as all the other men in my life. Well, you can go to hell, you sonofabitch!" She slammed down the receiver.

"I guess I'm not the only one having a tough day," I said lamely to O.J.'s inquiring expression, as I stared at the receiver.

"Hung up on ya?"

I nodded. "It's time for me to hit the streets anyway." I'd been sitting with my jacket on for the past twenty minutes.

The phone rang again.

"Child Protective, Mr. Richards."

"I'm sorry, Keith, I didn't mean it," Meg said. "My emotions are just all screwed up. Please forgive me. I just want you to know I'm still here, and if we can't be lovers, maybe we could still be friends."

That last word struck a chord in me. I knew the woman was in a lot of pain right now and desperately needed someone to trust. She was particularly vulnerable, and I didn't want her to believe all men were bastards; but if I went over there, even just to let her ventilate and then try again to soften the necessary termination of my involvement with her case, it would only prolong matters and make them more difficult.

I remembered Cathy telling me about a client she had (during the short time she worked in CPS) who liked her so much that he was continually calling in reports on himself, knowing Cathy would have to come to the house to respond to them. Eventually, Cathy had had to request the family be assigned to another, male, worker. I didn't want any such entanglement, and besides, cowardly as it may seem, I couldn't deny my attraction to Meg and didn't want to have to face that temptation again.

So, in one of the most guilt-ridden case decisions I've ever made, I simply hung up as gently as I could.

"These ring-backs are a pain," I said to O.J., wondering if she detected the tremor in my voice, but walking out before anything else could stop me.

■   ■   ■

I drove slowly to the Island Lodge, feeling like I was leaving a trail of slime behind me. Resorting to a bit of sour-grapes psychology, I told myself that Meg Riordan would not be able to understand me, and the job I did, as well as Gloria or Cathy could, and if I thought I felt like a slug now, I knew I'd feel even worse if we got involved. Professional ethics dictated that I'd done the right thing; still, I could not deny that the lady and her offer had excited me.

And now, with all these thoughts running laps inside my head, I had to go and do my job, presenting myself as a parental role-model with all the answers when it comes to children, investigating and counseling people on their relationships while wrestling internally with my own.

I parked the car opposite the motel room number listed in the report. I took a deep breath, slipped into my professional demeanor, and knocked on the door.

A demand, not a question, floated muffled through the door.

"Who is it."

"Social Services!"

The door swung open after a moment or two and a lot of shuffling around from inside. A scarred, not entirely youthful, female face peered out. "Yes?"

"Mrs. Jackson? I'm Mr. Richards, DSS. Can I speak to you for a few moments?"

An affirmative nod. "Jus' a minute." The door closed for a few seconds, then swung open. Keep your mind on the job, I kept telling myself.

The room was dark and smelled of sweat; the woman had a light sheen across her forehead. She sat on the unmade double bed, her torn yellow nightgown barely concealing her breasts. Her hair was dishevelled, her voice throaty and dreamy, though she didn't seem sleepy. And it was one-thirty in the afternoon.

The door to the bathroom closed a little more tightly, but I pretended not to notice. "Are Latoya and Tynesha here with you?"

"They with my mother. You from the welfare, right?"

"No, ma'am, I'm from Child Protective Services, and I wanted to discuss this report that was made against you."

"What report?"

I read it to her.

"Who called that in?"

"Sorry, ma'am, that's confidential."

"Then you can leave right now. You can't tell me who called it in, I got nothin' more to say."

"Okay, but you have a right to hear what the report is, and to give me your side of it. I have to investigate it, and I will, with or without your cooperation, regardless of who called it in."

"I got nothin' more to say."

I unclipped a printed piece of paper from my clipboard. "This is what we call a rights letter. It tells you some things you're entitled to know about the investigation, and has my name and number on the back if you should change your mind."

The bathroom door opened, and a large, strapping black man stepped out, naked from the waist up. "There some kinda problem here?" The ugly slash of an old scar ran from beneath his pajama bottoms diagonally up to his sternum, and he stood before me, arms crossed over his powerful torso like a bodyguard.

I held my ground. "Who're you?"

"I the babies' father. Now the lady done tol' you to git out, so git!" His expression showed he was prepared to back this up if necessary, and almost hoping he would have to.

I moved toward the door. "If that's the way you want it.

But I'll be back," I said. I paused once more with my hand on the doorknob, taking my final shot. "By the way. I'm not a welfare fraud investigator, but I'm sure income maintenance would be glad to know that you're all just one big happy family again." I gave a big smile and started to pull the door open.

"Wait a minute," Mrs. Jackson said. "I wanna hear the report."

I looked to the man, who simply turned away and went back into the bathroom. "We not livin' together," she explained after him, "we just *together*, you unnerstand?" I nodded and started reading her the report.

The rest of the interview went smoothly; I was able to do what I had to do, and even learned the address of the grandparents who were watching the children. For a brief moment, I allowed myself to bask in the satisfaction that I'd managed to put my own feelings aside, defuse a client's hostility, and get the information I needed.

We are taught early on that you cannot impose your moral value system on others, that people have a right to live as they want—within the structures of criminal law, child maltreatment guidelines, and local health codes. This doesn't mean you must abandon your own ethics and values, you just have to learn not to let them muddle your judgement. I believe value systems are a product of parental guidance, not socio-economic class, though the two are often confused. I'm proud of the values my parents instilled in me, and Morgan and Will will know them, too, if they don't already.

▪   ▪   ▪

I drove apprehensively over to the MacAvoy's. It had already been a rough week from the standpoint of being ordered off people's premises. I was also concerned because of Mr. MacAvoy's prior threats and Carla Simmons's concerns about his volatile nature, even though I wasn't doing this to harass; subsequent reports mandated subsequent visits.

I became aware that I was breathing hard and my muscles were tense, unconscious physiological preparation, I suppose, for the confrontation I was expecting. As so often happens, though, I'd gotten my adrenalin pumping in anticipation of something that ultimately wouldn't happen.

About two seconds after I got out of my car, Amanda MacAvoy poked her head out the door, and despite being highly agitated, was much more receptive to seeing me than I ever expected she would be.

She took one look at me and burst into tears.

"Oh, God. Why? Why does everything have to come down on me all at once?" she wailed, throwing her hands in the air, turning away, and sinking into a nearby chair inside. I followed her in, noting that the place looked even more neglected than it had on my previous visits. There was one notable exception: no children. I asked her where they were, in a voice I was sure was loud enough for her to hear, but she only continued sobbing.

All I could do was wait for her snuffling to subside, and once it did, she pulled a pack of cigarettes from the pocket of her faded housedress, lighting one with trembling hands. Where she was going to tap her ashes, I had no idea, but that problem had never seemed to bother my assistant director either.

"Mrs. MacAvoy, I want to apologize for having upset you folks the other day."

"This whole damned thing is upsetting me! I don't know how I let Jud talk me into getting involved..."

I kept silent for a moment to see if she would finish, but she didn't. I detected something I hadn't noticed on my other two visits—liquor on her breath.

"Involved in what, ma'am?" I prodded gently.

"Look." She dragged nervously on the cigarette dancing between her lips. "I've probably said too much already. But somebody's gotta help me—us." She paused a moment, probably trying to decide how much to tell me while she regained some bit of composure.

"I take it Mr. MacAvoy is not here."

She nodded. "After you were here the other day, two men came and talked to my husband. They all left together, and I haven't heard from Jud since. He was supposed to be going away for a day or two anyway, so I just figured the men needed him a day early. I tried to call Lenny but I couldn't get through." Tears started racing down her cheeks again. "It's not like Jud to be away this long. I . . . I tried to tell him we were getting in too deep . . ."

I sensed a widening crack in the dam holding back her emotions and felt that it would soon burst and she'd tell me everything. She needed to unburden herself. It didn't matter at this point who I was, or what I represented; I'd be hearing this if I were the mailman. She buried her face in her hands and began wailing through her sobs.

"I tried to tell him we didn't need the money that bad, that there were other ways . . . I knew there'd be trouble from the start. I never trusted those people, and I knew things could never go as smoothly as they said—"

I wanted to grab her by the shoulders and shake the answers I needed out of her. What people? What things? I resisted the urge, and instead tried a different tack.

"Mrs. MacAvoy—Amanda—I really want to help, but you've got to tell me everything. I need to know what's going on if I'm going to be able to help you. Or your daughter."

She looked up at me as if I'd slapped her. "My daughter?"

"Yes. Your daughter Jenny."

Despite the redness of her eyes, despite the eyelashes stuck together by teardrops that had yet to course their way down her face, despite the misery etched into the skin around her mouth, she gave me a look that bothers me still. It's the look of parents who suddenly realize that their children have been involved in some grown-up undertaking and think they know all there is to know about it, while still having so much to learn. Or unlearn. The look is part compassion, part worry, part comprehension of the enormous task lying before them. It's a look that says "You poor dear, there's still so much you don't understand, and I'm not sure I can bring myself to explain it all to you."

I realize now that for that instant, Amanda MacAvoy knew exactly who and what I was, and was somehow taking pity on me for being so ignorant.

"Why don't you sit down, Mr. Richards."

"Thank you."

Once I was seated on the edge of the sofa, pen poised over clipboard, I asked, "So who are these people who came out to see your husband yesterday?"

She lit another cigarette off the smoldering butt of the first. "I don't know their names. I think they work for Lenny, the man my husband set this all up with."

Set what up with? Who's Lenny, and how could we contact him? Where's Jenny, really? Easy, I told myself, only ask one question at a time.

"What did they look like?"

"Both seemed skinny, about medium height, with brown hair." She looked at me with impatience. "I mean, I really didn't expect I'd have to give a police description of 'em, ya know?"

"It's okay, I'm not the police. Anything else you can remember?"

"Umm . . . the one guy has a pretty bad complexion. I can't remember much else about the other."

"Did they say anything to your husband?"

"They talked, but I couldn't make out what they were saying."

"Okay," I said, scribbling quickly to get this all down. "Who is this Lenny, and what did he and Jud set up?"

"Well, he's just 'Lenny,' and he's some kind of lawyer or something."

"And what was the deal they made?"

"Well, you have to understand, Mr. Richards, things haven't been too good for us the last couple of years. Jud got hurt on the job, and they didn't give him hardly nothin' in compensation because they said the accident was his fault. He hasn't held down any kind of real job since then, so when Lenny's offer came up, Jud said we had no other choice but to take it."

"What was the offer?"

"See, Jud was talkin' to Lenny about gettin' somebody to represent us legally for Jud's workers' comp. case. He wanted to appeal the settlement, get a better lawyer, and somebody told him that this guy Lenny could help. Jud was only looking for enough money to help us get by, but Lenny said there was a better way, one that'd get us a lot more money."

She was reaching for the pack of cigarettes again when her head jerked around to the front door as though someone had yanked on a leash attached to her nose.

I'd heard it, too. It was the unmistakable sound of a car door slamming, and the subsequent squeal of its tires indicated a hasty exit.

"Does this have something to do with Jenny's where-abouts?" I asked, hoping for some connection to the child before our conversation was over, but I was too late. Before she could say another word, the front door opened, and she rushed over to her husband with an expression on her face that combined the best of joy, relief, and eternal salvation.

"Jud!" she screamed at him, snaking her arms around his waist, "Oh Jud honey, I'm so glad to see you. I was so worried. I was so scared, I thought they hurt you. Where have you been? Are you okay?"

In her excitement, she'd dropped her cigarette on the floor. Before it could burn anything, I retrieved it and snubbed it out in the ashtray.

"What the fuck is *he* doing here?" he asked, glaring hotly at me.

She lifted her head as though she'd only just realized I was there. "He stopped by and I was just finding out if maybe he could help us."

He pulled her arms by the wrists from around his waist, held them, and shook her roughly as he asked, "What did you tell him? Huh?"

"Nothing, Jud, nothing, baby, just that you weren't here, and I didn't know where you were, that's all."

"That's right, sir. We received another report, and I'm obligated to try to discuss it with you. Your wife was just telling me how worried she was when you came through the door. But if there's more you'd like to tell me, maybe I can help."

"Don't need your help. I'm fine, everything's just fine. We

got it all under control. I don't give a shit about your fucking reports, and I want your nosy ass outta here, or I personally am gonna kick it out!"

The woman began unbuttoning his shirt, slipping her hand inside and rubbing his chest. "C'mon, Jud, let's go inside. I've missed you, baby, we'll make everything all right."

He was still glaring at me, however. "You don't take a hint too good, do you, Mister?" He did go inside, and Mrs. MacAvoy followed him; seconds later, her wailing voice floated out to me, near hysterical: "Jud, don't! This won't solve nothin'! Please put it away, Baby!" He reappeared with her arms wrapped around his neck, and the fingers of his right hand wrapped around a steel gray revolver.

Now I'm no expert on guns, but between the determination in his eyes and the fear in her voice, I knew this was no time to try and call a bluff; this interview was *over*.

"That's not necessary, Mr. MacAvoy. Let's just be cool, here, okay? I'm leaving," I said, backing slowly toward the door. To my knowledge, no social worker in the history of Pelham County has ever been shot in the line of duty, and I wasn't going to be the first.

My hands were shaking, and I dropped my clipboard in the doorway; as I bent over to pick it up, I thought of the family I would never see again if this small act provoked him sufficiently. For all the times I'd pondered different ways I thought I might die, this one had never crossed my mind.

The next sound I heard was not the crack of a pistol shot, but Jud MacAvoy's depraved laughter. "Don't suppose you'll forget this little reminder again soon, hey, Mr. CPS Social Worker? I'll put a bullet between the eyes of the next one o' youse to set foot on my property!"

I walked backwards all the way to the car.

The man had been right about one thing; I wouldn't soon forget. The next time I needed to visit, it would be with a police escort; but as things turned out, I'd just had my last interview with Jud and Amanda MacAvoy.

CHAPTER
TWENTY-ONE

I called the office, found there were no new cases or messages for me, and chose to stay in the field for a while. Not wishing to answer a lot of questions or relive the whole incident right now, I said nothing to Lynne about Mr. MacAvoy's little demonstration. There would be plenty of time to discuss it when I returned to the office.

I decided to drive to Bellport and pay a visit to Charlene Simmons, Jenny's mother. I didn't know what I would say when I got there, and it was quite likely she wouldn't be home anyway.

The house was in a ghetto-like neighborhood called Pace Park. While I always expected my clients to be living in the worst-looking house on the street, and the Simmons place would have qualified on most blocks, on this block all the houses looked as bad. Tall, sporadic clumps of weeds and dandelion stems swayed amongst splintered boards and empty beer cans. An old bicycle frame sat rusting upside down in the yard, having long ago lost its handlebars, wheels, and pedals to some enterprising neighborhood thief. Brown plastic bags of garbage lay piled in the mud against the house, some of them split and spilling out their reeking contents like moldy melons that had been dropped from upstairs windows. New paint hadn't visited the place in decades, and disrepair was a way of life for the inhabitants. Broken windows would provide ample air-conditioning this coming winter, and the front door wiggled loosely in its frame as I knocked. Illegal entry would have required nothing more than a hearty shove, but there probably wasn't anything inside worth stealing anyway.

"Yes?" Charlene Simmons answered my knock, a smaller, sadder-looking version of her sister. The printout had told me she was four years younger than Amanda, but she looked ten years older—twenty-eight pushing forty. The joy of living had been evicted from her eyes many years ago and desperation had dwelt there ever since.

"Ms. Simmons, I'm Mr. Richards from Child Protective Services. Can I speak to you a moment?"

"Come on in."

The interior of the house made the exterior look good by comparison, and the stench from the woman not only forced me to keep my distance, but had me wiping my nose with the back of my hand every few seconds so I could inhale the cologne I splash there every morning for just such occasions. It was the only way I could breathe without gagging.

"What have the kids been saying this time?" She led me into a filthy kitchen and sat down at a small, rickety table. There was another empty wooden chair, but she didn't offer and I didn't sit. Her face wore the weary tolerance of someone who'd dealt with upsetting situations her entire life and was resigning herself to dealing with yet another one.

"I wanted to speak to you about Jenny."

A momentary glimmer flashed in her eyes, then was gone. "What about her?"

"She is your daughter, isn't she?"

"Was."

"I'm afraid I don't understand."

"I gave her up for adoption."

"Why was that?"

Her mouth scrunched up into a scowl she probably only used on the terminally stupid. "Take a look around you, mister. I got no job, no money, nothin' worth nothin'. No man with the right time of day comes back here more than once, even if he gets what he's lookin' for. If you ever saw my Jenny, you'd know this ain't no kinda place to be raisin' her in. She got two older brothers out runnin' the streets right now, and they got no better future than I got. Shit, they'll be in jail before she's old enough to want to know who they are. This was the only way I could give her the kind of life she'd never have around here."

"You mean a better home? Nicer clothes? Material goods?"

"Well, yeah, them too, but mainly I'm talkin' about hope. Worthwhile-ness. Self-respect. Things I ain't had in years, things her brothers ain't never known. We wake up every day reminded of who we are and where we come from. Dogshit to ratshit to horseshit. Different piles, same smell. I wanted better than that for her."

"Wasn't she living with your sister for a while?"

"My sister...." She bowed her head as her voice trailed off. At first I thought perhaps she didn't understand, and I was going to explain; then I realized her voice had cracked, and I let her have a moment to compose herself. She got up, took out a pack of cigarettes, shook one filtered end between her lips, and tossed the pack back into its worn cupboard over the stove while turning on the nearest gas burner. Then she touched end to flame, inhaled deeply, and with the heels of her shaking hands, pawed at tears she hadn't wanted to shed, at least not in front of me.

Finally, with her back to me, she said, "Yeah, she stayed with my sister a coupla weeks, so what?"

"So it just explains why she was there when the referral came in."

She spun around to face me again. "What referral?"

"I was originally called in on the case to investigate burns on Jenny's hand."

The woman's chin dropped to her chest as she shook her head. "Oh, that lousy son-of-a-bitch! I'll fuckin' kill him!"

"Jud MacAvoy?"

She nodded. "Maybe me and my sister ain't nothin' but poor white trash, but we never been no child abusers. Can't say the same for that scumbucket she married, may he rot in hell."

"Ms. Simmons, did you ever have any contact with the people who set up Jenny's adoption?"

She went to another cupboard, took down a juice glass with a chipped rim, which looked like it had been allowed to dry dirty, and poured herself a shot of Old-something-or-other from a bottle in the same cupboard. "'Scuze me for not offerin' you any, but I know you're on duty." She knocked that one back, poured another and sipped it, bringing glass and bottle back to the table. The long ash on her cigarette fell to the floor as she sat down again.

"No, I never seen 'em. Mandy talked about some guy Lenny a couple times, but that was all."

"Do you know whether there was ever any money involved?"

"If there was, I never saw none of it, and my sister probably never did neither." The juice glass emptied itself down her throat again. "She probably never saw no money from that cheap, lazy, no-good..."

Another moment of silence passed as she poured some more.

"You willingly turned your child over to a man you hate in the hopes he would provide her with a better life?"

"It was Mandy talked me into it. She said they knew a really nice family who would take good care o' Jenny, give her nice clothes and shit. I didn't do it so that bastard could abuse her." A look of dark suspicion seeped into her eyes, the most fire I would see there. "He ain't—you know—*bothered* her, has he?"

"Not as far as I know. The last time I saw them, they each told a different story of where Jenny went to live, and the only thing they agreed on was that she was gone. In fact, I didn't see any children at all. Do you have any ideas?"

She swallowed again, right from the bottle this time, and the fire was doused, replaced by a spacey, far-off look.

"Nope," she said, as if in a trance, "Don't care, neither. I'll pray for Jenny, and Mandy, too, I certainly will, but that's about all I can do for them now." Another swig, and I realized I had learned all I was going to from Ms. Charlene Simmons.

"Well, thank you, ma'am, you've been very helpful." I got as far as the front door when she called to me, her voice thick and slurred.

"Mis-tuh. You make sure my li'l girl's in a good home, y' hear me? Don't wanna see her, she's better off not knowin' where she came from. But you see to it they take good care o' her."

"I'll do my best, ma'am."

"Jus' see to it," she echoed softly, staring unfocused at a mound of kitchen garbage as the alcoholic haze enveloped her.

I drove out of the neighborhood feeling like a freed prisoner, marveling at just how sweet the air tasted, how radiantly the sun shone. I had a strong desire to see my wife and children, and couldn't wait until five o'clock rolled around so I could go home and give them each an appreciative hug.

I had a few more pieces to the MacAvoy puzzle now, but I was still trying to figure their proper locations. Funny thing about Aunt Sarah's jigsaw puzzle, though. Despite having studied all the pieces very closely that summer to try to differentiate the pictures and having put in many hours memorizing what the completed scenes would look like, at this moment I could not recall whether the bridge or the forest had been face up in the final solving. This was a typical example of concentrating so closely on something that you don't see the forest because too many trees are in the way. I just hoped I wasn't missing something on the MacAvoy case for the same reason.

■　■　■

"Daddy, how come you're working so late every night?" asked Morgan as I tucked her in. "I miss you."

Guilt! Shame! With her simple but direct clarity of vision, my own daughter was pinning me to the wall, and all I could do was apologize and try to explain. Though discussion of this topic would keep her up later than usual (and that was probably part of the reason she was asking it at this time), I felt she had a right to a straightforward answer.

"I know, sweetheart, and I'm sorry. It's just that there are a lot of children out there whose mommies and daddies aren't doing such a good job taking care of them. You know how sometimes you're doing your homework when Mommy says it's time for dinner? You have to stop everything to eat, then go back after dinner and finish. Well, I can't do that, because then

I'd have to leave again after dinner. So I just work until I've finished what I have to do, so that once I'm home, I'm home for the night."

"But sometimes you don't come home at all, and I don't see you."

"I know, sweetie, and I don't like it any more than you do. But some little boys and girls don't have a great mom or dad like you and Will, and if I have to stay with them for a while to make sure they're okay, I wind up getting home late to you guys. If a policeman was arresting some criminal, you wouldn't want him leaving right in the middle of things because it was time for him to go home, would you?"

She shook her head, wearing an expression in the night-lighted semidarkness that nonetheless bespoke understanding beyond her eight years. And reluctant acceptance. After a moment, she asked, "Do you have to arrest people?"

"No, but sometimes I have to take them to their grandma's home, or to some other relative, so they'll be safe, and sometimes, if the judge says it's okay, I have to put them in a foster home."

"Alissa says her cousin has a foster brother. What's 'foster?'"

"That means Alissa's aunt is willing to have somebody else's children stay in her home, and she'll take good care of them. 'Foster' means 'take good care of.'"

"Would you ever put me or Will in a foster home?"

"Only if something happened to me or Mom, because we're already taking good care of you. Besides, even then, you'd probably go and stay with Nana for a while. But don't you worry about it, sweetheart. Mom and I aren't planning to go anywhere. That's why I might come home late sometimes, but I always come home."

"Daddy? How come you were crying the other day? I thought daddies weren't supposed to cry."

"That's not true. It's okay for daddies to cry, they just don't do it very often. Maybe they should. I was just feeling sad because there was a little girl I was trying to help, and I worked very hard to do that, but she died anyway."

"Was somebody mean to her? Like give her a bad touch or something?"

I smiled and wrapped my arms around her. "No, baby. Her mommy and daddy wouldn't let the doctors do an operation on her, and I had to go to court and get a judge's permission for the doctors to save her life. But by the time we did all that, the little girl died, and I was feeling sad for the little girl, and sad for myself, too. I tried so hard, and failed, anyway. But that won't keep me from trying just as hard for the next little child who may need my help."

"And listen, since you mentioned it, Missy, um—"

"No, Dad, nobody's bad-touched me."

"I guess I ask you that a lot, huh?"

She nodded. "But if somebody did, would I have to go to court?"

"You might. Why do you ask?"

"Because they showed us a movie in school about what you always say, about telling somebody if you get bad-touched. The girl in the movie had to go to court and tell what happened. I don't think I'd like that."

"It can be scary sometimes. But sometimes the judge will let you talk to him in a private room called his chambers, and sometimes they let you talk into a video camera so they can play the tape in court, and you don't even have to be there."

I did not mention all the newspaper clippings Gloria had saved for me about the recent debate concerning whether videotaped statements denied an accused person the constitutional right to face his or her accuser. Let Morgan understand the rules first, before learning about the exceptions.

"Like when you taped us at Christmas?"

"That's right. But it's not a game, or a skit like we do here sometimes. The people at my job only tape children if they're telling the truth, if it really happened." I didn't want my daughter or her friends to get the idea that this was mere play-acting; I'd once spent two days on a bogus sex-abuse case where the girl finally admitted to making up a story about her stepfather molesting her because "all my friends had stories to tell, and I wanted to tell one, too." Besides, with possible charges still pending against me on the Hart case, I was particularly sensitive to false allegations.

"Will says if anybody tries to bad-touch him, he'll just 'kick 'em in the crotch' and run away. He's so funny."

"He's right, though, especially if somebody is trying to force you to get in a car or to go with them. You do whatever you can to get away, and start screaming 'Fire!' as loud as you can. That will get people's attention."

"Why can't I just yell, 'Help?'"

"Because a lot of people will be afraid to do anything if you just yell for help. And by the way, you just remember that Mom and I will never let anybody you don't know pick you up for any reason. So if some stranger says me or Mom are in trouble, or in the hospital, or something, and that we said for you to go with them, don't you believe them, they're just trying to trick you. Okay?"

"Okay, Daddy." I gave her a reassuring hug and a kiss goodnight.

"Don't you worry too much about it, Missy. Millions of children all over America live their whole lives and nobody tries to bad-touch them, or steal them away, or anything, and it probably won't happen to you or Will, either. I just want you guys to know what to do in case it ever does." I was concerned that I might have given her too much grist for the worry mill, but her huge yawn reassured me that she wouldn't spend the night awake and afraid to go to sleep.

It's a sad fact of life that children must become savvy in the ways of the world at an earlier age than ever before. I used to think that the loss of innocence was something that occurred randomly during the teenage years; now I understand that for today's generation of children, it's a process that for self-preservation's sake must begin as soon as a child can differentiate between good and evil.

Why in God's name do people practice such horrors as sexual abuse, abduction, and chronic physical abuse on children? We've supposedly come a long way from the days of the cave man; different jungles, different inhabitants, different obstacles, but in some ways, we're just as barbaric. Human beings have asked themselves, "Is nothing sacred?" almost since they first learned how to formulate a question; I've come to realize that in a society where such atrocities are perpetrated every day, truly, nothing is.

Is this a cynicism felt by most parents once they enter their thirties? Has my job shriveled the optimistic outlook I used to carry?

I don't know anymore.

But I can tell you this: my children will be as prepared for survival in today's world as I can teach them to be.

CHAPTER
TWENTY-TWO

Most people who have to report to work Monday morning after a weekend off are probably singing the same "I can't believe I have to work tomorrow" blues, but in CPS, the feeling is intensified. Co-workers have admitted they have more fights, tend to yell more at spouses and children, and are generally in more lousy moods on Sunday evenings than any other time of the week. I simply call this phenomenon the Sunday Night Dreads, and I find it much like anticipating a trip to the dentist.

This particular evening found the Dreads upon me once again, bolstered by an argument with Gloria about my punishment methods (she thought I'd punished our son too harshly for talking back to her—working in CPS does not mean you have all the answers when it comes to raising your own kids), and two items I'd just picked out of the Sunday papers.

The first was an account of the lead story, what the press was calling the "Bloodbath in Brentwood." This was a nasty case Buddy Hollister had been involved with on Friday. The father, who'd had a history of gunplay and tragedy stemming back to when he accidentally shot his older sister when he was seven years old, had finally fallen over the precipice of madness and had shot and killed his wife, his mother-in-law, his nine-year-old stepdaughter, and last, himself. Due, in part, to Buddy's intervention, a sixteen-month-old baby had been saved, yet when interviewed at the scene, Buddy tearfully blamed himself for not being able to get the father to hand over the nine-year-old.

Newsday slanted the story to reflect the tragedy of it all, rather than harping on the shortcomings of the agencies involved, since they had at least saved the baby. Still, a sidebar contained an interview with a grown son of the father who stated that his father had been a victim of an uncaring and ill-equipped system. The son did not mention why it was that he chose to live out of state.

The second article, which included a picture of the writer, sent me into a rage of frustration and helplessness. It was a face I'd seen once before.

"Oh, my God," I said, to no one in particular, "she's hung me out to dry. Administration's going to take one look at this, and —"

"One look at what?" echoed my wife.

I passed the article over to her. "Recognize the columnist?"

She nodded. "Sam Bishop. The one you were talking to at Joanie's wedding." Gloria was silent as she read, then asked, "Did you really say all these things?"

"Only some, and not in the context quoted. I was mainly bitching about how tough the job is. She makes me sound like an incompetent lush."

"Look at the bright side. When the commissioner reads this, you'll be fired and will have to go out and find another job, and the children and I can have back the sweet, loving man Keith Richards used to be, and he can have back his peace of mind and his sanity." She put her arms around me over the back of my easy chair and kissed the top of my head. "Maybe now you can get one of those really easy jobs, like air traffic controller, or psychiatric ward manager."

"This will absolutely blow any credibility I have with my clients."

"How many of your clients regularly read *Newsday* columnists?"

I kissed her appreciatively. "See? That's why I keep you around, I need your perspective. Not to mention your great sense of humor."

■ ■ ■

The reaction in the agency was no joke, however. The article was clipped and circled in red on my desk when I walked in the next morning, and as I walked by people in the halls or clustered at their desks, buzzing voices stopped until after I'd passed. One or two came by to offer condolences and to give me their vote of confidence, but others reveled in my discomfiture.

I had just signed off from the computer, and was tearing off the hard copy I'd printed out when a voice behind me said, "Well, well, if it isn't the star pensioner himself." I turned around to see Rosalie Schimpf and another woman I only knew as Noreen standing behind me. Rosalie was a clerk on an income maintenance team; Noreen was a data entry operator. They were best friends, which was surprising since Noreen was generally well-liked by everyone, whereas Rosalie was a rumor-monger who only got a story as accurate as she needed for the most dramatic impact as she retold it. Not who I needed to run into at the moment.

"Morning, ladies," I answered, admitting nothing but curious to know what they knew—or thought they knew. "I'll be out of your way in just a moment."

"The way I heard it, you're supposed to keep out of everybody's way until further notice, which hasn't been given yet. The way I heard it—"

"Rosalie, let the man do his job in peace!" the other woman cut in. "Honestly, sometimes you're such a magpie."

"Machine's all yours now," I said, walking away briskly.

"Awful big hurry for someone who can't do his job right," she goaded, but I didn't answer. I wondered if she'd heard something I hadn't.

One of the unjust aspects of the job was that we always had to bend over backwards to protect the confidentiality of reporting parties, as well as the families under investigation, but when it came to the private lives of the employees, we worked in a goldfish bowl. I walked through the building back to my office with the feeling that the whole place was watching me and snickering behind my back.

I buried myself in paperwork, managing to get the Zifarelli case all caught up and sending the file on to a monitoring team, which would check on how the children were doing since their return to their father. I knew they would probably make one visit, be treated to a glimpse of Mr. Zifarelli's temper, find nothing worth continuing the case for, and close the whole thing out.

It was amazing how much work I was able to get done that morning with everyone giving me such a wide berth. I even managed to follow up on two cases before lunch, wondering all the time if the top-level administration had read that hateful little opinion piece yet, and what their reaction would be.

In the afternoon, we received a subsequent report on Carmen Ortega, one of my clients whom I'd visited last week. We first received allegations (from a paternal grandmother) of drug abuse, ed. neglect, lack of supervision, and generally being unable to care for all her kids, because although she was only twenty-four years old, she was the mother of six. The two oldest each had a different father from the rest; her youngest three were triplets, and shared a common father with the next oldest.

I had to see her in jail because she'd been charged with petit larceny for shoplifting a $200 bracelet. There would be a hearing next Monday to decide what the department store owner wanted as restitution. In the meantime, I needed to know what Ms. Ortega's plan was for the care of her children, especially if next Tuesday morning still found her a guest of the sheriff's department.

The thing I disliked most about interviewing a client in jail was that despite my reasons for being there, and despite the fact that I knew that a few hours from now I'd be dining in my own home a free man, for as long as I was in there, I too was a guest of the sheriff's department and was locked up as securely as any felon. Though the officers there had come to know me, they had security measures that were there for a reason, and I still had to first gain clearance from the warden's office, state my business, and flash my ID; then proceed to the visitor's entrance, flash my ID again along with the pass from the warden, spit out my gum, empty my pockets and walk through the metal detector, wait for someone with a key to open the first steel gate to let me in, wait for a second person to open a second gate, show my ID again, be ushered into the visiting area on the near side of the long, solid block/table bolted to the floor, and wait for the client/inmate to be escorted down to me. Once the interview was finished, I'd have to repeat the process (save the trip to the warden's office) in reverse order.

I also didn't like being appraised by hardened criminals— something like what women must feel when they're heckled as they pass a construction site, like you're meat on a block, or something. As usual, I kept these thoughts and feelings hidden, only showing my professional face, and hoping my police image would help me avoid problems.

Finally, Ms. Ortega appeared, and I tried to forget my surroundings for a moment by immersing myself in my purpose for being here. The reporting party had claimed *she* should be caring for the children, and "not some stranger," a comment I took to mean she was against the children being placed in foster care. But Carmen had arranged for a friend of hers in the neighborhood to care for her children, banking heavily on the hope that she'd be released on her own recognizance for a fine and time already served; if the judge was a real hardnose, perhaps some hours of community service would be thrown in as well. Carmen did not particularly get along with the grandmother of her four youngest, and felt the woman, who lived in a neighborhood similar to Gordon Heights, merely wanted the children in order to double a Public Assistance grant already including four children (the paternal aunts and uncles of Carmen's children).

Despite her incarceration, Ms. Ortega did have the right — and, in fact, the responsibility—to plan for her children in her absence. While we were interested in knowing what her plans were, we could do nothing until the plan she put into effect was found to be unsuitable; only then could we step in to make a more appropriate one (with the judge's approval, of course). If we did not show that we had first afforded the mother such an opportunity, the judge would order us to do so, anyway.

In this case, the plan sounded fine—until Carmen let slip the small fact that Mrs. Linda Gomez, her choice of caregiver, already had fourteen children of her own, and twelve of them were under eighteen years of age!

"Are all of your children with her right now?" I asked, incredulous.

"Of course not," she replied, and as I breathed a sigh of relief, she added, "the two oldest are in school."

My agenda for the rest of the afternoon thus presented itself.

▪   ▪   ▪

Despite all my self-reprimands over the years about prejudging any situation before I'd seen it for myself, I had to admit as I drove to Mrs. Gomez's house that I'd already prepared myself for taking custody of the children, and I doubted we had an emergency foster home in the entire state that could take in half a bus load of kids. I also wondered how many homes we would otherwise need to accommodate them all—and how many trips it would take me to transport them with my little Toyota Corolla. Amazingly, forty-five minutes later I left her home not only alone, but feeling confident that the situation was at least stabilized for the time being. Though I'd waggishly dubbed it my old-woman-in-the-shoe case, Linda Gomez was anything but old, impressing me with her youth, vitality, and knack for knowing exactly what to do with so many children.

Two things about the situation made it more-or-less acceptable for a short-term basis. Although on the surface it seemed an impossible task for any one person to manage (New York State, for example, will not license a day care facility unless it has a ratio of one adult for every six children, or better), one of the keys was that of the eighteen children I had to be concerned about, fifteen of them were girls—generally better behaved and less likely to climb, wander off, or wind up in trouble than boys. The other was that four of Mrs. Gomez's children were aged twenty, eighteen, seventeen, and sixteen, respectively; and all the younger ones seemed to listen well to the older ones. Thus, Mrs. Gomez was able to delegate many of the supervisory and mundane day-to-day tasks to the older teens, while attending herself to the more serious and spontaneous tasks—cleaning up spills, applying salves and/or bandage strips, choosing clothes and changing them, etc. Her twenty-year-old was a great help, especially during the day, when two of Ms. Ortega's children and ten of Mrs. Gomez's were in school, leaving only six young children to be cared for between them—much better odds than during evenings and on weekends.

Mrs. Gomez was also one of those bubbly, let-it-roll-off-your-back type of people who possessed a big heart, a positive outlook on life, and a deep-seated love of children. She was loving, tended to the children's needs, and had the house as reasonably clean as could be expected. The children all acknowledged that between Mrs. Gomez and her twenty year old, nobody was starving. I was also shown two large pantries full of food, which she and Ms. Ortega had split the costs for. There was plenty of formula and enough disposable diapers for the three infant triplets and Mrs. Gomez's thirteen-month-old. When I observed the older children arriving home from school, changing clothes, and perching themselves at various spots to begin homework before being allowed to play, I had to commend the lady and wonder if she hadn't been an orphanage director in another life.

The situation was under control, I thought; none of these children could be said to be at risk, I didn't see one of them suffering or neglected despite the numbers, and all in all, I had to admit they were enjoying better care than some other children in families I'd observed with only two or three siblings. Besides, what better plans could the agency provide on such short notice? If Ms. Ortega was not released on Monday, of course, other plans would have to be made—no one could tolerate such an arrangement forever. But I felt the current situation was in hand for the time being, and I was optimistic that things would work out.

"Thank you for being so understanding," Mrs. Gomez had called after me as I left. I wondered if a thesaurus had ever listed in its pages "gullible" as a synonym for "understanding." Between the accusations of my touching the Hart child and the damaging Bishop *Newsday* article, this made a third Damoclean sword to hover by a hair's-breadth over my head. God forbid anything should happen to any child on any of my cases, because these three situations would be the additional fuel to be thrown upon what could be the funeral pyre of my career.

■ ■ ■

A bunch of us were gathered together in the office the next morning, deciding what to do about Marsha McKay, one of our co-workers. Marsha had been called yesterday afternoon to rush out on a personal emergency. It seems her mother had been involved in an automobile accident, and by the time Marsha had arrived at South Shore Hospital in Bayshore, her mother had died. Now we were collecting money for a floral arrangement, and discussing what funeral home her mother would repose at and how to cover Marsha's caseload for the few days she'd need off.

By contract, an employee was entitled to four working days off (or five calendar days, whichever was greater), called "pass days," for a death in the immediate family. Since Marsha had been called away on Monday, that was part of one day, and technically, she could be expected to report to work on Friday, although most of us would also take that additional day as sick time or something. Only problem was, between her divorce, a bout of pneumonia, and a problem with one of her own three children, Marsha didn't have a lot of leave time left, so part of the discussion was speculation as to whether she'd return Friday or not. Thursday being a payday this week, we figured we might see her then, although somebody pointed out that that might well be the day of the funeral.

Lynne was going around collecting money, and as we dug into our pockets, the phone rang. "Keith? It's a detective for you, line three," called Joe Picante over the buzz. "Sergeant McKenna. On the MacAvoy case?"

"This is Mr. Richards."

The deep voice on the other end identified himself and explained that he worked for the Youth Bureau of the police department. "I'm currently investigating missing persons reports on two cases I believe you're involved with. One is a young girl named Jenny MacAvoy, and her mother, Amanda?"

"Yessir."

"The other is a fifteen-year-old boy named Joseph Browne?"

My mind flew to a case record buried under a stack of others, which I had neglected due to other caseload demands. (It always amazed me that you could spend a whole week writing up and processing 98 percent of your cases and yet on the following Monday morning your first phone call would be about one of the neglected 2 percent.)

I fumbled through the stack, pulled out the record, placed the palm of my hand on my forehead in dread anticipation—the Browne fatality! I'd had three negative attempts at contact in the nearly four weeks I'd had the case. I'd been forced to prioritize it downward, since I still had time to complete the investigation within ninety days, and had figured that the child in question was not at risk. Unfortunately, this did not give me a chance to check out the other children in the family, including this older brother, another hole in the dike of my caseload left unplugged for too long by virtue of too many holes and not enough fingers—not too mention too large a dike to begin with.

"I'm investigating a fatality on a sibling, yes," I said.

"What can you tell me about either case?"

The multitentacled specter of blown confidentiality rose before me like the Audrey plant in *Little Shop of Horrors*, yet it was our policy to cooperate with the police, so I gave him what information I had that I felt he might need for his job, including a warning about both Mr. MacAvoy's temper and Mr. MacAvoy's gun.

"That may not pose any problems for me," he said. "I was out to the house yesterday, and the place was deserted! No toys in the yard, no furniture of any kind in the house when I peeked through a couple windows, and a pile of trash heaped together at the curb."

"No laundry on the line?" I asked, trying hard to believe they'd cleared out in the three days between my ejection and McKenna's visit.

"Nothing," he stated. "They were lock-stock-and-barrel gone. I spoke to a neighbor who said they'd moved out the day before, and a check with the post office confirmed they'd left no forwarding address. That's why I wanted whatever info you might have had."

"This was the kind of case where you end up with a whole lot of suspicions, but not much proof," I said. Though it might be a while before I could finish up the necessary paperwork, in my mind the MacAvoy case had just shifted from the active investigations pile to the closed bin.

"Since I've had no contact with the family, I haven't any info on Browne, unless you'd like to hear the report itself."

"Why don't you fax me a copy, with the reporting person, so I can contact them for info," he suggested, and after I promised I would, he asked, "You wouldn't have worked on a Mikkelson case as well, would you?"

The case name rang a bell. "No," I said, recalling a conversation I'd had with Cathy a while ago, "but I can give you the number of someone who might be able to help you."

Cathy had had difficulties securing school records for three children she'd had to monitor in their foster care placements, and thinking of that conversation now, an idea suddenly occurred to me. "You know, Sergeant, you ought to see if the schools can compile a list of recently enrolled children for whom they are having difficulties securing past school records, or where none seem to exist. They also should be able to come up with a list of those who've been unexplainedly absent for a long period of time or who've been said to have moved, and no request for forwarding records has been received from any new district. You could then cross-reference these designated children against personal, identifying information contained in the listings from one of these national computerized clearinghouses such as ARMY (the Association for the Return of Missing Youngsters) and get a greatly narrowed-down list of crossmatched children and current districts. Then it would simply be a matter of circulating recent photographs and descriptions to the schools. It seems to me you could locate a lot of missing kids that way."

"I see two problems with that," said McKenna, "at least on a national scale: not enough money, and not enough manpower."

"Like everything else, right?"

"Right. Besides, though that might help me on this case, what about preschool children?"

"I've felt for a long time that kids should be routinely fingerprinted at their first medical check-up, and again when they're enrolled in school, and a national file kept somewhere, like the FBI does on criminals. Then, when we need to run checks on cases like this, the info would be in place, and positive IDs could be made."

"And we'd all live happily ever after," said the detective. "Well, you've given me an idea or two, anyway. Thanks for your cooperation. Think you could transfer me now to Cathy Whiting's extension?"

"Sure thing. Keep me posted, okay?"

It was good to know the police were on the MacAvoy case. If not for the report on the official state form, those two short interviews I'd had with Jenny (especially the one in the fog) would have seemed like dreams.

She'd been scared, and unsure of herself, but that was common in children that age, especially when they talk to me. (Many refuse to say anything, covering their heads with pillows or burying their faces in their mothers' chests.) Jenny never did corroborate Mrs. MacAvoy's story of being burned by spilled coffee, and the burns had showed an immersion pattern, not a splatter one, though Jenny had never admitted that her hand had been held in scalding liquid, either.

But it was a question that she had asked me that came back to me now. She'd wanted to know if I was the man coming to take her, not "away," or "to foster care," but *"to her new home,"* as though somebody had briefed her about moving on. Yet a simple adoption would never explain the discrepancy in the MacAvoy's stories, their ultrasensitivity and closed-mouthedness, or what Mr. MacAvoy had gotten them into with Lenny.

Only one explanation seemed to make all the puzzle pieces fit at this point, though like so many other crimes you read about every day, it's difficult to imagine that you or someone you know is actually caught up in it. The more I thought about it, the more it seemed that perhaps Jenny had been the merchandise in some sort of illegal, black-market adoption, and

Lenny had been the middle man between Jud MacAvoy and someone on the other end. All I could do at this point was hope that wherever Jenny was, it was in a decent home along the lines of what Charlene Simmons had intended for her.

Still, the thought haunted me, and in my mind's ear I heard a criminal's advertising spiel, delivered in a carney sideshow hawker's voice:

"Step right up, Ladies and Gents, get yer red-hot children here, fresh off the street, guaranteed to be your slave, your lover, your pet, whatever you want. We're Quick 'n Quiet, and we've snatched more kids than CPS! You say you want black? We'll deliver. You say you want white? No-o-o problem! We got 'em blonde, we got 'em brunette, and for a slightly higher fee, we can even get 'em redhead. Have the family you've always dreamed of. Pose the little darlin's in any kind of picture you want. Got a job that needs doin'? Kick your feet up and let one of our kids get it done for you! Full paperwork and documentation included, all sales final. Quick 'n Quiet is an equal opportunity procurer!"

Again I began to despair at just how low people can stoop when conscience and compassion are devoured by greed, and humankind pays homage only to the Almighty Buck.

CHAPTER
TWENTY-THREE

I finally was able to set up a lunch date with Cathy. I'd passed her in the hall, I realized I hadn't spoken with her since our conversation over coffee, and we agreed to meet for lunch. Simple. Easy. I wasn't even suspicious that something might come up.

I should have been.

"Oh, there was a big blow-up on Mikkelson," said the woman who answered Cathy's phone, "and she had to go to family court this morning.

"But isn't Marge Sternberg the CPS worker on the case?"

"That's right, because Cathy said something as she was leaving about Marge being on vacation and her having to wing it by herself."

"Did she have any idea when she'd be back?"

"Who can ever tell about court? We don't expect her until at least this afternoon, if at all."

There was silence, and I prepared to hang up. Then, as if the woman had been doused with ice water, she said, "Oh! Are you Keith Richards?"

"Yes, ma'am," I answered, as patiently as I could, since I'd identified myself at the beginning of the call as I always do.

"Cathy left a message for you. She said she'll try to call you from court when they get a break. Um, excuse me for asking, but isn't Keith Richards a member of the Rolling Stones?"

"No relation," I said tiredly, "thanks for the message."

I busied myself with catching up on dictation and writing two UCRs (Uniform Case Record—an expanded, standardized case-reporting system of forms required by New York State to be completed at specific time intervals, criticized by workers for its redundancy, volume, and the excessive amount of time required to complete it). I also noted two more cases as they came in, both made anonymously and both alleging dirty houses, improper or nonexistent supervision, and drug abuse. Though I'm sure one or two of every twenty of these we receive may have truth to it, usually this type of anonymous report is what I call a zap referral—made solely to zap it to someone for a variety of reasons. These same allegations made by a mandated source at least usually contain some truth, or some reasonable explanation as to why they were made, but zap referrals are a major waste of time and tax money. They're also why I believe the State Central Registry should not accept anonymous referrals. If a reporting party does not wish to give his or her name, then the situation should be referred to the police. If the police find the situation reportable, then they can make the referral, and if we get as far as court, we'll have someone we can subpoena for eyewitness testimony. It will also keep down the number of spiteful, untrue, zap referrals.

Ironically, Cathy called while I was transferring the Riordan case to the undercare unit for follow-up. The judge had guaranteed all morning business would be concluded by 12:15 to insure his making a 12:30 luncheon speaking engagement. Cathy asked if I could meet her at family court, and we'd go to lunch from there.

A full court calendar made parking space outside the court as hard to find as seating space inside, and the lot was jammed full when I got there, so I parked at a bank across the street, dodged the traffic along the always-busy Veteran's Highway, and after passing through the metal detector, again found myself at the big desk in front of the main lobby. It stood like a sentinel before the doorway leading to the corridors, much like a sergeant's desk greets you upon entry to a police precinct house.

"Help you?" asked the uniformed officer at the desk. His job was to log in people whose presence was necessary at the various proceedings, keep out those whose presence wasn't, and generally insure security and a smooth flow of people traffic.

The CPS workers' association had been pushing our administration a long time for better ID cards. The ones we had consisted only of our picture, the county seal, the last four digits of our Social Security number, and the county executive's name stamped under everyone's picture. This was one time I was thankful for the inadequate ID; despite the latest improvements in security devices (that had been installed after a client pulled a gun on a judge in court), it's still relatively easy to gain admittance.

"Yes," I said, flashing my picture briefly, "I'm here on the Mikkelson case."

"Name?" he asked, flipping through papers on his schedule clipboard.

"Mike Sternberg," I said, to save myself a long explanation.

"Sorry, don't see you list—oh, here you are, 'M. Sternberg.'" He checked off the name with a flourish. "Courtroom 104. Through this door, a left, down to the end, a right, follow it around, right again, second courtroom on your left. Got it?"

"Left to the end, right to the end, another right, and second on the left."

"That's it. Judge already called them in, so just check in with the officer inside."

"Will do."

So there I was, in that crowded, smoky corridor, keeping my eyes open for familiar faces, and one in particular, trying not to inhale too deeply.

I found Courtroom 104 with no problem. As it was just after noon, I ducked into the nearest men's room to freshen up and kill a few minutes. When I was finished, I checked with an officer who had appeared in the hall, and learned that the proceedings in 104 were on schedule, and they expected to break for lunch in about ten minutes or so. Would I like to have a seat in the lobby?

Sure, I said, but on the way I changed my mind and stopped by the social services office to call in. Surprisingly, there were no messages for me, and no new cases; I really could go to lunch without feeling too awfully guilty. I'm usually trying to cram so much into such a limited amount of time that to have a few minutes with nothing to do, prior to going to lunch, seemed alien indeed. I checked back to 104, noting the door was still closed, but the officer had disappeared. I also noticed the courtroom across the hall had already recessed, with the door chocked open, and no one around. Obviously, lunchtime rated very high on everybody's priority list around here.

Succumbing to both temptation and curiosity, I went inside and took a tour of the facility. I sat in the juror's box, imagining myself the foreman, standing before a packed courtroom, about to deliver a momentous verdict. I'd only gotten this far twice during any of my five previous jury duty summonses, and once the lawyers heard that I worked for social services, they exercised their right to peremptory dismissal, and I was excused.

I made my way to the judge's bench, murmuring softly, "Your Honor, I'm approaching the bench whether you like it or not." For a brief moment, I sat in the tall leather chair and looked out over the courtroom, with its high, sky-lighted ceilings and oak-paneled walls, the now-empty jury box on my left, the court clerk's table in front of me.

I was struck by the similarity between being here and being in a pulpit, where what I did and said affected all those before me while they held me in the highest regard. Justice and religion are siblings conceived of the same parents: sired by the human need for structure and order, a need which transcends life or death; born of a mother who demands that the good be rewarded while the evil be punished. After sitting up here in their fine robes day after day, presiding over the sea of human aberration, it's little wonder many judges begin to view themselves as gods.

"Can I help you with something?"

My thoughts were quickly brought back to earth by a court officer, who was not so pleased with my newly acquired position, and did not ask this in a questioning tone.

"Er, . . . I was just leaving." He checked over the judge's bench and chair once I'd vacated it, then eyed me suspiciously until I was out of the room. Fortunately, Courtroom 104 had just recessed, and I caught up with Cathy in the hallway, grabbing her elbow and affecting my best derelict-type voice: "Give you a lift in my car, little girl?"

"That's not even funny," she growled, and I knew immediately what kind of morning she'd had. I quickly dropped the affectation.

"So how'd it go?" I asked as we reached the parking lot.

"You know, some of these judges really have no idea what's going on," she fumed. "They think we social workers are always to blame, always incompetent, and all we do is sit around all day drinking coffee and reading newspapers. The lawyers do their best to deflect the blame off their clients and onto us, like their clients would be great parents if only we did our jobs better. And the stupid judges buy that crap!" She was sputtering now, and I stayed silent, letting her ventilate.

"You work for weeks and months beforehand to prepare a case, trying to act in the child's best interests, you think you're finally going to get the kids in a home where people really care about them, and one disparaging remark from an attorney blows your case away! Makes you wonder why we even bother." She paused for a moment. "And you know what else?"

"Yes?"

"I miss talking to you."

"I miss you, too."

"Sorry to let this all out on you, but . . ."

"That's what I'm here for," I soothed. "This has been a crazy week."

■   ■   ■

"Another thing that's got me annoyed is our commissioner," she said, once we were seated in the restaurant. "Administration has been after Tricia to certify two new homes so we could place some kids out of the institutions they're in. The kids are ready for discharge as soon as we have a place to put 'em, and a foster home placement won't cost nearly as much as an institutional placement does. Then the commissioner decided she would open up a dozen foster care slots we don't have and let

New York City place some of their kids out here. A PR move if ever I saw one; we don't have the places for our own kids. So now, my kids are still waiting to be placed."

"I hadn't heard about this."

"Well, we try to keep our appalling lack of resources a secret." The waiter came, we ordered, and he brought us each a complimentary glass of wine. "We also had charges of sexual abuse leveled against one of our long-time foster fathers by a teen formerly placed there; CPS should be checking it out even as we speak."

We clinked glasses and sipped. I totally understood her need to get it out of her system, having been in the same mood so many times myself.

"But the worst—the worst!—was this idiot of a judge who returned the Mikkelson kids to their natural mother this morning. You remember the case. One of the mother's boyfriends beat on the eight-year-old, putting him in the hospital, and Mommy never lifted a finger to stop it. She never visited the kid once after he was admitted; the police arrested her for endangering her baby and her six-year-old when they found her weaving down Main Street at eleven-thirty at night, drunk out of her mind.

"So there I am, covering for Marge, who wrote the petitions but is on vacation. We get the petitions in court, bust our bananas to find a home with three slots so that when the child in the hospital gets out we can keep them all together, get medical check-ups for them to make sure they're all right (the oldest two needed immunizations because Mommy never took them), and get them enrolled in school.

"Mommy makes two AA appointments, gets on a waiting list at the clinic for counseling, goes before the judge, turns on the tears about how she misses her kids, and that—that *asshole*—falls for it and orders the kids returned to her immediately!"

"But with ongoing DSS supervision, of course," I said dryly.

"Of course. No doubt we'll be there to catch her at the wee hours tonight, or next week, when she steps out to wherever it is she goes at night and leaves the children home alone—because she won't want the kids with her when she's picked up for public intox!

"Honestly, we get three children who really need our help, we bend over backwards to get all the elements of the system to do what they're supposed to do, and one pompous, ill-informed jackass bangs his gavel and undoes it all. Plus, he said he didn't see how being intoxicated in public constituted endangerment, and instead of yelling at the mother, he blasts Glenn Goddard, for traumatizing the children by taking protective custody in the first place!"

"And this was Glenn's first removal, right?"

"You got it. Now he's going to be gun-shy the next time he's in a protective custody type situation."

"Or is called upon to testify."

"That too." She shook her head. "Makes you wonder how some of these guys get to sit up there."

"By the way," I said, "I got a call from a detective about a Mikkelson child who's missing or something?"

"Yes, there's an eleven-year-old who's been on runaway status for weeks. Mother thinks she's with a distant relative or something."

"That relative doesn't happen to live in North Carolina, does he?"

"I don't know, why?"

"I had a similar situation on my MacAvoy case, and McKenna wanted info on that, too." I played a hunch. "Is there anybody named Lenny involved with Mikkelson, by any chance? Mrs. MacAvoy kept referring to some shady character named Lenny."

"Mrs. Mikkelson's attorney is Creighton Leonard, if that's any help."

"I don't know, could be. I've got this crazy idea that maybe Jenny MacAvoy was involved in some sort of illegal adoption or something. At this point, all I can do is to turn over any info I get to the police and let them worry about it. We have enough to do with the children who are still around," I said, not entirely believing it but wishing to change the subject. "Did you happen to read Samantha Bishop's column in last Sunday's *Newsday*?"

"Yes, I did. Pretty nasty stuff. Any reaction yet from administration?"

"Not yet, but I have the feeling they're not going to take too kindly to it. You would hope that on the face of something like this, they'd back up their staff, but I'm not counting on it."

"Whatever made you talk to her in the first place?"

"I didn't know who she was!"

"Well, you'd better watch your backside."

"Speaking of which...." I suddenly remembered. "How's it going with your client romance?"

"Not well. Or very well, depending on how you look at it. I saw him again over the weekend, and I was going to break it off, but I wound up having such a good time, I just couldn't."

"The deeper you get involved, the harder it's going to be."

"I know, I know. It's just that we get along so well, he's really a nice guy, and after a morning like this one, you start to wonder if the job is worth all the sacrifices it demands."

"I'm afraid the only advice I can give you right now, Ms. Whiting, is to practice what you preach—watch your backside."

"That's what we'll do!" she said excitedly, clapping her hands like a little girl, "we'll form a Backside Watchers' Club! We'll draft a charter at the next CPWA meeting, elect officers, collect dues—"

"Buddy can come up with a secret handshake."

"Right! And at the end of the year we'll hold a gala Backside Watchers' Ball! No administration allowed."

"We'll have to come up with an official song, though. 'Blue Moon'? 'Moon over Miami'? 'Moon River'? 'Shine On, Harvest Moon'?"

"How about, 'Someone to Watch Over Me'?" she asked, and it was good to see that dazzling smile back in place.

We laughed through the rest of our meal, having shed the agency armor for a few precious moments, reminding ourselves that we are people deserving of respect and dignity regardless of the job we do or how well or poorly we do it.

"Keep me posted," she said as she got into her car, preparing to head back to family court.

"Non illegitimi carborundum!" I yelled after her. It's Latin for "Don't let the bastards wear you down," and I had no way of knowing it was advice I'd very soon need to follow myself.

CHAPTER
TWENTY-FOUR

WASHINGTON, MARVENE, read the case folder
waiting for me.
    "Oh, no," I said when I recognized the name.
    "You've got forty-five minutes to get to the school and see
this kid," said Cecil.
    The report stated: "Marvene has a 2 in. laceration on her
jawbone, underneath her rt. ear. Ch. stated 'Poppa did it' after
having had a fight with her mother. There has been an ongoing
history of neglect and domestic violence in the family. Unk. if
younger sibling affected."
    As I drove to the school, I remembered part of the "ongo-
ing history of neglect." Three or four years ago, I investigated
allegations concerning Marvene's younger brother, Marvin.
Marvin had broken his leg in a fall from the third story of the
family's home, and I'd interviewed him in the hospital.
    As it turned out, he hadn't fallen. He'd jumped.
    Lying there in a traction bed, in a cast from the waist
down, Marvin related the story of how his mother had gone in
to nap one Sunday afternoon, leaving the then nine-year-old
Marvene to supervise five-year-old Marvin. They had been
watching one of the Superman movies on television, and Marvin wanted to see if he could fly, with Marvene's encouragement. Marvene had taken precautions: she told Marvin to wait
until she got back, ran downstairs, spread a blanket on the soft
earth below to cushion his fall, and raced back upstairs to

watch her brother learn the hard way that Newton's demonstration of gravity is far less illusory than Christopher Reeve's
aerial acrobatics.

Of course, we'd indicated the mother for lack of supervision and inadequate guardianship, and she'd called us thereafter to protest in language that would have embarrassed even
the most colorfully expressive marine drill instructor. Still, the
whole case had me scratching my head at the limitations of
both the girl who would encourage such folly and the boy who
would attempt it, not to mention the mother who was more
concerned with venting her spleen on us than with preventing
any repeat occurrences.

The children had made mention of physical fights and arguments they'd witnessed between the parents, but as I recalled, the father had moved out nearly a year before Marvin's
fall, and it hadn't seemed at the time that there was anyone
who would put up with the mother's temperament. Perhaps
she'd found herself another boyfriend, or the father had moved
back in; I made a mental note to find out more about "Poppa"
when I questioned the child.

School staff was now informing me that the mother apparently was working two jobs, and though they admitted they
didn't know that much about what child-care arrangements, if
any, she had set up, they were concerned, due to the family's
limitations and past history, that the children might be at risk
if left alone after school.

The interview itself didn't take all that long, however.
Marvene pointed out, upon hearing the allegations, that her father had died two years ago in some drug-deal "payback" (her
word—I wondered where she'd heard it?) and that there was no
man living in the house.

"Who's 'Poppa?'" I asked.

"My grandfather," she replied.

"Is that your mother's mother's husband, or your father's
mother's husband?"

"Ain't nobody's husband, they ain't never been married.
Him and my Gramma was livin' together for awhile, but not
no more."

"Is Gramma your mother's mother?"

She nodded yes. "See, he been good to all of us, and he bes like a grandfather, so we calls him 'Poppa.'"

"Does he live with you?"

"Next door. We stays with him after school while my momma working."

"Did Poppa cut your face like that?"

"No."

"Well then, how'd you get cut?" I noticed the laceration, as described, but it seemed almost healed. This hadn't just happened last night.

Marvene looked me squarely in the eye with a defiant pride. "I was in a fight."

"Then why'd you say Poppa did it?"

"I didn't say that."

"You never told anyone you got that cut from your poppa?"

"No."

"And when was this fight?"

"Last week, or somethin' like that."

"Here in school?"

"Uh-huh." She sighed as though she was starting to get bored. "Hey, look, I'm missin' gym. Can I go now?"

"Sure, but let me ask you one more thing, because it's my job to make sure everything's okay with you. You said you're not related by blood to this 'Poppa,' but he watches you and Marvin after school, right?"

She nodded.

"And he takes good care of you?"

She nodded.

"Marvene, has anybody been messing with you? You know, giving you bad touches, or touching you in private areas, trying to get your clothes off, anything like that?"

"Uh-uh. Can I go now?"

"Sure."

I planned on stopping by the house to see Marvin, since the odds were that Ms. Washington would be at one of her two jobs and I'd have to make other arrangements to see her. Maybe

I'd get real lucky and he'd be with "Poppa," so I could interview them both. I never got the chance, though; when I called in for messages, I was told that Roxanne wanted to see me as soon as I could get back to the office.

This was not a good omen. You only get summoned back to the office if there's an emergency, a higher-up demands to see you, you're suddenly needed to testify in court, or the office staff wants to throw you a surprise party, and today wasn't my birthday. Despite my resolve to forget about the sex abuse allegations made against me, my first fear was that the administration must somehow believe that they now have enough of a case to charge me formally.

Roxanne was curiously low-key, however. She sat with a confident, catbird's I've-got-you-now smile wrapped around her latest cancer stick, knowing I was in deep, career-threatening trouble, and all she'd have to do was sit back and enjoy it.

But maybe I wasn't being fair to her, maybe there was more to her than that. I could usually find some redeeming qualities in my clients; maybe if I looked hard enough, I'd find some in Roxanne, too.

"How does it feel to have your name in the papers?" she asked, fairly exploding with gloatful glee.

"Oh. Right," I said, understanding what this was about now, and feeling somewhat relieved. I knew some sort of official reckoning could be expected eventually, might as well get it over with. "It's not my name there that's got me upset, it's the other garbage that was printed along with it. I guess you've read the article?"

"By now, I would think everybody has. You weren't timid about what you told that reporter."

"I didn't know—." Something made me stop. If a stranger at a reception could twist my words and misquote me, what would a boss who didn't like me be capable of? Suddenly, I was no longer willing to trust blindly, or to make spot assumptions about the depths of maliciousness to which people might or might not stoop. "Listen. Is this just a preliminary little chat? I mean, am I going to have to explain it all again to administration in a formal hearing or something?"

An assistant director is technically the first level of admin-istration, and I could see her bristling at my nonrecognition of such. "Brandon and somebody from Central Office are waiting to speak with you in his office."

"So what was this? A cozy little chat to see if I said any-thing informally that you could charge me with?"

"You do me wrong, Mr. Richards!" she said with mock in-dignation. "As your administrative superior, I merely wanted to get your side of the story first before we spoke to the director and the deputy commissioner."

She was obviously impressed by everyone's titles.

I wasn't.

"There's not much story to tell. No, I'm ready to meet with them now."

"I must ask if you would prepare a written version of what happened and bring it in with you."

"No, I'm putting nothing in writing at this point." If I was going to be barbecued, I wasn't supplying any matches.

"Very well. Let's go."

The march into Brandon's office was disturbingly familiar. It had been less than ten days since a similar hearing had been held, and that problem hadn't yet been resolved either, so far as I knew. At least this time, Roxanne hadn't been so quick to lock up my file drawer.

The deputy commissioner had not been present last time, though, and I also saw, upon entering Brandon's office, that they hadn't bothered to include Cecil Perry this time. Instead, they had given Cecil's chair to Jim Clarke, the public relations liaison. That probably meant this hearing was about the Bishop article, as opposed to the alleged sexual misconduct, though you never knew for sure. Somehow, I took comfort in that, though making the agency look bad for any reason was an of-fense probably punishable by death. Maybe I'd get off easy, and they'd only cut out my tongue.

"Keith Richards," Brandon began, "this is Deputy Com-missioner Lionel Fredericks." The tall man from Central Of-fice nodded grimly, and for a moment I was relieved that the seriousness of the occasion would at least spare me the usual Stones comment. I'd heard Fredericks's name before, but I hadn't known he was black. Then again, such highly placed administrators only get one carefully guided tour of the place when they first start, and are usually never seen again, unless something like this comes up.

"I believe you already know Jim Clarke, our PR liaison." Another nod of acknowledgment. I hadn't done anything deserving of a handshake, and none were offered.

Brandon paused a moment, waiting to see if either man wished to say anything, but they both kept silent, letting Brandon conduct this meeting, or hearing, or trial, or whatever it was.

"Keith, I want to start off by informing you that the charges pending against you regarding the Hart case have been dropped. Although there is evidence that the child was molested, the mother admitted she could not be sure you were responsible. However, we have other fish to fry here."

Despite my relief that I had been exonerated in the one issue, I was still in hot water, and Brandon's choice of words wasn't particularly comforting.

"I assume you've read Samantha Bishop's article in last Sunday's *Newsday*?" he continued.

"I have."

"Before we start asking specific questions, is there anything you wish to say?"

"Am I on trial here? Is this some sort of formal hearing?"

"Yes and no. You've committed no crime, so far as we know, so it's not a trial. But the agency has a right to conduct a disciplinary hearing, to discuss the situation with you. Then, we'll meet with the commissioner to decide what, if anything, is to be done about it."

"I'm feeling kind of ganged-up on, here," I ventured, nervously. "And no offense to Mr. Fredericks, but how come I don't get to meet with the commissioner herself?"

"She's out of town right now."

"Can we sort of get this moving?" said Clarke, looking at his watch.

"Of course," answered Brandon. "Keith, did you or did you not say those things to Ms. Bishop?"

"Some of them, but I was quoted out of context."

"Did you say we were—" he referred to a copy of the article before him, "'conducting witch-hunts?'"

"I believe I said that *in certain cases* I felt that way, yes."

"Did you state that 'almost all our cases are bullshit and busywork'? "

"No. I said something to the effect that we do get inappropriate referrals, and that certain types seem like busywork. I think I was complaining about the overlap of functions between us, school attendance officers, and the probation department."

"Did you make those statements about burnout and workers who—and I quote—'don't give a shit'? "

"I was referring—" I glanced at the Central Office people hesitantly, but ruffling their feathers was the least of my concerns now—"to the feeling we workers often have that our own administration cares nothing about us. And the statement about burnout was not mine. I was quoting a remark made to the papers by our previous commissioner."

"Is it true you're only doing this job for the paycheck and the pension?" asked Fredericks.

"Aren't we all?" When my flip answer failed to break the tension as I'd hoped, I smiled, looked at the floor, shook my head. "Did you make the statement about 'treating people like lepers in order to save children'? " Brandon pursued.

I sighed deeply. "Look, folks, I was at a wedding reception, on my own time. I was introduced briefly to this Bishop woman, who seemed interested in what I do for a living. I'd had a few drinks and decided to let off a little steam. Some of the comments I made I really do feel strongly about, but she twisted both my words and my context, and made me look terrible. She never even told me she was a reporter until she was leaving! You should be going after her for slander, libel, misrepresentation. Force a retraction. Have her fired. You should be stringing *her* up, not me. All I did was allow myself to be duped into looking bad."

"I'm afraid it's not quite that simple," said Fredericks. "You've made the whole department look bad. Do you know how many calls the commissioner has already received from the press, from legislators, and even from the county executive's office, demanding to know what the hell her people are doing out there? We're going to have to justify every second of time, every paper clip, every policy and procedure we've ever made! Didn't anyone tell you that statements to the media must go through Mr. Clarke's office first?"

I was getting angry now, but it wouldn't serve my cause to throw a tantrum, so I struggled for self-control. "I thought this was just an informal chat about my job. People are usually quite interested in hearing about it, though nobody wants to do it. Had I known she was from the press, I would've told her to find some other poor bastard to interrogate. It's not like I was consciously trying to make us all look bad. I think I follow procedure around here as well as the next guy."

"That hasn't been my experience," blurted Roxanne. So much for her redeeming qualities.

"Ms. D'Angelis, I'm perfectly capable of handling this hearing," Brandon said. "Please don't make me have to ask you to absent yourself from the room."

"Sorry," she murmured, giving me what would be my only satisfaction of the afternoon.

"Mr. Clarke," I said, "is your office going to demand a retraction from *Newsday*? An apology? Are you making an official statement to the contrary? Something?"

"We'll wait until the commissioner has been apprised, and then we'll follow her directive. I suggest you do the same, Mr. Richards," said Clarke.

"If all you decide to do is hang me out to dry, you'll authenticate the statement about our administration not backing up its workers. I trust you gentlemen will point that out to her."

"Mr. Richards," Fredericks continued, "I must inform you that discussion of any agency business with outside contingencies constitutes a breach of established protocol punishable by either suspension without pay, or dismissal, at the discretion of the commissioner. I'm not certain you understand the seriousness of your actions."

"I hope the record would reflect, sir, as I've already stated, that I was tricked, ultimately misquoted, and/or quoted out of context."

"As you've already stated," Fredericks echoed. It was clear to me that nothing I could say would earn any bonus points with him; the whole mess had given him both extra work and extra headaches, and all he wanted was the most expedient resolution.

"In the meantime, Mr. Richards," he said, gathering papers into a briefcase, "you will do nothing other than what is stated in your job description, which does not include speaking to, or antagonizing, anyone outside of this room about this matter. Do I make myself clear?"

"Yes, Mr. Fredericks, I believe everything is crystal clear."

▪   ▪   ▪

Although work was the last thing I felt like doing right now, it was only just after three o'clock, so rather than spend any more time in the office, I decided to follow up on a case involving a woman charged with inadequately supervising her four-year-old son. The mother had turned her back, her boy had run into the road. A car was coming. She had run after him, grabbed him, and carried him back up the lawn. "Unknown if child was hurt," the report stated.

Whenever I see the word "unknown" used this way in the narrative, I get annoyed at the people who take these reports at the State Central Registry: it's like allowing free speculation by a reporting party who realizes the referral is weak, so adds a few "unknown" comments to spice it up a bit. "Unknown if mother has a lesbian girlfriend who might be abusing children." "Unknown if father has past history of murder, or was on drugs at the time." "Unknown if this referral will result in removal of the children, but let's call it in and see." And of course, the caller had wished to remain anonymous.

Although I was sure I had the right address on this particular case, one of the problems we encounter here in Pelham County is that despite being only sixty-five miles from New

York City, some areas are very rural. The house-numbering system is inconsistent, and families often have their mail delivered to a post office box or a cluster of mailboxes on the road, so unless they're kind enough to post their name on a wooden goose in the front yard or something, you can't be sure you've got the right house. Another drawback to anonymous referrals is that you have no RP to call back for more explicit directions and can spend a lot of time just trying to locate the right family.

Again there was no answer to my knock. Again I left a note asking the mother to call for an appointment. Again I walked away wondering if "Anonymous" was watching my attempted visit, excited to see me "going after" the mother, disappointed to see me leave when the "alleged perpetrator" and her son weren't home.

Three other cases panned out the same way, and I was just as glad. It would have been most difficult to keep my mind on an investigative interview with the thought of those two Central Office toadies mindlessly kowtowing while the Lord High Commissioner decided my fate.

Didn't this job have pressure enough?

CHAPTER
TWENTY-FIVE

The next morning's itinerary reaffirmed my basic belief that everything balances out in this world. Despite the hearing in Brandon's office yesterday, I'd enjoyed a nice, relatively leisurely day, one where I could actually sit at a table in a restaurant, converse over lunch, chew my food thoroughly, and relax for a moment afterwards (as opposed to doing fourteen things while I wolfed down a sandwich at my desk or while driving to a next appointment—or skipping lunch altogether). Now it was time to pay my dues for such a relaxed time-out.

Gloria and I both overslept, which meant instant double craziness in getting everyone out to their appointed rounds. Morgan and Will were sluggish, and my wife and I couldn't keep them moving as we normally do because we were so preoccupied with our own personal routines. (Saturdays, of course, they're up at the crack of dawn, because it's the only day any grown person can sleep in.)

Hurry to toilet and shave; hurry to wash hair in the sink, dress, and put in contact lenses; hurry to set table for breakfast, hurry to get the kids dressed, kiss Gloria goodbye as she leaves first; hurry to eat, hurry the kids to eat, hurry to wash dishes; hurry to get teeth brushed, hair combed, lunch made, jackets on, car loaded; make sure kids have what they need for school, don't forget the stuff I need for work, drop off Morgan at school, drop off Will at nursery school. Then settle back for the relaxing ride to work in rush-hour traffic, during which I invariably think of an item one of us has forgotten—an unextinguished light, an unlocked door, a faucet that one of the kids has left running in the bathroom.

It's an early morning song sung by millions of families in America every day. (I would suspect the tempo is even quicker for single parents.) By the time you walk through the doors of your job, you feel as though you've put in a full day's work already, just to get there!

On this particular morning, though, the craziness had only just begun.

■   ■   ■

The phone rang as soon as I walked in the office, and I answered it, wondering why everyone else was clustered at Buddy's desk and ignoring the ringing. After taking a message, I learned that the Civil Service Department had just posted the results of the senior caseworker and supervisor's exams taken almost ten months ago by everybody in the agency with enough experience to qualify, which explained the groups of people congregated at desks, scanning lists of names and rankings hastily copied from the master list.

Musings and speculations abounded as people tried to figure how this would affect staffing changes, who had scored high enough to keep the provisional jobs to which they had already been appointed, who would be "bounced" from those positions, and who would replace whom. For example, Mark Vlasic, the senior caseworker who often helped our unit with court petitions, was a provisional appointee, and though he had done an efficient, competent job for nearly two years, he had not scored particularly well on the exam, and thus would likely revert to being a caseworker as soon as administration effected these changes. Cecil Perry, on the other hand, a permanently appointed senior caseworker who had merely been acting supervisor in Woody's continuing absence (doing a supervisor's job at senior worker pay), had earned himself one of the top five scores on the exam. Thus, he would probably be made a permanent supervisor someplace, though not necessarily in Woody's slot.

Out of nearly 125 people who'd passed the senior test, it was felt that you had to score in the top 35 or so to have a chance at a promotion, at least within the next year. (The actual score was nowhere near as important as its relation to the other scores, so that as long as you passed, position on the list was what really mattered.) Of those 35, approximately 40 percent were current provisional senior caseworkers who would now be allowed to keep their present positions, but as permanent appointees. This meant that perhaps twenty people might have a chance of moving up, once civil service's slow-moving wheels were set in motion.

Although I had not seen a copy of the list, I overheard some of the scores. Cathy had scored in the low 40s and would probably just miss out this time around. Buddy Hollister, Rick Beconsall, Marsha McKay, Joe Picante, and Norma Vezey had all scored lower. Tricia Smollins was 21st. Another pleasant surprise was O.J., who, having acquired the necessary qualification of two years experience only three days before the testing date, scored 17th. Ironically, on the supervisor's list, Bill Kahn's name appeared 2d, meaning he would have finally gotten out from under Martha Hubbard's thumb, had he lived a little longer.

In the middle of this clustered chaos, I noticed two new cases in my IN bin, a bunch of memos, and several phone messages. One case was a referral from a hospital social worker involving a child admitted with respiratory distress who also had a large, swollen, purplish mark between his eyes. The child was too young to speak, but the mother had been "acting crazy" in the hospital and the staff felt the child might be at risk if discharged to the mother without an okay from CPS.

The second case was called in by a seventeen-year-old girl who had moved in with a girlfriend's family because of alleged abuse by her stepfather and an "uncaring attitude" by her mother. Since the teenager wouldn't even be home at her friend's until later this afternoon, I decided to see the child first.

As I started to scan the memos, the phone rang and I answered. It was one of the persons who'd left a message, very upset over the letter she'd received and wanting to know what this was all about. I explained to her that a report had been made and I wanted an appointment to discuss it with her. I had managed to calm her down and was setting date and time when Lynne told me I had another call holding on her line.

I finished setting that appointment and completed the transfer of the second call (a school principal demanding information on results of a case he'd called in last week—his implication being that we'd done little or nothing to protect the child he'd referred, and done it too slowly). John Markham, a caseworker assigned to our county registry unit, walked in to remind me that my presence was required at an expungement hearing (an appeal process for indicated cases) the next day. I made a note of the hearing in my book, while trying to appease the principal, who kept making remarks like "Aren't you listening?" or "This is so typical of the CPS attitude," or "What is it you people do? It certainly isn't protecting children!" I thought about offering to trade jobs, but let it pass as an intrusive beep sounded in the receiver, meaning there was yet another call trying to get through on my line.

As politely as I could, I told the principal I'd try to stop by his student's home sometime today, wondering at once whether or not I'd actually get the chance. He expressed a similar doubt, then did me a huge favor—he hung up on me. The waiting call automatically kicked in, giving me no chance to ruminate on the prior discussion, and the caller was a teacher I'd kept missing, who was returning my call for about the fourth time.

Lynne put a form requiring my signature in front of me and I signed as I spoke to the teacher. Mrs. Ryan was calm and helpful, giving me background information I needed, and I was so grateful to be able to converse with someone who related to me as another human being, let alone a fellow professional, that as the contact was ending, I told her I wanted to have her children. She laughed, then said she had a class coming in and we rang off; I'd spent a half-hour talking with her without realizing it.

I turned my attention back to the memos. Designated period for conversion of health insurance coverage plans. Announcement of the DSS Christmas Party particulars, seven weeks in advance. Two fliers asking donations for employees whose relatives had died, one of whom was Marsha. An informational bulletin clarifying a previously clarified point in the procedures to be followed in regards to the county attorney's office and their mandates under the New York State Social Services Law and the Family Court Act.

The last memo, from the top administrator in the building (which I scanned while taking a phone message for Buddy) was dated five days ago and read as follows:

"I am pleased to announce the assignment of two security guards to our building to help prevent recurrences of recent incidents of violence in the office directed towards workers by clients.

The respective directors' offices should be informed by 4:00 P.M. of the day prior to when the violence might be expected. Coverage will then be arranged for, but can only be guaranteed between the hours of 1:00 P.M. to 4:00 P.M. Where possible, all appointments where violence is expected should be set between these hours, in one of the two interview rooms set aside specifically for this purpose.

Accordingly, these rooms shall not be used for interviews or purposes other than said expected violent encounters without prior approval of this office. A sign-up sheet will be posted for such approved visits."

At first, I thought someone had slipped me a dose of office humor, one of those printed gags that circulate in every office, like an x-rated version of a popular comic strip, or a proclamation that employees dying on the job will not be eligible for overtime, or a chronicle of how The Asshole rose over all other parts of the body to become The Boss.

"Have you guys seen this?" I asked a group of promotion speculators. "Is it for real, or some kind of joke?"

"Both," said Joe Picante, walking over and extending his hand. "Hey, let me be the first to congratulate you."

"On what?"

"You haven't seen the list yet?"

I shook my head no. "I've been on the phone since I got in."

"You're number 18, Keith old boy. There are approximately twenty-two provisional senior slots, and probably eight people who scored high enough to keep their positions. Five of those eight keepers scored better than you. There are two others in front of you who've taken jobs with probation, and Cindi Patchoulli is out on extended maternity leave. That, in effect, makes you tenth on the list for one of fourteen slots. *Amigo*, you're a winner!"

"I'll believe it when I see it in writing," I said.

"The writing's on the wall, my man! Or should I say, 'my man, Sir!'"

Buddy also came over to shake my hand. "Way to go, Rich. Who'd you copy off of?"

I remained pessimistic. "Yeah, right. Like administration's really gonna promote me!"

"Well, they've gotta promote somebody."

"Like I said before, I'll believe it when I see it in my paycheck." I was trying for cynicism, but ultimately lost the battle my face had been waging with the biggest grin I'd worn in months.

Which was erased once I took my next call. It was Martha Washington, and her call was anything but congratulatory.

"Mr. Richards," she demanded, her tone reminding me of a sprinter exploding from a starting block, "You got one hell of a nerve! You talked to my daughter Marvene on Tuesday at her school?"

"Yes, ma'am, I believe you gave your per—"

"I didn't tell you you could be askin' her all them different kind of motherfuckin' questions! Questions 'bout her father, questions 'bout who watches her, questions 'bout if I sexually abuse her?" Her tone rose here, like that sprinter hitting her stride. "What the fuck you tryin' to pull?"

"Mrs. Washington, it's my job to find out what the situation—"

"It ain't your job to be nosin' around, tryin' to find somethin' what ain't there! This was about a cut, motherfucker, not no sexual abuse!"

My hackles were starting to rise; I could feel my face getting hot as I fought to control myself. "I was just trying to be
certain you daughter was not abused in any w—"

"You got some goddamn set o' balls, mistuh, you know
that? If I'da knowed you was gonna be askin' Marvene about if
she was touched, or if somebody tryin' to take her motherfuckin' clothes off, I never woulda let you near her!"

"Mrs. Washington, did you call just to curse me out, or can
we set an appointment so I can discuss this report with you in
person?"

"I got nothin' more to discuss with you, cocksucker, and
I'm gettin' mighty tired of all your white-ass, sonofabitch,
motherfuckin' ques—"

Three "motherfuckers" and a racial epithet in less than a
minute told me it was pointless to continue this.

I'd heard enough and hung up.

The phone rang again, after about thirty seconds, and I said
to Lynne, "If that's Mrs. Washington, I'm unavailable," then
headed for the men's room. Even senior worker pay would be
nowhere near compensation enough for that kind of tongue-
lashing. There are limits to how much each of us is able to put
up with, and I knew when I'd reached mine.

■   ■   ■

I was determined not to let my venom from the Washington
case spill over onto other, undeserving clients, and my next
case helped take the fury out of my sails. Ms. Sharon Payneton
was a slim, twenty-three-year-old mother who had moved back
from Texas with eleven-month-old Raymond when her mar-
riage to the child's father had dissolved. She'd been accused by
hospital staff of excessive corporal punishment and bruises (because of an unexplained purplish mark between Raymond's
eyes), and for medical neglect when they'd advised her the
child should be admitted for observation of what turned out to
be the first stages of pneumonia, and the mother had refused.

Although my visit was unannounced, the small basement
apartment she rented from her mother was clean and orderly.
The child was dressed warmly, in clean clothes, and, save for

the raised, ugly, black-and-bluish mark about the size of a half-dollar at the top of his nose between his eyes, appeared healthy with good grooming and hygiene evident. The mother acted too scared to be angry, seemingly on the verge of tears as she spoke to me, but continued to attend to the child appropriately and warmly throughout the interview.

When I read her the allegations, her reaction was one I hadn't seen before: she started crying as she put a clean, warm outfit on the child, wrapped him in warm blankets, gently placed him in a large wicker basket in the middle of the floor, and cried, "There, then, take him if you're gonna take him! There he is! I can't stand it anymore! Everybody's got somethin' to say, except when I ask for help. I've been doing the best I can to care for him, but all you people want to do is snatch him away. All right, then, take him if you want him, but one thing you can't do is put down anywhere that I ever abused my child. *Nobody* can accuse me of that!"

She then buried her hands in her face, and, kneeling on the floor beside the basket, began heaving out great ponderous sobs, as though I were about to rip her very heart from her chest with my bare hands.

"Ms. Payneton . . . ," I began lamely.

"Is this what being a parent is all about?" she demanded, lifting her head, her cheeks streaked with tear-tracks. "You break your back to have him, get up in the middle of the night to nurse him and comfort him, run around to all the friggin' doctors in the world to get help for him; and all so CPS can take him away on the word of some asshole intern who treated me like shit?"

The sobs continued through my standard lines about having to do an investigation on each report that comes in, not knowing if a child is abused or not until we investigate, and the fact that the report in my hand initially only means that someone picked up a phone. These seemed to help somewhat, and her crying abated as she fought for composure.

"You know," she said, "when I had Raymond, I thought he was a gift from God. If I didn't care about him, I wouldn't have taken him to the hospital in the first place. In fact, my mother tells me all the time that I'm overprotective, but you can't be too careful with kids in today's world."

"Why don't you put him back in his crib for now?" I offered, wanting to put her at ease without making any promises.

"Can't. His diaper needs changing." I was able to observe, once she'd gotten her tears under control, her baby-talking, snuggling, playful method of changing what she called "Raymond's dirties," and if this all was an act she was putting on for me, it was worthy of an Oscar. Would that all my clients treated their babies as well as she did.

As I was about to ask about the bruise, she started explaining, "Raymond was born with some fancy-named syndrome, which is what caused that mark between his eyes. It is *not* a bruise! When I first saw him after birth, I thought the doctors dropped him or something. His pediatrician, Dr. Gottlieb, can tell you more about it. But he was away on vacation when Raymond had trouble breathing, so I took him to the emergency room. They took Raymond right into one of those cubicles, you know? When they were checking him, they clustered all around him, almost like they wanted to block me from being near him, wouldn't let me hold his hand or touch him. They asked me a lot of questions about his birthmark, and when I tried to explain, they got a real snotty attitude, and kept implying I'd hit him.

"When they were done, the resident who checked him told the nurse to stay with us both, and I felt like I was under guard or something. Then, Raymond pooped right there on the bed, and even though I had clean diapers with me, I went out to the nurses' station to get one of those wet wipes, and I saw the resident on the phone, going like this to one of the nurses"—she smacked the fist of one hand into the palm of the other—"and pointing to our cubicle! I was tried and convicted right there in the emergency room! I mean, I know they have to be on the lookout for child abuse when it happens, but aren't you supposed to be innocent until proven guilty in this country?"

"All I can tell you, ma'am, at the risk of sounding pompous, is that it's not abuse until we say it is. Can I ask why you didn't consent to his admission?"

"When all they seemed to be worried about was his birth-mark, and after they practically ignored his respiratory prob-lem, I wasn't about to let him stay in that place. I took him home, and got him to Dr. Gottlieb's associate, Dr. Madison, the next morning. Here's the bill to prove it." Still holding the boy, she extracted a piece of thin yellow paper from a pile on the kitchen counter and held it out for me. Dated the next morning, it was indeed a bill that had both doctors' names at the top.

"It doesn't seem as though you were treated very fairly at that ER."

"It was terrible! And now here you are. . . . " She stopped as another lump seemed to form in her throat. "Look," she con-tinued, "I know you're just trying to do your job, Mr. Richards, and I thank you for being so kind. You should give lessons to those people at Pelham General. But I don't think anybody can understand what it would mean to have Raymond taken away from me. He is my life, and I could never do anything to hurt him. If I actually was abusing him, I would be the first to give him up voluntarily. He's my heaven-sent gift."

I had her sign a release so that Dr. Gottlieb could talk to me about the child, then said goodbye to Ms. Payneton and Raymond as she played with him and his brightly-colored building blocks on the warm, carpeted floor. I really hoped the doctor backed up all that she said, because it sure seemed to me that Raymond was one child who didn't deserve to be any-where else *but* with his mother.

My next case was not so clear-cut.

It was one of those cases where, after spending almost three hours speaking first with the child, and then with the parents, I was no more certain as to how I'd ultimately deter-mine the case than when I first knocked on the door.

There had been two reports, made about an hour apart. Al-legations of the first one read: "There has been a history of do-mestic violence in the home for over four years. Ftr. often beats mother in chn.'s presence. Both parents drink heavily, and use drugs. Last summer, 17 yr. old Michelle was hit by ftr. for un-known reason. Child fell and hit her face on a bed frame, caus-ing a bruise on her rt. jaw. Parents have been threatening ch. recently, and ch. is afraid of recurrence. Ch. does not want to live at home. Additional Information—Source is mother of Michelle's friend, with whom Michelle is staying. Requests contact ASAP, also requests her address and phone be kept confidential from parents."

The second report had been called in about an hour after the first one. These allegations also mentioned domestic violence, but accused the parents of lack of medical care and inadequate guardianship for terminating attendance at counseling sessions they'd been going to.

The longer you do this job, the more catch-22s you come across, and this was one specific to counseling. What happens is that after weeks or months of slowly building up a trust and a rapport with a counselor, a family member confides some significant incident of abuse or neglect, hitherto hidden by the family. The counselor is then placed in the difficult position of being mandated to phone in a referral, seemingly betraying the trust the family placed in him or her in the first place. Since most competent counselors are honest with their patients and tell them when they are going to have to call in a referral, the family sometimes stops going to therapy either as a retaliation or because they feel they can never trust any counselor again. The cessation of therapy is, in turn, referable in many instances (especially if the counseling was court-ordered).

Such seemed to be the chronology of this case.

The seventeen-year-old presented the case very convincingly that she'd been a victim of cold, uncaring, abusive parents, and it was obvious that her friend's mother viewed herself as a sort of community social-work Samaritan in taking the girl in. Something in the girl's whole demeanor struck me as a little too pat, a smidgeon too practiced, and I wondered if someone had been coaching her in what expressions to use in speaking with authorities like myself.

The bottom line, as I told her (and later told her parents), was that at age seventeen, we cannot make her go back home if she doesn't want to, and although we technically can take protective custody of children up until they're eighteen, we almost never would in such a situation as this, where she has found a seemingly appropriate resource for herself and the parents consent to it (or know where the child is staying and take no further action). Thus, since the girl was not at risk, and the situation seemed stable, there was nothing much I could do other than speak to both households.

Still, my feeling that the girl was manipulating both the system and her parents was reinforced as I was leaving. As I let myself out the front door, I looked back down the hallway into the kitchen, and saw this poor, oppressed, downtrodden victim grinning and exchanging "high-fives" with her friend, like a jubilant athlete who has just scored on a big play.

While the parents did seem to leave a lot to be desired in the appropriate parental decisions department, and though I suspected that their marital problems and domestic violence were contributing factors in the tensions between them and their daughter, they had directed most of their violent actions at one another and were probably not the abusive ogres the girl had made them out to be.

I was convinced that, as in so many cases of teenagers who are struggling desperately to emerge as adults as fast as they can, the problems were not entirely the fault of the parents or of the child, but of both. I spend a lot of energy in this type of case keeping myself from playing referee, despite the family's desire to have me pronounce fault or absolve blame for each member. That's not my purpose, but even when I tell them that everyone is to blame to one degree or another, the people want me to establish who is more to blame than whom.

I hate these kind of cases because I am not that skilled at extricating myself from them quickly, after I've extracted the information I need, without appearing callous to somebody, especially when I won't take sides. What usually happens is that, particularly if they're my last case of the day and I can't use the excuse that I have another case waiting, I end up staying long past five o'clock because I've also never been able to simply say, "Sorry, it's after my quitting time, I have to go now." So there I was, at ten minutes after six, tired and drained, looking for a pay phone to tell Gloria I was all right, and I'd be home in a little while.

God, grant me the wisdom to make all the right moves with my own children, so we don't wind up in the same situation years from now!

CHAPTER
TWENTY-SIX

Friday morning found me alone at my desk, comforted by a few, avoided by most, dragging myself through the motions somehow. Cathy, Deanna, and Rick had offered some kind words, but there wasn't much you could say. I was the wrong horse for smart money to be backing. Everyone else was looking and pointing as I passed, trading whispered comments behind the backs of their hands. I didn't get too awfully mad at anybody, though; I knew that if someone else was sitting in the hot seat like I was, I'd probably be whispering, too.

I finally began writing up the MacAvoy closing. There wasn't any point in keeping it open, and it was a way of keeping my mind off other problems. By ten o'clock, people focused less on me and more on Marsha, who was kicking herself for having come to work the day after her mother's funeral, because there were four cases waiting for her when she walked in the door.

Around eleven-thirty, Cecil came out of the supervisor's cubicle, a case record in hand. "I've got another one for you, Keith, a priority. This one's a straight physical abuse, and may entail a medical exam of the child. He's twelve years old and told the school he's afraid to go home. Bruises about the head, chest, neck, and back. We've already faxed a copy to the police, and I guess your first step is to coordinate with them to see the child at the school."

"Not a sex abuse case?"

"No, but sounds like a nasty AB. Apparently, the father is supposed to come to the school this afternoon, and the school fears an altercation. Roxanne said she'd approve overtime for it if necessary."

This didn't sound good. "AB" stood for "abuse," the more serious of two degrees of abuse or neglect assigned to each case; fractures, burns, severe lacerations or welts, fatalities, and sexual abuse all carry this designation. ("MA" stands for "maltreatment," and cases carrying this designation are generally considered less serious.) In addition, overtime approvals were never given before lunchtime except in cases that obviously would run long and late. I sighed as I picked up the phone. Would Gloria and the kids have to eat by themselves again tonight?

One step at a time, Richards.

First I set up an appointment with the school. Next, I secured a camera. We actually have several for CPS use, including two 35-mm cameras, two instant cameras, and even a video camcorder for taping statements and interviews given in the office. Instants are fine for reunions, visits, and identification purposes, but if you really need to clearly show the color and size of the injuries, you use the 35-mm.

Bruises fade and injuries start to heal by the time you can appear before a judge, and the incurred injuries are usually downplayed—"I didn't hurt him that bad, Your Honor." Yet, severity of trauma is a major consideration in assessing risk, and often the deciding factor in whether or not to invoke protective custody. When you're called upon to justify your decision to remove, properly taken pictures will say volumes more in court than verbal descriptions ever could, and 35-mm photos are the most eloquent.

Next I called the police. As it turned out, Jeff McKenna had just started a tour of day shifts, and would be the detective with me on this case. I arranged to meet him at the school, making a mental note to find an appropriate moment to ask him about MacAvoy.

He nodded at me as I walked into the school's main office, camera in hand, and signed their visitor register.

"Keith Richards, CPS, this is Ralph Stedman, the principal," McKenna said, "And George Kontzamanys, vice-principal."

"What've we got here?" I asked, after we all shook hands and seated ourselves in the principal's private office.

Stedman spoke. "We've got twelve-year-old James Carmichael, who came to school today covered with bruises. He's in with our nurse now. He's been going downhill in his schoolwork lately, and we spoke to Mr. Carmichael on the phone last week about it. The boy says that last night, he got into it with his father about doing homework, and the old man just lost it. Started hammering away on him with his fists, yelling he'd kill him if the kid didn't start 'straightening up.' James says he's afraid to go home after school today.

"The father's just recently remarried, and the boy has said he doesn't like his new stepmother. She instigates many arguments, and never sticks up for James—probably afraid of Mr. Carmichael, who James says is a pretty big fellow. James also has said that he's witnessed his father beating up his real mother in the past, and this is what led to their divorce."

"Where's his natural mother now?"

"She's in Florida with friends, trying to make a new start, but she wasn't set up to have James live with her just yet. We weren't able to reach her at the phone number James gave us."

"What kind of kid is James, and how's he doing? I mean, is he all upset, crying, what?"

"No, he's pretty mellow, actually. He's like a Baby Huey. By his size, he could be a defensive end, but by his demeanor, he's really a cream puff. Doesn't give anybody any trouble, at least not here in school."

"So he's only been going downhill academically?"

"As far as we can see. He's always kept pretty much to himself, doesn't have a lot of friends. I don't know how much the father's temper has had to do with that, but I suspect it's quite a bit."

"Now I understand the father's coming to the school this afternoon?"

"That's right. Dismissal is at 2:30 and the father said he'd try to be here around then, and take James home with him after he meets with us."

I nodded. "Anything else I ought to know?"

"Mr. Carmichael is first vice-president at Pelham Savings and Loan," he said, "so if you have a loan or mortgage with them, I wouldn't let on, if I were you." He stood up and came from behind his desk, then moved his arms in an underhanded motion, as though he were tossing me an imaginary basketball. "It's all in your lap, now. I'm going to get me some lunch. I'm sure you'll still be here when I return."

I was sure I would be, too.

The vice-principal escorted McKenna and me to the nurse's office, introduced everyone, then left to attend to other matters. Mrs. Ingram had just finished her examination of James, who still had his shirt off as I entered, his torso sporting several mild bruises. His left arm had a small bruise the size of a quarter, two more dotted his chest near the shoulder below the collarbone, and the two largest had sprouted on his lower back.

What concerned me most were the dime-sized circles and slashes of color on or near his neck, especially the older ones, which had started to fade to brown. These were not caused by blows, but rather seemed to be the result of gouging; with the pictures I was taking and a doctor's testimony, we would try to substantiate not only that James had been choked, but that it had occurred on more than one occasion.

In a way, I was disappointed. The bruises didn't look as bad as they'd sounded in the report. While I was relieved for James's sake that he hadn't been hurt worse, I knew that even with the 35-mm, our pictures would not be graphic, making our case less convincing in court. We would have to rely on testimony to show the emotional climate in which James was living, and there was then much more chance of our concerns being downplayed. Though I'd made no firm decision as yet, I guess I was already trying to build an argument for taking protective custody, but this was no clear-cut case (most aren't).

James was a doughy, heavyset boy, large for his age. He was quiet and respectful in answering our questions, but made eye contact mostly with the floor, and his voice often bordered on the inaudible, almost as though he felt sorry for having to put us through all this. This was another point which I hoped to make—James's body language was totally consistent with that of the classic battered child.

I wished there was some way the judge could see this without having to drag the boy into a courtroom before his father; however, videotaped statements are seldom, if ever, used in emergency protective custody cases, especially where sexual abuse is not involved. Still, the two most telling statements he made to us were naming his father as alleged perpetrator and claiming he was afraid to go home as a result. I'd just have to hope the judge would trust my professional judgment and expertise for the rest.

Perhaps James was always a well-behaved boy, perhaps he was worn down from fear at what disclosure might bring, perhaps he'd suffered an internal injury that was taking its toll, but James went along with our statement-taking and picture-taking procedures like a trooper, and it was hard to understand what he might have done to deserve to be beaten. (The terms "beat," "hit," and "spank" are often erroneously used as synonyms, and should not be; in my experience, the first usually means abuse and the last usually doesn't, while "hit" can mean anything from a slap on the wrist to a gangland murder.)

Part of the prudence necessary when taking pictures arises from the need to take them in a sequence that will show an injury up close while identifying the child in question. There is also a whole procedure to be adhered to with the police department to get pictures developed, whether they are otherwise involved in the case or not, in order to demonstrate an unbroken chain of evidentiary custody. These procedures must be followed precisely to discount any arguments that the evidence has been substituted or tampered with, or is not applicable to the subject in question (i.e., the bruises pictured in close-up shots were on someone else's body, these are not the pictures Mr. Richards took on October 24th). James was patient and cooperative throughout, though perhaps somewhat "out of it."

After I finished with the pictures, James asked for a break in his statement-giving to use the bathroom, and I called my office. Since I knew that both Cecil and Roxanne would have to pass my report up to Brandon for a decision anyway, and since there would still be much to do if we did take custody, I phoned Brandon directly. He listened to my assessment, and told me he'd get back to me after he contacted both the judge on call and the county attorney's office. As I hung up, a secretary poked her head in the room to inform us that James's father had arrived and was waiting in the office. McKenna then called my attention to the small bathroom James had just used.

"I thought you might want to see this," he said quietly, nodding at the bowl as James dressed himself in the outer room.

What I saw raised the stakes a few notches. The contents looked and smelled like urine, but were tinged with pink, like a bit of catsup permeating a beer.

I'd seen worse. In one memorable case, the poor child's urine had consisted almost entirely of maroon-colored blood, and only prompt medical attention had saved her life. Still, with the bruises on James's lower back, it could mean kidney damage, bladder damage, perhaps a broken rib puncturing other organs, and I was taking no chances. Although my interview with Mr. Carmichael would be complete (to be certain all of his legal rights were attended to), I would keep it as short as possible; as soon as I got my call back from Brandon with verbal permission, James was going to a hospital. And I would be the one to take him.

"James, are you in a lot of pain?" I asked.

"My back's a little sore," he said.

"Do you feel dizzy, or like you're going to pass out, or like you might throw up?"

He shook his head no, and Mrs. Ingram did likewise, to confirm these were the same answers he'd given her.

"You said your father punched you in the back? With a closed fist?"

He nodded yes.

"How many times?"

He shrugged. "Couple."

"Okay. Will you be all right here with Mrs. Ingram while Detective McKenna and I talk to your father?"

I meant this rhetorically, but James nodded yes, then asked, "Am I going to have to go home?"

I gave him what I hoped was a reassuring smile, and squeezed his unbruised arm gently. "Not if I can help it, buddy."

On the walk back to the main office, I said to McKenna, "Ever notice that the most serious ones don't want to go home?"

"Yeah. I guess you're gonna take custody?"

"Unless I can talk the old man into giving it up voluntarily."

He shook his head. "Don't count on it. I know this guy, and even on a good day he's a snotty SOB to everybody. He doesn't have a real long fuse, and if he can't intimidate you with his size, he loses his temper."

"That's what I have you along for." I shot him a brief smile. "Listen, I meant to ask you—have you found anything new on MacAvoy?"

"Yeah, as a matter of fact. We're checking out a lead right now on a couple of kids who've been adopted recently. These kids fit missing persons descriptions, but we have to talk to them before we decide on anything. It's tricky, because the parents aren't keen on giving permission, ya know?"

"Even if a clean break is best for all concerned, you'd think the parents would at least allow the children to know where they came from."

"That's what I don't like about it. These parents all seem very hinky about everything. Nobody's cooperating."

I paused with my hand on the doorknob of the office. "Well, if you could get me some names, addresses, former names, dates, stuff like that, I'd be grateful."

"I'll see what I can do."

■　■　■

Ralph Stedman had returned from lunch. He introduced us as we set up chairs in a large semi-circle in his office. There were seven of us all together: Stedman and Kontzamanys, myself and McKenna, Mr. Carmichael, his new wife (James's new stepmother), and a school psychologist whose name I didn't catch. We weren't two minutes into our discussion before I had a pretty good notion of what James's home environment was like.

"So what's this all about?" demanded the father, his speech clipped and curt. "I left a very important meeting to come down here."

"We appreciate your concern and cooperation, Mr. Carmichael," Stedman began, "but we have more to discuss than James's academic performance." He introduced us all around. Wary nods supplanted handshakes as McKenna and I were identified.

"Police? CPS? What's going on here, Joseph?" said the woman, in a piercing, high-pitched voice.

"That's what I'd like to know."

"And how come James isn't here?" she prompted.

"Yes, where is my son?" demanded Mr. Carmichael.

They made an interesting contrast. Though both were exceedingly well-dressed, Joseph Carmichael was huge and, despite a bit of paunch at the middle, seemed like he possessed great upper torso strength, probably from working out at a health club. His red-on-red power attire, coral shirt and scarlet paisley-patterned silk tie framed by a charcoal-gray pin-striped suit, told me he was used to being in control and having his orders followed. As I'd passed behind him in setting up chairs, I'd caught a whiff of cologne that struck me as both sweet and pungent, but somehow offensive.

Mrs. Carmichael stood about two feet shorter; probably didn't have an ounce of fat on her slim, wiry body; and with a straighter, shorter haircut, she could have passed for James's younger brother. She was dressed in an ankle-length blue jersey dress topped with an oversized bright red sweater. The sleeves were hitched up her forearms and, together with her glasses and no-nonsense expression, made her look like an office manager of some sort.

I realized the others were looking to me to answer the man's question, my cue to take charge of the meeting.

"He's in another room, Mr. Carmichael," I answered calmly.

"Well, get him in here, Joseph," said the woman, "this is supposed to be about his schoolwork, and I think he should hear this." She poked him with her elbow, and I would have bet a month's salary she was the only person in the world who got away with jabbing Joseph Carmichael like that. And then, only sometimes.

"I'm afraid it's not that simple, ma'am," I said. "James came to school today with bruises about his chest, back, and neck. I've been called in to investigate the possibility that James has been abused."

The father looked at me as though I'd asked him to put all the bills in the register into a brown paper bag. "You are joking, right?" He glanced at his wife, who wore the same let's-not-give-this-credence-by-taking-it-too-seriously expression. "Do we look like child abusers to you?"

"James looks to me as though he's been abused, yes, and he told me his father beat him up for not doing homework."

Both parents looked knowingly at one another, and broke out in knowing, derisive grins. "That's absurd," said the woman.

"Ridiculous," added the father. "James is just trying to put one over on you people. Sure, I hit him. He's lazy, and a good swat in the rear is the only thing he understands. Are you saying I can't even discipline my own son?"

"Discipline is one thing, Mr Carmichael. Abuse is another."

"This is crazy, Joseph," said Mrs. Carmichael, as Mr. Carmichael stated: "But he's not abused. You call a spanking abuse? If anything, I'm too lenient. Had I tried half the garbage that I let James get away with, my father would have beaten me bloody." Almost as a throw-away comment, he muttered, "and did, sometimes, for reasons good and bad, and I still turned out okay. I'm a bank manager, for Chrissake."

He paused. I could have jumped in and pointed out that Child Protective Services was not created until the Family Court Act of 1979, and that a parent was now expected to conform to the laws set forth in today's society—but I didn't bother. It would have deflected the conversation off the issue at hand, and I wanted to keep the focus on James and his father, not the laws of the land.

So I kept silent, the other professionals following my lead, waiting to see whether Mr. or Mrs. Carmichael would speak next. I would have bet on the woman, and she didn't disappoint me.

"How can you people accuse this man of abuse? How can you say anything when you don't know what's going on? I manage my own business, and my husband is vice-president of Pelham Savings and Loan! We don't do abuse." When our faces remained impassive, she turned to her husband. "Tell them, Joseph. Tell them how you're trying to do what's proper for James, so he'll succeed in school, so he'll make something of himself in this world. Tell them how James just doesn't listen to you. Go on, tell them!" She nudged him again with her elbow.

"Carol, it's my son, I'll handle it, all right?"

"Just trying to help," she mumbled.

"Then let me do it!" he said, his exterior calm showing signs of unraveling now. "They don't frighten me, and nobody's taking James anywhere," he added, though no one had yet mentioned anything about custody or removal. The man turned back to us, pointing his forefinger at me like a weapon. "Now look here. James can be quite the little con artist when he wants to be. We've been having problems with him about lying, too, though he's never gone quite this far before. But I'm quite capable of handling my own son. Now where is he?"

I remained unflappable. "James says you beat him up and tried to choke him. By the nature of the marks and bruises I saw, I believe him. He says he's afraid to go home, and to be honest, I'm not sure I should let him."

"*You* should let him? Listen, mister, I don't know who you think you are, but you have nothing to say about this. It's my kid, and he's going home with me!"

"Mr. Carmichael, I'm sure you're aware that I have the right to take protective custody. My office is explaining the situation to a family court judge right now, and we're going to go by his decision."

"Judge? Court? Wait a minute. You folks are way out of line here. James is putting on a little stage play here, and you're all swallowing it!" He turned to his wife. "I can't believe this! I told you we should've put him away last year, or at least in private school, but no! 'Give it a chance,' you said. 'Let me talk to him,' you said. Well, here's what your 'chance' has wrought!" He looked at McKenna defiantly. "You going to arrest me, too?"

"Why don't we all just try to keep it calm here, okay?" McKenna said.

"Keep it calm?!" the father exploded, bolting out of his chair.

"Ea-sy," McKenna warned, rising just as quickly out of his.

Carmichael began to pace the room, like a bull waiting his turn to enter *la corrida*. "Keep it calm? You tell me you're going to snatch my kid, and I'm supposed to sit here and calmly accept it? How calm would *you* be if you were ganged up on like this? But I don't guess the parents' feelings count for much, do they?"

"Why don't you sit down, Joseph?" said his wife. "You aren't helping matters."

"Why don't you butt out, Carol? This isn't your goddamned kid."

When I first started as a caseworker seventeen years ago, they gave us a quickie course in social work theory, just so we'd have some idea of the more classic dynamics occurring in situations we'd be facing. (They'd probably love to mandate a master's degree in social work as a prerequisite, but then they'd find no one to do the job for the money they're paying.) One of the theories they covered was Kubler-Ross's five stages of grief, the process by which people come to accept the death of a loved one. Briefly, this includes denial, anger, bargaining, guilt/depression, and, finally, acceptance.

Though I'd been involved in some two or three dozen removals during this time, I'd never noticed until now how parents seemingly pass through those same five stages when their children are taken away. It's as though they're already grieving, albeit on a smaller scale, for the children they're about to lose. Thinking back on all the cases where I've needed to invoke protective custody, I realized this response was fairly universal in parents, although I supposed acceptance is only reached after many years, when and if there is no longer any hope for the children's eventual return. Most of the parents I've seen are still somewhere between anger and depression by the time I pass the case on to the undercare units for ongoing involvement. Maybe they should call it Richards's Theorem of Emotional Loss.

Despite the high degree of my intellectualizing, I realized I was letting my thoughts wander, probably as a defense mechanism for avoiding the unpleasantness of this whole scene, and I snapped my attention back. Mr. Carmichael was making promises (beginning the bargaining stage?) to the school officials.

"... wouldn't be taking time off from work to come down here if I didn't care, right? The whole reason this all started was because his schoolwork wasn't up to standards. If I didn't give a damn, I'd be closing on a huge business mortgage right now." He sat back down next to his wife. "I mean, I'm out there in the community, dealing with people every day. If this gets around that I beat my kid, no one will want to do business with me, I'll lose my job, and I won't be able to give him all the things he has now. Then we'll all go on welfare and I'll be accused of being neglectful, is that it?"

"My first priority is to ensure James's safety and well-being. Anything else is secondary," I said, paraphrasing the Major Maxim.

"Easy for him," the father said to his wife. "They all just sit here, making decisions to screw up people's lives. All they care about is covering their own behinds. 'Just doing my job, sir.' 'I'm sorry, Mr. Carmichael, but I'm just doing my job.' You people make me sick to my stomach."

"Aren't you entitled to have your lawyer here?" the woman asked. "I mean, this can't be legal. They've got to read you your rights, I know they do. My girlfriend Sarah went through this, and she told me. She retained Siben and Siben, and they smeared CPS all over the courtroom."

A secretary poked her head in the doorway.

"Excuse me, Mr. Stedman, there's a call for Mr. Richards."

"Thank you, Sheila. Let him take it inside, and then you can go."

"I'll be right back," I said. The principal shot me a knowing look as I left the room; he'd been party to a few removals in his time.

"Keith? This is Brandon. What you have to do first is to offer the parents a chance to consent to placement voluntarily. If they refuse, you then inform them you are invoking protective custody, and inform them about their rights to ask the child's return at a 1028 hearing on Monday."

"I doubt they'll go for it."

"You've been through this before, Keith. You know you have to offer them the opportunity. Then get back to me." He rang off.

I knew this all had to do with covering the parents' rights, as well as an attempt by the county to reduce or eliminate our liability in the remote chance the child became hurt somehow while in our custody. I also knew that I would be asked in court if these procedures had been followed, and there would be hell to pay if they weren't, so despite the seeming ridiculousness of it, I did it all.

I offered. The parents refused. I called Brandon back.

"Okay. We've received verbal approval from Judge Thornton to take protective custody. I've got Tricia Smollins working on a foster home for the boy right now, and I'm going to put Cecil on the line so you can give him the reasons you felt protective custody was necessary. He'll need that info for the petition we have to file in court on Monday morning.

"As soon as you're done with Cecil, you've got to take the boy to Rocky Glen Hospital for an exam. Depending on the nature and extent of his injuries, he may have to be admitted. Then get back to me from the hospital with the results. Here's my home phone number."

I jotted it down, stuck it in my pocket, hung up. Then I went back inside, ready to say the words every parent dreads, and fortunately, only a handful ever actually hear.

"Mr. and Mrs. Carmichael, I'm informing you that I have received judicial approval to take protective custody of your son, James."

"I can't believe this bullshit!" Mr. Carmichael exploded from the chair again, forcing McKenna to block his path. I continued resolutely; I was required to inform him of a number of things, but I didn't have to be sure he'd heard and/or agreed with them, nor did I have time to allow for him to ventilate.

"There will be a hearing in Family Court, Part Nine, Judge Thornton, Monday morning at 9:00 A.M. Your presence is not required, but you have the right to be there to require us to show just cause, and to petition for the boy's return home. You probably should have a lawyer representing you, though that is also not required. If you are not there, the judge will automatically approve our petition. This is a copy of the formal notification, a copy of which will also be mailed to your address, and there are telephone numbers on the back in case you need to reach us for any reason."

"This is wrong," the woman said.

"I'm not sitting still for this," the man said, starting for me. "I ought to thrash your ass right now!" I was already standing and braced to defend myself, but McKenna interceded.

"Don't make me have to get ugly," the detective said, moving between us. "This man has the right to do his job, and I'm going to make sure he gets to do it."

"It won't help things if you get crazy, Joseph," the woman said, showing rationality and insight I hadn't thought her capable of.

"I'm sorry, Mr. Carmichael, but I think it's the best thing for James right now. I'm going to take him right to the hospital for a physical exam, and then he'll be placed in a foster care resource over the weekend, pending the outcome of the exam."

"My lawyers will nail your hides to a tree!" the man said, backing off somewhat. "This is America, not Nazi Germany."

There was nothing more for me to say. The parents had been informed of, and offered, everything to which they were entitled. It was finally time to focus on James's well-being. The father's sudden outbursts, coupled with the dynamics I'd observed of his relationship with his wife, made me concur with James's fear of going home all the more.

"You haven't heard the last of this, Richards!" he called after me as I left. "I'm going to haunt you like a bad dream!

You'll wish you never heard the name Carmichael by the time I'm fin —"

I closed the door to the office, muffling the rest.

It wasn't anything I hadn't heard before.

I made a mental note to call Gloria from the hospital to explain the situation, knowing I still had a long night ahead of me.

It would be an even longer one for James.

CHAPTER
TWENTY-SEVEN

The principal's office overlooked the main parking lot, which was where I'd left my car, so that as I walked James out to it, I could feel his father's eyes boring into my back. That didn't bother me so much as the notion that as we pulled away, my license plate was being recorded. Add to that the fact that the judge who'd approved the removal was Thornton, a family court judge with whom CPS workers (including myself) had had particular difficulty, and it made me feel like fate's dart board.

James said nothing during the drive to Rocky Glen, but he wasn't wearing his happy face. We checked into the emergency room, where I explained the situation. The nurse gave me a form on a clipboard to fill out, then asked us to wait. She said she would have a resident assigned to begin James's exam "momentarily."

We took a seat after I called Gloria. Then we waited. After twenty minutes or so, I asked the nurse if there was a problem. She spoke to another person, then asked me alone to follow her. I was introduced to a resident doctor; young, slim, manicured beard, glasses. The nurse explained I was from CPS and wanted a physical exam for a child client. We were interrupted by another man in a suit and tie, and the resident began talking to him. The nurse instructed me to tell the resident the nature of the complaint, and said she would be leaving for dinner. My watch read 5:45.

I waited another ten minutes, and the men seemed to be enjoying an anecdote. I approached the resident again, to ask how much longer before James could be seen. He looked at me, then back to the other man, who said, "We'll be waiting for you." The doctor gave me an icy smile, then walked off in another direction. "The boy is pissing blood!" I called after him, but I was ignored. He had not spoken a single word to me. I did not see the resident with the manicured beard again.

The nurse came back from dinner, incredulous that James hadn't been seen yet, and promised some action. People were coming and going at a bustling pace, and I heard comments about somebody retiring and "a hell of a party if you can make it." Emergencies were wheeled in and out: someone who'd dropped an engine on his foot; a twelve-year-old who'd cut off several toes with a lawn mower; a car crash victim; the loser in a knife fight behind a nearby shopping mall. All were seen ahead of us, by a different young man I also had figured for a resident, especially when he made the comment about there "only being two of us covering." He appeared as harried as I was frustrated. Other patients lined the hallways, similarly worried about their conditions, tired of enduring pain, bored with waiting.

James was not a complainer, but when I asked him how he felt, he said he was hungry, his lower back hurt him, and he had to go to the bathroom. I accompanied him, used the urinal next to him, and saw what came out when he urinated. This was no pinkish tinge anymore. This was more like cherry soda. He said it hurt him to pee.

James denied hearing any noise when he was hit (i.e., a rib cracking or something), but in showing me where it hurt, I noticed the bruising on his lower back had gotten worse. As we walked out to the hallway again, he explained that his father had punched him there yesterday, and when he'd complained this morning, his father had said, "You think that's bad, I'll give you something to complain about," and had hit him there again, only harder.

That did it. It was time to get bitchy. I realized we'd been waiting nearly three hours, and somebody was going to see this boy, now, if I had to tackle the next doctor who passed by.

I marched to the nurse's desk, noted the new face sitting there. She had just come on at eight o'clock, she explained, and would get someone right away. "Don't tell him I'm from CPS, tell him the child is bleeding profusely and in great pain," I called after her.

Someone with a stethoscope was introducing himself to James within ninety seconds. "I'm sorry," she explained, "but one of the department heads had a retirement dinner this evening, and we were short on staff during the last shift."

The new doctor began issuing orders for a gurney, Foley catheter, an IVP, and a cystogram. People started scurrying to comply. James was assisted onto a gurney and wheeled into an examining room.

"This is what I'd expected a couple hours ago," I said to the nurse. "Who were the residents on duty the last shift?"

She consulted a clipboard on her desk. "Drs. Kramer and Goldfield," she replied.

"Well, I hope one of them enjoyed the party, because he obviously had no intention of letting something so trivial as an abused child urinating blood impinge on his plans. The other poor guy had to bust his hump to try to cover." I was starting to lose it now, the pressures of the day catching up with me. It wasn't this young woman's fault, I knew, but she was there, and I couldn't stop.

"The SOB wouldn't even speak to me, just turned his back and walked away. He knew right then he wasn't going to give up his dinner, or his good time. We'd just have to wait for the shift to change. After all, what's one more CPS case? No prestigious contacts to be made there. No prospect for career advancement there. He let this child's condition worsen while he was out there whooping it up! Is this the level of dedication we can expect from the new crop of 'professionals' this place is churning out? And how come Samantha Bishop isn't here to write up a piece on this?"

I was thankful James was in the other room being examined. His day had been tough enough without witnessing his caseworker cracking up.

"Are you all right, sir?" asked the nurse.

"You know, I've had clients who were referred to Albany

for possible abuse in half the time it took to have this already abused child seen! I wonder how commonly such prejudicial practice is observed in treating DSS children covered only by Medicaid?"

"I wouldn't know that, sir. I only just came on."

"Listen, when you jot down a list of the child's complaints, include possible hunger. We had to wait here through dinner."

"Neither of you has eaten?"

"No, we weren't on the guest list." I took a deep breath, reached over, and squeezed her shoulder gently. "I'm sorry, it's not your fault. It's been a long day. I'd just appreciate it if you would pass my concerns up to the shift supervisor. It's too dangerous to let stuff like this go unreported."

"Yes, sir, I'll do that. And we'll see if we can't rustle you up a sandwich or something."

I thanked her, went to the cashier, made change for the phone, dialed a familiar number again. Explained the situation. Took a guess at when I'd be home. I told her I'd make it up to her. Told her I missed her—terribly.

"Mr. Richards?" the nurse interrupted. I nodded. "The boy is asking to see you, and Dr. Babroit would also like a word with you."

I rang off with Gloria.

James wanted reassurance, and the doctor wanted permission to perform some test procedures, starting with X-rays. I gave both. While the X-rays were being taken, the nurse brought a tray for me with a turkey sandwich, an apple, vanilla pudding, orange juice, and a container of milk on it. I wolfed everything down, thanking the nurse profusely and apologizing for my earlier rudeness. "I just couldn't let the boy wait around any longer," I explained between mouthfuls. They may knock hospital food, but to me it seemed like a gourmet feast, and it was vastly preferable to receiving your dinner through a small IV tube, as James's condition would necessitate.

"That's okay, Mr. Richards, I don't blame you for being upset," the nurse said. "You must see some pretty tough cases." I merely nodded in agreement as I finished the last of my tray. "I used to think working the ER was the toughest job in the world," she continued, "but nobody could get me to do your job."

"I've had about enough of it myself this week, " I conceded.

The X-rays proved negative. Dr. Babroit said he wanted James kept at least overnight, for observation and more tests in the morning. He didn't think the boy's bladder or urethra were injured, but was certain the boy had suffered renal trauma and raised the possibility that James might require surgery, depending on the morning's test results. If the bleeding had been caused by one or two small blood vessels being ruptured, it would be a much simpler matter; they needed to rule out the possibility of more serious damage to James's kidneys and bordering organs.

"It's just as well you keep him here," I muttered. "I don't know if we would have had an appropriate foster home for him, anyway, and his medical needs have to be the first priority."

I signed the papers to have James admitted and left the number for emergency services. If surgery was necessary, they'd need permission slips and other forms signed, and tomorrow being Saturday, ES would have to handle things.

As James was being wheeled up to his room, I called Brandon at home, and explained everything to him.

"Thank you, Keith. You did a good job today. Your decisions were correct, you handled yourself well, and you didn't complain about having to work the overtime to stay with the case." I checked the clock over the desk I was sitting at. It was nearly ten-fifteen.

Such praise from my director was nice to hear at the end of a long day, but I didn't get to enjoy it for very long.

"Er, I'm afraid I have some, ah, unfortunate news on top of everything else, though, Keith. While you were taking the boy to the hospital, we received word from the commissioner's office. I know this isn't the best timing, but . . ." He sighed deeply, like someone about to tell a paraplegic he'd have to have an arm amputated. "It's been decided that you're to serve a one-week suspension, without pay, for your unauthorized conversation with Samantha Bishop of *Newsday*. You'll have the right to appeal the loss of pay upon your return, but the suspension is to begin immediately. I'm instructed to be sure you understand that you're not to report to work on Monday morning."

I was dumbfounded. I might have become angry at a different time, under a different set of circumstances. But after all the tensions of a long, extremely emotional day, I found myself drained of everything else but tears, and I fought hard to hold them back. One must maintain a professional image and all that shit.

Most days you feel as though you're walking a tightrope between children's and parents' legal rights, the mandates of the job as set forth by law, the physical and emotional demands of the work, and the dictates of your own administration. There are penalties and sanctions for everything, and you run around trying to keep everybody satisfied; then suddenly, you're zapped when you least expect it because the agency looks bad and they need someone to pin it on. Suddenly, all the other stuff becomes secondary, and the Major Maxim goes right out the window.

"Keith? Are you still there?"

"Yes." My voice had turned to gravel. "But what about James? What about follow-up, with him and with his family? What if they need me to testify in court? What about all the paperwork necessary to authorize payments for his placement and medical costs? Who'll notify his school, and find a foster care resource once he's discharged from the hospital? What about my other cases, or getting my notes dictated, or meeting the deadlines coming due next week, or already passed? Who's going to handle all that without any knowledge of my cases? Is it all going to sit for a week until I return?"

"I'm sorry, Keith. I don't agree with any of this. But it's coming down from Central Office, and there's nothing we can do about it right now."

What was this 'we' stuff? *We* weren't being suspended, *I* was. *We* wouldn't have to return in ten days to the leech-like shame and stigma of official reprimand, *I* would. This wouldn't sprout up in *our* personnel folder, and the loss of pay wouldn't be coming out of *our* pocket.

"I understand," was all I said.

"When you return a week from Monday, you're to report directly to my office. We'll take care of your case notes, your overtime for tonight and such, at that point. If we need you for anything else this coming week, we have your home phone number."

"Yes. I understand," I repeated, and hung up, wondering as I sat in the quiet room whether Roxanne had my case file locked up yet.

"If you need me for anything else this coming week," I said to the silent phone console, "you can all kiss my ass and go to hell."

Then I went upstairs to say goodbye to James.

At least somebody involved with this agency would be treated fairly, and with the respect and dignity a human being deserves.

CHAPTER
TWENTY-EIGHT

I t'd been a while since I'd had a vacation, perhaps too long—
a classic case of not realizing, until you're in the middle
of one, how badly it was needed. Although on Saturday I
was able to keep busy with jobs around the house, by Sunday I
was starting to feel very sorry for myself. I went to an early
church service, alone, and prayed for guidance, help, and the
strength to make a proper decision.

Who needed this friggin' job? At least someone working on
the stock exchange, dealing in commodities and hundreds of
millions of dollars, would reap rewards for jumping through
their hoops of stress, anxiety, and frustration. What did I have
to show for nearly eighteen years with Social Services, eight of
them with CPS?

Eighteen years of getting bills paid. Eighteen years of calling myself a civil servant, and of automatically being considered incompetent just by virtue of who I work for. Eighteen
years of seeing children in pain, families in turmoil, people desperately wanting to pursue the American ideal of the happy
family—a mommy and a daddy living in perfect harmony with
their 2.4 model children—and watching them run into the
stumbling blocks of having been ill-prepared for parenthood by
their own upbringings, crippled by the plagues of substance
abuse and domestic violence, and dwelling in utter despair due
to the chasm they've come to believe exists between what

their lives are and what they should be, because of what Madison Avenue and the media have taught them.

I don't know how people last at this job as long as they have. One fellow has been with DSS as long as I have, all of it with CPS, and is still managing to do an effective job. I don't know how he hangs on, how he's been able to bear it all for so many years. It gets to everyone, sooner or later, and it was getting to me. Maybe this little forced vacation was a message that it was time for Richards to consider a career change, start looking around, find some other method of supporting his family. Maybe it was time to pass the flaming torch on to someone else, and make my own self and family my first priority for a change, instead of worrying about strangers day in and day out.

But what else could I do? I had a bachelor's degree in health education, and eighteen years experience knocking on doors, assessing situations, and offering advice, but not much else. I'd have to consider a substantial pay cut, because I'd be starting over. I'd need square-one training at anything other than social work, and even if I stayed in the social work field, the experience was all I had to offer—no Master's of Social Work degree, no Certified Social Worker accreditation, not even any supervisory experience.

Where had the time gone? It seems only yesterday I'd been a bright, energetic young college grad, eager and full of zeal to set the world right. I recall being in the initial training sessions, noting how most people there were older than I, trying not to let my youth and naivete show as they taught us about having a "positive impact" on the lives of people in crisis. That's what I'd wanted to do, though the notion had no concrete label until the training session. I wanted to impact positively on people, make the way of the world smoother and less troubled for my having passed through it. I could not recall coming to any particular crossroads along the way and having to choose (at least not up until now), but looking back, it sure seemed that I'd taken a wrong turn somewhere.

Maybe that was why I now found myself back in church, after not being much of a worshipper for many years, because subconsciously I'd realized how lost I was and needed guidance. Maybe I was looking for comfort I could find nowhere else. But one church service wouldn't turn my life around. I left feeling better about my soul than when I entered, but the problem of my job still remained.

I passed the day miserably, not speaking to my wife, avoiding the kids. I wanted them to come to me for a change, put their arms around me and ask, "What's wrong, Daddy?" When they didn't, I was hurt and felt neglected. Of course, my intellect told me this was an unreal expectation of an eight-year-old and a four-year-old, but my emotions blinded me to my intellect, and resentment sprouted.

Monday I kind of bummed around, kicking the dog, slamming cabinet doors, trying to bolster my own self-confidence. I looked in the mirror, and noted with horror that a miserable, tousle-haired, pushing-forty reject with three-day-old stubble looked back. I'd seen drunks who looked better. I convinced myself that if I was going to look the part, I might as well act the part, and downed two double scotches by ten-thirty that morning. I dozed while scanning the want ads.

One-thirty found me with a headache and three hours more stubble on my chin, but no better prospects.

I went to the public library and signed up for a career counseling appointment. I scanned more want ads. I waited for someone to come along and say, "You look like a bright, articulate, personable sort of fellow, and you're not that old. How about working for me, nine to five, full benefits and pension, no experience necessary, and I'll double your present salary?" I hoped in vain.

When Gloria came home, I was glad to see her, and promptly showed her how much by ranting about her shoddy housekeeping standards because she hadn't vacuumed in the past ten days. She replied that she had to work for a living, too; I then bestowed my recognition of all the contributions she made to the family by belittling her career in speech pathology, screaming that she was the Queen of the Bullshit Jobs, and storming out of the house.

I drove to the Bald Hill Overlook, one of my favorite contemplative spots, with a view of both the north and south shores of Long Island on a clear day. I wallowed in self-pity for a while longer, shed a few tears, felt a little better. It suddenly

important to me to show how good and caring a work-
and I drove up to Rocky Glen to see how James was
he'd undergone surgery on Saturday morning and was
genuinely glad to see me. I didn't mention my problems with
my own agency; they sort of paled by comparison with his.

Indicative of this was the fact that in the four days he'd
been in Rocky Glen Hospital, he'd been visited once by his
stepmother, once by Mrs. Ingram (the school nurse), once by
the emergency services worker, and now once by me. His father had not appeared, though I didn't know whether he'd been
warned away or not by the ES worker.

I left the hospital feeling good that my visit had bolstered
James's spirits, but realizing once again that for all the difference we think we make as workers, we are merely people doing
jobs that hundreds of others could do. I've often said that if I
died tomorrow, somebody else would take my place and life
would go on as though I'd never poured the time, effort, and
caring into this job.

Just like Bill Kahn.

Now, having seen James, I realized that even after we'd
shared such a rough day together last Friday, another worker
had taken over on Saturday, had authorized the surgery, and
had easily continued handling the case without me. Of course I
was being unreasonable, because the primary concern was
James's well-being. But it became important for me to know
Keith Richards had made a difference, that the job had been
done a little better, a little more empathetically, a little more
personally because Keith Richards had done it, and my visit today made me realize I'd been kidding myself. James's worker
might have made a difference, but Keith Richards hadn't.

I felt myself slipping into my grains of sand funk: you
know, we are all just grains of sand on an endless beach, each
so insignificant and worthless compared to all the others, each
powerless to resist the forces of tide, weather, nature, or time.
What is our purpose here on the earth? What was my purpose?
Would I never accomplish anything to lift me above being
merely someone with the same name as a rock star? Was I put
here to both live and set an example of utter futility?

I went home, avoided any contact with my wife or children, and went to bed without any dinner, a fitting punishment for the parent in me to impose upon the child in me.

It was a long time before I was able to get to sleep, though, and even then I slept fitfully.

▪ ▪ ▪

"You did it then?" I asked incredulously, sitting at my kitchen table and sipping a cup of tea, "You found her?"

"I'm pretty sure," McKenna said. "The description matched, down to her given birthdate. It's apparently a legal adoption, finalized about two months ago. The child I saw is fine, healthy, and living under the name of, er...Donna Buchanan."

"Did she have any kind of burn marks on her hands? Like hot liquid splattered them?" He admitted he hadn't really noticed, but gave me the name and address of the school he'd visited her at and the home address of the adoptive parents.

"Do you have any problems with me seeing this Donna Buchanan at school? I should be able at least to give you a positive ID."

"It couldn't hurt," said McKenna, "but do you have the time to go and see this kid? I don't."

"I do. Probably tomorrow morning."

"Hey, how'd that boy make out at the hospital the other day?"

"He was admitted for surgery on a ruptured kidney his old man gave him. He's in good shape now, but we're still looking for a foster home for him, last I heard. The home we originally were going to place him in took three sisters the next day, filling James's slot and that entire home. It's just as well he's in the hospital for a few days."

For the first time all week, I had something to attend to where the main purpose wasn't to kill time. This was just what I needed, a little trip on my own, to remind myself that I do make a difference, to see with my own eyes a success story with a happy ending, created at least in part by my efforts. All I wanted was to observe Jenny from the back of the room, or through a two-way mirror—whatever would disturb her least. I'd made a promise to Charlene Simmons and wanted to be certain that I'd made good on that promise.

The girl was having a snack with her classmates, squealing with laughter as the boy across from her smeared the insides of a peanut butter and jelly sandwich all over his mouth. Whoever she was, this Donna Buchanan, she was a beautiful, blonde child exuding delight at the boy's entertainment. I almost wished I could adopt her myself, right there on the spot.

But she wasn't Jenny MacAvoy.

The physical likeness was striking, and I could see how easily the two girls could be confused, but her hands showed no burn scars, and her eyes no emotional scars, no haunted look, that look of a lifetime of doom realized before the age of six. I'd seen the look in too many children's eyes over the years, but it simply wasn't in Donna's eyes, and never had been.

The entire drive back to Bald Hill and the four hours I spent parked there are all a blur, a melting watercolor enveloping and choking me with the visions of eighteen years of failed efforts. Even when I returned home and allowed myself to dine with my family, I was silent, staring into space as though I'd taken a megadose of antihistamine.

After everyone was asleep, I sat in the dark living room, watching from my easy chair as the blue numbers of the VCR's digital clock changed, the minutes silently, coldly, relentlessly ticking by. The overnight storm they'd been predicting all day hit now, the winds howling and the rain bombarding the roof and windows.

"I don't know if I can do this anymore," I said aloud to the numbers in the blackness as they changed again. "But how can I continue to support my family? I have good benefits through the job, but I'll have to take a substantial cut in pay. Then, again, if I'm so stressed out that it puts me in an early grave, how does that help my family? Whaddya think, Dad? What should I do?"

I'd never hesitated to seek out my father's advice when he was alive; it is a practice I refuse to abandon just because he died three years ago. He still talks to me when I need him to; I just have to listen a lot more carefully. In asking his advice now, however, I started reminiscing about his death, a tangent I allowed myself to follow in order to escape, at least for the moment, a set of questions the answers to which might be painful, might involve a change I wasn't quite ready to face.

I empathized with Marsha McKay, because when Dad had died, there had been cases waiting for me upon my return, too. At least I had a loving spouse to lean on during that time, whereas Marsha, with her recent divorce, was not so fortunate. I wondered if Marsha had gotten any support from friends at work—I'd certainly been too wrapped up in my own problems last Friday to offer much sympathy—yet the condolences of co-workers had meant an awful lot to me at Dad's funeral. For all the wakes I'd ever attended, wondering if it really made a difference to show up, mutter some sympathetic cliches and say a prayer or two over the departed, burying my own father made me see how much it does help, how important it is to realize in the midst of your grief that there are people who care enough to interrupt their busy schedules just to comfort you by their presence and kind words.

I recalled that the day Dad was laid to rest, the Beatles' "Eleanor Rigby" echoed over and over in my mind, and it further strengthened the resolve I'd forged at age sixteen when I'd first heard the song: that I would not allow the importance of my life to be washed away by a lonely, insignificant death. That was when I first knew I wanted to do something with my life, to "positively impact" on the people and environment around me. The gap between that resolve and what I'd accomplished since was one of my chief sources of torment now.

The electricity must have gone out briefly, because I was suddenly aware that the blue VCR clock light was blinking 12:00 over and over. I sat there, nodding off, too depressed to be bothered with resetting it. The electricity would just go out again at some point in the future, and I would have to reset the clock again, so what was the point?

It was still blinking in the morning when the kids woke me up, and the family's usual weekday morning routine was begun once more.

■   ■   ■

"Miserable," Gloria said into the receiver on Wednesday night, "absolutely miserable. It's good you called, Cathy, maybe you can talk some sense into him." She handed me the remote phone, and I took it into my den and closed the door.

"Your wife tells me you're not taking this too well."

"She's right. I'm not very good company this week."

"Then I'm glad I phoned, instead of dropping over. Everyone at work just thinks you're on a week's vacation, except for Rick, Deanna, and me, who found out the story from Buddy. I was voted spokesperson, and I'm supposed to tell you we think this whole thing sucks. Rick says that he's seen people getting away with stuff so bad it makes what you did look like jaywalking by comparison."

I didn't feel like keeping up the pretense of a cheerful disposition. Since I couldn't think of anything fitting to say, I kept silent.

"C'mon, Keith, snap out of it. Doesn't it help to know your friends are behind you, and miss you?"

"Mmm." I murmured, not at all convinced.

"I was talking to a Detective McKenna yesterday. He said you gave him a great idea for tracking down that little girl you were looking for, and it helped him find one of my Mikkelson kids."

"It wasn't her."

"What do you mean?"

"It—wasn't—her. I went to the school to see the child, and it wasn't Jenny. I haven't bothered to call McKenna back yet."

"Oh," she said, struggling to keep her cheeriness afloat. "Well, at least you helped him find one of my kids. That's something to be proud of."

"Right."

There was only awkward silence for the next moment or two, but I could feel Cathy's exasperation growing. I wanted to thank her for calling, to say something so she wouldn't get discouraged and hang up. Just having her share time on the other end of the line helped, and I probably should have told her so.

But I didn't.

When she finally broke the silence, it was not in the way I'd expected.

"You know, Richards, your problem is that you feel too much. Your clients manage to tap a deeply-sunk well of emotion within you. You're so used to pouring out your empathies for your clients while keeping your own problems on hold, that now that you have the chance to feel sorry for yourself, you're taking a bath in it. You're wallowing around in self-pity like a pig in slop."

"Not a pretty sight, is it?"

"No, and you've got some nerve. You're rejecting the people around you who are trying to be supportive, and acting like nobody on earth could be suffering as much as you are. You think you're the only one who's ever been stung by the hornets of official reprimand?"

"What are you talking about?"

"I'm talking about snapping out of it. I'm talking about getting your head on straight, so when next Monday morning rolls around, you can get your ass back into gear and do your job."

Another silence. Then I said, "When next Monday rolls around, it might not be my job anymore."

"Why? They're not going to fire you for this."

"No, but I'm thinking about telling them what they can do with their job. Packing it in. Hanging up the clipboard. Calling it a career. I mean, who the hell needs all this aggravation? I can find some other job, one that's less stressful."

"One that pays less."

"True, but maybe there will be rewards in other areas. Such as job satisfaction, actual accomplishments. Not having to feel as though nothing you've done has made the slightest bit of difference in the world."

"It's your move to make, but I think you're grossly overreacting." She affected a bratty child's voice. "'They bounced me out for a week, so I'll show them. I'll quit, and then they'll be sorry.' Don't you think that's kind of immature? You're going to brashly throw away almost twenty years experience?"

"How am I gonna face everybody at work, snickering behind my back, looking at me like a leper. I don't know if I can face that."

"So then it's your pride that's hurt, eh? Let me tell you a little story."

"Is it going to take long?"

"Who cares? It's not like you have to get up for work tomorrow, so shut up and listen.

"Back when I'd been here only about ten months, I had a case involving a mentally deficient mother with her child in foster care, and I had to conduct an in-office visit. They had just started some renovations on the building that week, including the room we had to use for visitations, so there were ladders, ceiling tiles, and some other construction materials stacked against the wall of the room. Now this mother, of course, wanted to buy the kid's affection, so she brought him every kind of candy in the world.

"So here I am, trying to hold a conversation with a woman who could barely ride the train in from the city by herself, while her four-year-old, already hyperactive son is running amok, all pumped up on a sugar high. She's watching him, and he's bumping into some of the construction stuff, trying to play with some of it. I'm getting worried the boy might hurt himself, or us, and I suggest to the mother that perhaps she should pull the reins in a little. Trouble is, she obviously doesn't know how. She does say some ineffectual stuff like, 'Joey, you really shouldn't touch,' and 'Maybe you should sit down now,' but the kid keeps running around and knocks into a ladder resting against the wall. It crashes to the floor, just missing his foot. Mom says nothing, so I grab him and tell him he's going to get hurt. I find a coloring book for him, which holds his attention for nearly three seconds. Then he's running around again.

"The child loves the attention, though, and starts deliberately running into the ladder. Mom says nothing. Kid starts to climb up his mother's back. She shakes him off, then continues to sit there, stupor-like. I wondered if she might be on drugs. The kid starts hitting her and running away. She does nothing. I grab the kid, and start hugging him, figuring if he wants attention, I'll give him attention and affection while I explain what's right and wrong to him.

"The kid turns around and kicks me! The mother says, 'Yeah, he kicks me, too,' but does nothing else. So I shake him a little, tell him he's bad, tell him we're going to end the visit if he can't behave. He squirms away, then runs by to see if I'll chase him, which I don't do. Then he runs by again and hits me as he passes. Still, I try to ignore him. Finally, he runs over to the ladder, picks it up, lets it fall to the floor again with a crash, then runs away again. I calmly get up and straighten the fallen ladder, he comes over and hits me again, but this time, I grab his arm, spin him around, and give him one good swat on the rear while sitting him in a chair. I mean, enough is enough!

"The boy was as good as gold after that. He still bugged his mother for attention, but there wasn't any more of that crazed, running around, aggressive hitting or kicking behavior. And he stayed away from both me and the construction stuff.

"The visit ends, mom goes home, I return the boy to his foster home. Next morning I come in to find I'm being brought up on charges of child abuse because a passing supervisor saw me hit the boy. I mean, I'm talking about one slap on the fanny, with a bare, open hand, and the kid was fully clothed! Mom said and did nothing, and my punishment modified the child's behavior as intended. I couldn't understand why everybody was so alarmed.

"The bottom line was administration was so afraid of possible repercussions that they wanted to have themselves covered and be able to say they were not only aware of the incident, but had taken corrective measures. So, despite no complaints being made or actions taken by the mother or anybody else outside the agency, I was suspended for a week without pay. They told everybody I was on vacation, like they're doing for you, but I just know that supervisor chirped the story into a few select ears, because years later people were still asking me about it, saying that they'd 'just heard the story,' or some such thing. So I know what you must be feeling right about now."

"You mean they punished you out of fear of what might happen?"

"Exactly. They also stipulated that I was never supposed

to have contact with children in any future job assignments, but they forgot all about that when they needed all the experienced workers they could find to form a new foster care unit. That was nearly seven years ago, and I've been here ever since."

"But you're one of the best, most caring workers we have."

"Didn't matter back then. Doesn't matter now. When butts are on the line, the only prerequisite to being made scapegoat is vulnerability, and I had plenty of that, along with a dollop of naivete."

"You know, when I was first assigned to CPS, one of the first things Brandon Ericsson said to me is, 'Don't worry, you're not alone out there.' Sad fact is, you really are. It's like you're walking through a giant mine field of human emotion without maps or guides, and nobody will tell you anything until you've made a wrong step and blown your foot off. Then a battalion of people appear to make sure you suffer quietly, don't leak out the truth of what happened, and don't get any blood on the agency's image."

"And yet," Cathy said, "there are good people there, people who know what they're doing, and who do a great job. Look at Faye Highstreet, my supervisor. Or Sheila Doyle, your other assistant director in CPS. They're both knowledgeable, fair, supportive when necessary, but don't sit on your shoulder every minute of the day, waiting for you to foul up. They're interested in getting the job done, but it's no skin off their noses to treat you like a professional, to give you credit for the experience you have. We need good people in the agency, Keith, to offset the jerks. That's why it'd be a shame for you to pack it in right now."

"So I should stay on because Roxanne D'Angelis needs workers who have experience at being whipped?"

"No. You should stay on because of all the good you do in the job. Because if you quit now, people like Roxanne will use that to illustrate their claim that you were no good anyway. You should stay on because you have a family to support, a lot of trained experience under your belt, and because I'd hate to lose one of the people I trust and admire most in the whole place. But most of all, do it for yourself. You know you do a great job, you know you make it easier for your innocent clients to get through the system, you know you've helped a lot of kids over the years who really needed a competent worker to come along when you did."

"But what do I have to show for it? I never see the end result of my efforts, and I seriously doubt I've made any big changes in anyone's life. The system ties my hands in helping those who really need it, while to those who don't really need help, the system's just a plaything. So many times I've asked myself in the field, 'What the hell am I doing here?' I appreciate your optimism, Cathy, but I'm afraid I can't buy into it. I'm just a burned-out worker with a tainted image. Damaged goods. What kind of difference can I make in anybody's life now? What kind of difference have I ever made?"

"I think you know the answers, Keith, or you at least know where to find them. You just have to want to look deeply enough inside yourself, and right now, I think you're afraid of what you might find." She paused, and when I didn't respond, added, "All I can say is, if you want to quit, then quit, nobody's stopping you. Lord knows, you've paid your dues. But this is one friend and co-worker who'll miss you something fierce, as will all the kids still out there who need your help."

"I'll miss you, too," I said sincerely. There was truth in her words, but it didn't make my choices any easier.

CHAPTER
TWENTY-NINE

Of all the places you might dream of being when the hand of God touches your life, few grown-ups ever think of a toy store. I sure didn't. But there I was, a few days later, wheeling around an early November shopping basket full of toys and games at a local toy store.

Though feeling very much like Santa Claus, I was thinking about work, and specifically, about the agency policy-makers, likening them to bombardiers in wartime. They do their jobs, generally insulated from the victims far below. Sight their target, drop their load, return to base. They never see, on ground level, the havoc wrought by their actions and never take the time to find out, because it isn't their concern. They've done their job; dealing with the aftermath is someone else's problem. They know all there is to know from ten thousand feet.

"Hi," said a tiny voice from behind me in an aisle loaded with Barbie dolls and accessories. It didn't quite register at first that the voice was talking to me, but then it was repeated, snapping me out of a fog the way it once led me into one.

"Hi!"

I'd heard the syllable used in this manner before, by children who know you and want to attract your attention, but who don't know or remember your name, and are years away from merging verbal skills with social graces. I turned around slowly, and there she was.

She'd grown some in the months since I'd seen her, and put on a bit of weight, too, making her look less waif-like and attesting to the proper care and nutrition she must have been receiving. Same blonde hair, same blue eyes, same look of burdens shouldered prematurely, though tempered now by a joy I'd never seen in those eyes before. Her burned hand was bandaged.

"Hi," I answered back, stifling the urge to call Jenny by her name, lest I cause the woman whose hand she was holding even more suspicion than she already must have felt. "How are you?"

"Fine."

"You know this man, Wendy?" The woman's arm slipped protectively across the child's chest, and Jenny grabbed the arm as she explained, "He's my friend, Mommy. He saw me before."

So there we were, two strangers grinning awkwardly through our wariness of one another, each willing to trust the other based solely on a little girl's endorsement, each with a flood of questions we didn't quite know how to ask. I must have looked like some sort of shabbily-dressed, unshaven derelict, though it had obviously made no difference to Wendy, and I believed the woman sensed this. She, on the other hand, was neat, attractive, and well-dressed, and the Barbie dolls and clothes already in her basket, coupled with the protective affection I'd already witnessed, told me this woman had no problem providing for the girl, either materially or emotionally. Though I'd really had nothing to do with it, I was certain that this was exactly what Charlene Simmons had intended for her daughter and wished that she could see this somehow.

"I'm Keith Richards, and I was Wendy's worker several months ago."

"Worker? As in caseworker?"

"Yes, ma'am. Child Protective Services worker, actually."

"Andrea Beaumont." A warm smile was followed by a petite, well-manicured, braceleted hand being offered for a handshake, which I took.

"Do you live locally, Mrs. Beaumont?" I asked.

"Right here in Setauket," she answered, and then, apparently figuring Wendy's joy at seeing me was endorsement enough, added, "Perhaps you can help us, Mr. Richards. My husband and I adopted Wendy about two months ago. Although he handled all the legal details, we were told very little about Wendy's background. We weren't given immunization or health records, have no idea how she burned her hand"—I watched as Jenny/Wendy turned her face into the woman's waiting embrace—"you can see she's very sensitive about it, and anything you might be able to share with us would be greatly appreciated."

"Why the bandage? Last time I saw her hand, it appeared to be healing normally."

"When Wendy first came to us, one of the blisters became infected after it broke, and it hasn't responded to any of the medications the doctor's been trying. Since she won't talk about it, and we felt it best not to press her, we have little idea how she suffered the burn."

"I have a doctor friend who is wonderful with children, and with whom I was trying to arrange an appointment for Jenny—sorry—Wendy, when she disappeared. That was probably around the time she came to live with you."

"Jenny? Disappeared? I'm afraid I don't understand."

"Mrs. Beaumont, I think you, your husband, Wendy, and I have a lot to talk about," I said, giving her my warmest smile and reaching in my pocket.

Though I'd spent the last nine days writhing under introspection and self-doubt (not to mention wallowing in self-pity) and had been feeling inclined toward serving DSS notice of my resignation, I never gave a thought to what I did next. It was a small act that had become reflexive from eighteen years of repetition.

I wrote out my office phone number on a scrap of paper and handed it to Mrs. Beaumont, inviting her to call me on Monday morning for an appointment. It wasn't until later that I realized I'd committed myself, and I wondered if perhaps I shouldn't have been committed in another fashion (i.e., to a nice padded room someplace).

"In the meantime," I continued, "I can try to secure copies of her records from the health clinic where she was most likely treated. When you call me for the appointment, I'll give you Dr. Bronson's phone number."

The woman gave me her number as well, pointing out that it was unlisted. "I'm so glad Wendy recognized you, Mr. Richards."

"Keith."

"Thank you, Keith. My husband and I will be thrilled with any information you can provide us."

"Believe it or not, Mrs. Beaumont, I'll bet I have as many questions as you do!" There were smiles all around as Wendy/Jenny gave me a big hug.

"Keith Richards. Isn't he a rock musician with The Who?"

I just smiled and shook my head. Some things never change.

"Rolling Stones," I corrected.

∎ ∎ ∎

As I drove out of the parking lot, I saw Mrs. Beaumont buckling Wendy into a seat belt. They noticed me, too, and waved, Wendy holding up her bandaged hand—the one for which I was finally going to be able to secure medical care.

Then we returned to our own lives again, leaving me to ruminate on my belief that what happens in this world is governed by more than just random chaos, that things happen for a reason, and that God has a plan for each of us. For the rest of the day, and all of the next, Cathy's words and Wendy's wave kept coming back to me. And I resigned myself to where I'd be, and what I'd be doing, come Monday morning.

It would be back to the bullshit. Back to the paperwork. Back to the nicotine reek of Roxanne's office, and the questions of my co-workers regarding my absence, and the complaints of both reporting persons who think we do too little and alleged perpetrators who feel we should be in someone else's home catching the real child abusers.

But just maybe, in another seventeen-odd years, I'll be party to another success story like Wendy Beaumont's. Maybe I'll orchestrate timely medical care for the next Corrie Martinez, maybe I'll prevent the next Mrs. Pressman from throwing her child in the car like a rag doll and dumping her on some hospital doorstep months later. Maybe I can intervene before the next James Carmichael urinates blood, before the next Cindy Riordan is raped by her father. Perhaps I can get the next Stephen Nuñez in a stable environment sooner, or teach the next Marvin Washington the difference between Hollywood and the real world *before* he tries to fly like Superman.

Hopefully, with God's help, I can help innocent people navigate their way through a CPS investigation more smoothly, and teach others not to use the referral system to snipe at someone with whom they're involved in a neighborhood, family, or custodial dispute. And maybe, just maybe, I can help a fellow worker through a tough time, being supportive when it seems nobody else in the world understands what's going on or gives a damn.

I took my family out to dinner, a partial apology for the bitchy way I'd been acting. Something I'd felt vaguely for a long time had crystallized into an intact, coherent concept: for all the broken, tension-filled, dysfunctional families I see, I must do all I can to ensure that there isn't one more in the world, that I've at least got my own family together and living in an atmosphere of honesty, trust, warmth, and love.

My own family will be the example for each of my children to carry with them, the model upon which they will raise their children when the time comes. And while I don't mean to imply that mine is the one true standard by which all other families should be judged, it does afford me the chance to try to do things right, to avoid mistakes I've seen my clients make with their children and their spouses, and to practice what I preach. I hope that twenty years from now, when my children are grown, I haven't fallen victim to the same mistakes I've sworn through the years not to make, and that, looking back, my theories and practices of child-rearing always remained in Morgan and Will's best interests.

And I hope that somewhere along the way, I can pass those ideas and techniques that work best along to other families who need the help, improving the quality of life for their children, too.

CHAPTER THIRTY

A lot happened in the three months after my suspension. Cathy broke off her relationship with her prospective foster parents' son. Buddy Hollister, not having scored high enough to be appointed senior caseworker, accepted a position with the probation department. Tricia Smollins was made a senior worker under Martha Hubbard, taking Bill Kahn's old court worker position. Not surprisingly, Cecil Perry became the permanent supervisor of my old unit once we got the official word that Woody was retiring. But I was long gone by then.

I had asked for, and received, a transfer to another unit, but not without having to put in many evenings of overtime to clear up my backlogged caseload. When there were only about three weeks left before I would actually start my new assignment, Roxanne was ordered not to give me any more new cases, and with yeoman effort, I finished up the backlog. The key was not having any new cases coming in.

One of the things that made the transfer so desirable was that although I was still working in an investigative unit, it was one which was covered by Sheila Doyle, the other CPS Assistant Director, and supervised by Ron Harvey. Both of these new bosses not only knew the job implicitly, but, as Cathy had pointed out, had reputations for being fair to staff and treating them as the professionals they are. I was assigned a new catchment area, farther east on Long Island, but after what I'd been through under Roxanne *sans* Woody, it was like paradise. I was now where neither her smoke nor her supervision could touch me.

The nosy questions about my "vacation" were a pain, but they faded after a few weeks. With being assigned cases out east, there was much more travel time involved, so I was simply not around the office as much as before to face such questions. And the icing on the cake came after I'd been in the new assignment about two months.

In a marvelous example of how the civil service machinery cranks on day after day, blissfully oblivious to most of what goes on around it, I was promoted to field senior caseworker in my new unit, because the person who'd been doing the job provisionally could not be reached on the list established by the promotional test; I could be reached; being highest on the list of those in my new unit, I was simply promoted in place. What made it doubly interesting was that when our other senior was promoted to supervisor of an undercare unit, we needed a court senior worker, and that slot was filled by O.J.

Of course, there were those who smiled congratulations in my face and remarked behind my back to others that they couldn't understand how my being suspended had resulted in a promotion. They failed to look at the two occurrences as separate, coincidental events, neither being monumental enough to have much influence on the other. I was an experienced worker who had happened to land in the right unit at the right time, and though a lot of people feel that you take a promotion any way you can get it, people from other parts of the agency were not exactly beating down doors to become CPS workers. For me, it was a major turnaround in my situation, and enabled me to make a new start, extricated from the tangled morass of problems that had dragged me down in Woody's unit.

Besides, I thought I'd earned it. Between the time I'd logged in CPS, let alone the agency, and the quality of the work I'd done, I felt there were much worse choices for a senior position (Sam Bishop's article be damned!) and obviously, so did administration. It was a megadose of confidence, without which you really cannot do this job. When your confidence is gone, you can't carry the authority vested in you to conduct investigations and take necessary actions. You can't hold your own in a courtroom. And when you start to wonder if every little thing you do on the job is correct, you wind up spending so much time monitoring yourself that the job doesn't get done properly.

As a field senior worker, you are supposed to get the more difficult cases, especially the sex abuse cases. While no one has ever addressed the issue of whether or not senior workers should handle higher numbers of caseloads, your time is often robbed because you're also expected to cover the unit in the supervisor's absence. While you're not approving time off or travel voucher payments, you are responsible for prioritizing and assigning cases, ensuring they all get a twenty-four-hour contact (ours is the only county in New York State to enforce such a policy), dealing with irate RPs who call demanding immediate action, making case decisions on smaller problems (and seeking appropriate administrative help on larger ones), and trying to ship out or close out cases that the workers have completed.

I'm like a corporal in the sergeant's absence; in charge one day, a grunt the next. Where yesterday I was the one complaining about being assigned more new cases, now I get the complaints from the workers when I must assign cases to them. If we get a nasty situation handed to us, I must either delegate it to another worker (who won't want it) or else handle it myself (which backs you up very quickly if you take on too much at once).

But I do have more freedom to make my own case decisions, a certain autonomy I never knew before. I like the inherent assumption that I know what I'm doing on a particular case, though like anyone else around here, I'd better have a good explanation ready if the spam hits the fan. The extra money helps, too, though it's only about $50 more per biweekly paycheck.

I also can't deny the little satisfied smile at the corners of my mouth when I pass Roxanne in the halls, knowing that my very presence is a reminder that her favorite ne'er-do-well whipping boy succeeded just as soon as he got out from under her thumb, a perk I relished even more the first time I sat across from her at a supervisor's meeting I attended for Ron. To her credit, she's never said anything derogatory to my face since my promotion, though she's never offered any congratulations, either.

I had my appointment with the Beaumonts. I don't know much more now than I already knew about how they came to adopt their daughter. They were rather vague about it, and since it apparently wasn't handled through our agency, I didn't press the issue. Perhaps Mr. Beaumont did arrange for Jenny/Wendy's new life through the black market, I could never be sure, but it seemed to me that at least in this case the end justified the means. They did explain that they wanted a new name for her to help break ties with her old life, and chose Wendy. Although the name means "Wanderer," the Beaumonts vowed to end her days of wandering and provide her with a loving, permanent home.

Wendy's appointment with Dr. Bronson resulted in a new course of treatment for her hand, which is nearly healed now. I was able to secure her medical records, scant as they were, and thus avoided having to make the child repeat what inoculations she'd received as Jenny MacAvoy. The record now contains a written diagnosis confirming my initial suspicions that her hand had been immersed in scalding water, not splashed upon, and although we've heard nothing from them since, the MacAvoys were both indicated for burns and inadequate guardianship (due to domestic violence in the children's presence). We have since closed the case, and Jud and Amanda's whereabouts, as well as that of the baby Carlotta, remain unknown.

The job goes on.

Cases roll in and roll out, relentless as the tides, as people continue to abuse or neglect their children and other people continue to refer them. Still others continue to waste time and money by trying to manipulate the system to gain an edge in custody or visitation hearings, force a teenage parent to accept responsibilities, retaliate against parental restrictions, or simply snipe at a troublesome neighbor or in-law.

Overreactions continue to abound in less serious cases, while hesitations and delays in reporting continue on certain critical ones. Schools and hospitals continue to report everything, appropriate or not, so that their posteriors are protected. Judges continue to decide the fates of families in oak-paneled courtrooms, while foster care resources continue to dwindle.

And CPS continues to shoulder the burden of its bum rap. We continue to be blamed for taking custody in cases that don't warrant such action, while everybody knows of a case "where child abuse is really going on, and CPS does nothing." Workers continue to investigate, testify, and determine cases as they become even further bogged down in the quagmire of paperwork and the responsibility of too many cases. Staff turnover continues to plague administrators, who can barely keep the status quo on staffing levels, let alone increase it, because nobody wants "to become the next Bill Kahn."

Keith Richards continues to bear the brunt of threadbare Rolling Stones jokes, taking each day one at a time, and making sure his children get a huge hug at the end of it. As my mother prayed that her children would grow up to become anything but registered nurses (as she was), I pray that my children will choose something other than social work for their careers. I also pray that I have done a proper job preparing them for the challenges they'll face as parents in a new century.

Perhaps by then lawmakers and administrators will have discovered the inequities and injustices we face every day in this system and will have ironed out at least some of them. Perhaps the job we do today will impact positively enough on the families of tomorrow that the actual occurrences of abuse or neglect are greatly reduced. Although even the Bible states that "the poor will be with us always," perhaps we can improve upon everyone's quality of life, one day at a time, one family at a time, one generation at a time.

Such are the thoughts we routinely put on hold while we go about the daily business of getting our jobs done. Such are the reasons many of us find the strength to continue. As each day passes, we sigh, and perhaps we grieve, waging an internal wrestling match no one ever sees; and we go home and either write up our resignation, or put it behind us, trying to get a good night's rest so we can do it all again the next day.

Tomorrow's Sunday, thank God; I've got another day to recharge my batteries. Yet, even while I'm watching football or playing a game with my children in my cozy living room, I know that abused children will get no time off unless someone like me can give it to them, that the phone will be ringing in the State Central Registry, and allegations made, and reports written, which will be waiting for me to check out come Monday morning.

Somewhere a child will be crying, and I'll have to find out why. I'll arrive on someone's doorstep, brandishing my Excalibur clipboard, my white steed parked at the curb, my vested authority representing either a knight's shining armor or the cloak of doom to whoever answers the door.

Back at the office, some administrator will decide on some new policy or procedure; someone will evaluate the quality of the job I've done; other workers will decide they've had enough and either take a leave, transfer out, or quit. Old reports will sit waiting for their paperwork to be completed, new reports will keep pouring in, and work will keep piling up as those of us who stay on will ask ourselves for the thousandth time how much more of this we can stand.

Then we'll sigh deep sighs, roll up our sleeves, don professional demeanors, and begin another week doing the job nobody wants.